The official history of the first war between Tsar Alexander I and Napoleon in 1805, using original military and diplomatic documents and the testimonies of witnesses and participants from the war.

First published in 1844, the history describes the causes of the war and the state of the opposing armies before tracking the march of Kutusov's corps into Austrian territory and the concurrent Austrian disaster at Ulm. It then looks at the Tsar's diplomatic efforts: Emperor Alexander's journey abroad; Prussia's changing relationship with Napoleon; the Treaty of Potsdam; and the Tsar's relations with Britain and Sweden. Returning to the Danube theatre the history covers: Kutuzov's retreat from Braunau to Krems, the actions at Lambach and Amstetten, the Battles of Krems and Dürnstein; Kutuzov's march from Braunau to Znaim; Bagration's march to Hollabrun; and the action at Schöngrabern.

After a consideration of operations in the Tyrol and Italy, the narrative shifts to the arrival of Buxhoeveden's corps and the Austerlitz campaign including the action at Wischau and the pre-battle manoeuvring and dispositions. Austerlitz itself is then considered in detail: Napoleon's dispositions; initial operations by Dokhturov, Langeron and Przhibyshevsky; the defeat of the coalition centre; Kamensky's battle; the exploits of Prince Volkonsky; the actions of the coalition cavalry; the defeat of the Russian Guard; Bagration's operations; the defeat of Langeron and Przhibyshevsky; Dokhturov's exploits; the coalition withdrawal; casualties of the coalition and French armies.

The narrative of the primary theatre of war concludes with the arrival of Essen's corps, the Tsar's return to Russia, the Peace of Pressburg, and the march of the Russians through Hungary and Galicia. However, details are also included of subsidiary operations in Hanover under Tolstoy in conjunction with the British and Swedes, and in the Mediterranean under Lacy at Naples and Corfu.

Born in Russia in 1789, after the death of his father Alexander Ivanovich Mikhailovsky-Danilevsky used his inheritance to study in Göttingen from 1808-11, on returning to Russia he became a civil servant.

During the War of 1812, he joined the militia and participated in the Battle of Borodino, after which he served in the Quartermaster's Department and was present at many battles from 1813-14.

From 1815-20, he was head of the General Staff library but returned to military service until 1832, when he was commissioned to write Russia's official military histories.

He died in 1848 during a cholera epidemic in St Petersburg.

Peter G.A. Phillips is a retired soldier and civil servant who served for 27 years in the British Army Intelligence Corps (in Germany, the Falkland Islands, Northern Ireland, Hong Kong, Bosnia, Iraq and Afghanistan), including working as a Russian, German, and Serbo-Croat linguist, before working for five years as part of a Civil Service team training UK military personnel to serve in diplomatic missions worldwide. He has been translating Russian military histories of the Coalition Wars since December 2019, initially as a hobby, having been encouraged by renowned Napoleonic historian Dr Alexander Mikaberidze following a chance encounter on social media. He now lives in the Philippines with his Filipina wife of 33 years. They have two adult daughters.

1805 – Tsar Alexander's First War with Napoleon

The Russian Official History

Alexander Ivanovich Mikhailovsky-Danilevsky

Translated by Peter G.A. Phillips

Helion & Company

Helion & Company Limited
Unit 8 Amherst Business Centre
Budbrooke Road
Warwick
CV34 5WE
England
Tel. 01926 499619
Email: info@helion.co.uk
Website: www.helion.co.uk
Twitter: @helionbooks
Visit our blog at http://blog.helion.co.uk/

Published by Helion & Company 2022
Designed and typeset by Mach 3 Solutions Ltd (www.mach3solutions.co.uk)
Cover designed by Paul Hewitt, Battlefield Design (www.battlefield-design.co.uk)

Original text published as *Opisanie pervoj vojny Imperatora Alexandra s Napoleonom, v. 1805-m godu [History of the first war between Emperor Alexander and Napoleon in 1805 written under Supreme command by Lieutenant-General and Member of the Military Council Mikhailovsky-Danilevsky]*, St Petersburg, 1844

Cover: Fight for the Banner, oil on canvas by Wiktor Mazurowski (Public Domain)

ISBN 978-1-915113-85-6

British Library Cataloguing-in-Publicationv Data.
A catalogue record for this book is available from the British Library.

For details of other military history titles published by Helion & Company Limited, contact the above address, or visit our website: http://www.helion.co.uk

We always welcome receiving book proposals from prospective authors.

Contents

List of Maps

Introduction – Alexander Mikhailovsky-Danilevsky and His Works

Alexander Ivanovich Mikhailovsky-Danilevsky holds a distinct place in the Russian historiography. An eyewitness to the historic events of the Napoleonic era and direct participant of the later Napoleonic campaigns, he went on to write official Russian histories that remain among the finest sources on the period. His studies of Russia's wars against Napoleon in 1805, 1806-1807, and 1812-1814 represented some of the earliest attempts to produce scholarly analysis of the campaigns and still remain valuable sources on the subject. The present publication is the first English translation of Mikhailovsky-Danilevsky's original study of the 1805 Campaign[1] offering numerous interesting insights and perspectives on that momentous campaign when the Russian army first confronted Napoleon.

Alexander Ivanovich Mikhailovsky-Danilevsky was born on August 26/September 6, 1789 in St Petersburg.[2] His father Ivan Danilevsky (1751-1807) was a common Ukrainian Cossack who defied the odds to climb the notorious rigid Russian social ladder. Showing scholastic aptitude, he was accepted into the Theological Academy in Kyiv and excelled in his studies so much that a local nobleman, Brigadier Peter Miloradovich, recruited him to tutor his son. In 1778, Miloradovich dispatched his son, Gregory, and his nephew Mikhail (the future general and hero of the Napoleonic Wars) to study in Europe and instructed Danilevsky to accompany them and supervise their studies. Danilevsky made the best of this opportunity, enrolling in courses at the University of Konigsberg, where he attended lecture of Emmanuel Kant, and the University of Gottingen, where he completed a doctoral degree in medicine. Returning to Russia in 1785, Danilevsky, reinvigorated and more ambitious than before, left the Ukranian countryside for the bright lights of the imperial capital, where he opened private medical practice and secured the rank of court counsellor.[3] He also began working at the famed Noble Loan Bank (Dvoryanskii zaemnyi bank) where he quickly excelled and rose to the position of the first director and member

1 There does exist an earlier translation, by George Nafziger, but it is based on the French edition published in 1841. See *Austerlitz: A Russian Account of the 1805 Campaign*, translated and edited by George Nafziger (West Chester OH: Nafziger Collection, 2005).

2 This date is shown on his tombstone in St Petersburg. However, some sources refer to his birth in 1790.

3 This was a civilian rank of the 7th class in the Table of Ranks, a system of ranks that tied a person's social standing to service in the military, in civil service, or at the imperial court. Each category listed fourteen ranks. For a common Cossack man to reach a court councilor's rank was a remarkable accomplishment indeed.

of the Board of Control. Along the way Danilevsky also acquired a new last name, albeit as a result of an unpleasant incident. During the reign of Emperor Paul I, a certain Danilevsky authored an impertinent letter to the czar who was enraged with the tone of this missive and demanded its author to be punished. While searching for the culprit, the imperial authorities came to suspect Ivan Danilevsky who was detained and repeatedly interrogated despite steadfastly professing his innocence. At long last, he was able to convince the authorities that they had detained a wrong person. Informed of Danilevsky's misfortune, the czar comforted the unfortunate man by promoting him to the civil rank of Active State Councilor, the fourth highest civilian rank that was equivalent to a major general, and decreeing that 'Mikhailovsky' – the emperor had just moved into the new Mikhailovsky Palace – should be added to his surname to prevent any future mix-ups.

Young Alexander Mikhailovsky-Danilevsky followed in the footsteps of his father who understood the value of education and was determined to ensure that his son got the best one possible. The boy was first enrolled in the Lutheran St Peter's College, one of the best schools in St Petersburg, where he studied for ten years before graduating in 1806. Along the way, Ivan facilitated his son's career by enrolling him in state service at the tender age of eleven when young Alexander became a clerk at the Noble Loan Bank; in 1803, he was given the rank of collegiate registrar (kolezshkii registrator, fourteenth civilian rank) and two years later, that of college assessor (the eighth rank in the Table of Ranks). In 1807, Ivan Danilevsky passed away leaving his son a vast inheritance of some 100,000 rubles, a remarkable sum considering his own humble beginnings. Young, ambitious, and rich, Alexander quit his job at the bank and traveled to Europe to improve his education, just as his father had wished on his deathbed.

For the next four years, just as Europe was in throes of the Napoleonic Wars, Mikhailovsky-Danilevsky crisscrossed the continent, studying at his father's alma mater, the University of Gottingen, and visiting various German states, France, Switzerland, and Italy. After completing his study of law, politics, and history, Mikhailovsky-Danilevsky returned home where his education and talents were noticed by Minister of Finance Count Dmitrii Guriev who recruited him for the chancellery of the Ministry of Finance. Mikhailovsky-Danilevsky served barely a year in his new administrative capacity when the news arrived of Napoleon's invasion of Russia. He immediately quit his job and volunteered to join the militia force (opolchenye) that was being raised in and around the imperial capital. The St Petersburg militia was commanded by General Mikhail Illarionovich Golenischev-Kutuzov who quickly noticed the young and gifted man and selected him as one of his aide-de-camps.

Thus began one of the brightest pages in Mikhailovsky-Danilevsky's career. After Kuzutov was appointed the supreme commander of the Russian force, Mikhailovsky-Danilevsky followed him everywhere, receiving the baptism by fire at Borodino, for which he was given the Order of St Anna (4th class), and witnessing the surrender of Moscow in mid-September 1812. After Kutuzov reorganized the Russian army headquarters at the famed Tarutino Camp, Mikhailovsky-Danilevsky became the commander-in-chief's right-hand man, effectively directing the field chancellery, where he was responsible for correspondence and managing the *Journal of Military*

Operation (zhurnal voennykh deistvii), the official account of army's movements, operations, and battles. In his capacity, he had become '*istoriograf armii*', as one contemporary aptly put, the official historian who kept the record of the Russian army's accomplishments.

In October 1812, Mikhailovsky-Danilevsky fought at Tarutino (Vinkovo) where he was seriously wounded in the right arm, which compelled him to leave the army to recover; he subsequently received the Order of St Vladimir (4th class) for his actions during this battle. After four months of convalescence, he returned to the army in February 1813 and resumed his responsibility as Kutuzov's aide-de-camp. After Kutuzov passed away in April 1813, Mikhailovsky-Danilevsky received an invitation to join His Imperial Majesty's Suite for the Quartermaster Service and granted the military rank of staff captain. Serving in the Main Staff (glavnyj shtab, the precursor of the General Staff), Mikhailovsky-Danilevsky was entrusted the responsibility for conducting foreign correspondence (he was fluent in French and German) and managing the *Journal of Military Operation,* which Emperor Alexander personally supervised. As Mikhailovsky-Danilevsky noted in his memoirs, '[back then] I usually spent all day on horseback, traveling here-and-there, and at night I was busy writing the Journal based on generals' reports, orders that were given to them, and the so-called dispositions.'[4] Participating in the campaigns of 1813-1814, Mikhailovsky-Danilevsky was present at all major battles and earned several awards, including a gold sabre with inscription 'for gallantry' and the Prussian Pour le Merite for the battle of Lutzen; the Order of St Anna (2nd class) and the Austrian Order of St Leopold (3rd class) for the battle of Leipzig; the diamond signs of the Order of St Anna (2nd class) – for the capture of Paris.

In the late spring of 1814, Mikhailovsky-Danilevsky was asked to join the newly established General Staff, where Prince Peter Volkonskii, the new chief of staff of the Russian armies, came to appreciate the young officer's mastery of foreign languages. In his new capacity, Mikhailovsky-Danilevsky accompanied Emperor Alexander during his travels for the next few years and attended the Congress of Vienna, where he served as the emperor's private secretary. Alexander appreciate his service, promoting to colonel (September 1815) and appointing him as a flügel adjutant (1816).

Understanding the importance of keeping record of historic events he had witnessed, Mikhailovsky-Danilevsky secretly kept journals where he described his daily observations and confided his inner thoughts and assessments of events and personalities. In 1814-1818, he wrote an autobiography entitled *Réflexions sur les années 1812, 1813, et 1814 autant qu'elles me concernent*, and began writing the first history of the 1812 campaign, which remains unpublished but is very interesting considering personal insights that the author possessed. Seeking to 'immortalize my name,' as he had privately admitted, Mikhailovsky-Danilevsky also began selecting letters, written during the campaigns in Germany and France, as well as at the Congress of Vienna, for publication, and published articles, essays, and excerpts

4 Alexander Mikhailovsky-Danilevsky, *Memurary, 1814-1815* (St Petersburg: Russian National Library, 2001), 29.

from his journals in various periodicals including *Syn Otechestva, Russkii Vestnik and Otechestvennye Zapiski.*

In 1817 Mikhailovsky-Danilevsky married Anna Pavlovna Chemodanova, the heiress to a rather wealthy Russian noble family, a decision that scandalized the contemporary society because he had been already betrothed to another, albeit less affluent, woman. Mikhailovsky-Danilevsky obtained a furlough and took his young wife to Moscow, where the couple celebrated the birth of their first child in 1818.[5] Dreading leaving his wife and son to return to the military responsibilities that he came to dislike, Mikhailovsky-Danilevsky kept postponing his departure and ended up overstaying his leave by five months. The imperial rebuke was fast. Mikhailovsky-Danilevsky, though promoted to a major general, was given command of 3rd Brigade of the 7th Infantry Division in Poltava, a small and dreary town far from the capital and the court. While serving there, he befriended local officers who later participated in the Decembrist Revolt of 1825, which further tainted him and made his position in the army untenable. In May 1826, he requested to be discharged from the army.

Mikhailovsky-Danilevsky spent the next four years arranging the affairs of his growing family[6] and observing the conservative reaction that the new Emperor Nicholas unleashed in the wake of the failed revolution. Official investigations revealed nothing compromising for him so he was ultimately absolved and restored in the army in 1829. Just in time for another war. In 1830, a powerful rebellion began in the Russian-occupied Poland and Mikhailovsky-Danilevsky was appointed Duty Officer to General Ivan Diebitsch who commanded Russian forces sent to crush the revolt. He accompanied the Russian army on campaign and was seriously wounded at the Battle of Grochow on February 25, 1831, forcing him to leave the army and return to St Petersburg.

While recovering from his injury, Mikhailovsky-Danilevsky completed his memoirs that were published to great public acclaim. Emperor Nicolas himself came to appreciate the skill of his quill and, in September 1834, instructed him to write the formal history of the Russian army's campaign in France in 1814. This request effectively turned Mikhailovsky-Danilevsky into the first official Russian historian of the Napoleonic Wars and granted him unparalleled access to the Russian military and state archives; to facilitate his research, Emperor Nicholas promoted Mikhailovsky-Danilevsky to lieutenant general and appointed him as the Senator and member of the Military Censorship Committee, effectively giving him the seniority and clout needed to circumvent any administrative morass that he might have encountered while seeking documents needed for research.

Mikhailovsky-Danilevsky took full advantage of his new position and authority, producing a steady stream of histories of the Napoleonic Wars. Demonstrating incredible work-ethic, efficiency, and commitment, he completed a two-volume history of the 1814 Campaign in 1836, a four-volume account of the Russian Campaign of 1812

5 Anna Chemodanova passed away in July 1832, at the tender age of thirty one, due to the complications of giving birth to her sixth child.

6 The family welcomed Ivan in 1818, Lidia in 1821, Leonid in 1823, Antonina in 1829, Maria in 1830 and Anna in 1832.

in 1839, and that of the 1813 Campaign, in two volumes, in 1840. Over the next three years he produced multivolume histories of Russia's wars against Sweden and the Ottoman Empire before turning to the earlier Napoleonic campaigns and writing the first in-depth Russian study of Emperor Alexander's first and second wars against Napoleon; the 1805 campaign study was published in 1844 while the history of the Polish campaign of 1806-1807 appeared two years later. Hardly taking any respite, the historian then plunged himself into writing and editing the six-volume study of Emperor Alexander and his companions, and researching the history of the 1809 Campaign when Russia and France fought together against the Austrian Empire. Yet this proved to be the historian's last endeavor – Mikhailovsky-Danilevsky was adding last touches to this study when an outbreak of cholera epidemic claimed his life on September 9/21, 1848.[7]

These publications brought Mikhailovsky-Danilevsky fame and recognition[8] but also elicited much discussion in the Russian society. Contemporaries were well aware of the tight censorship that surrounded the publication of these official histories as well as of the fact that Mikhailovsky-Danilevsky was required to present draft manuscripts of his works to Emperor Nicolas who personally edited and revised them. Thus, many Russian participants of the Napoleonic Wars – General Ivan Paskevich, Count Alexander Chernyshev and Prince Peter Volkonskii, to name just a few[9] – lamented the fact that Mikhailovsky-Danilevsky steered clear of criticizing Russian commanders, frequently suppressed facts that were damaging to the Russian cause, and reserved a decisive role in these wars to the monarch, with the army commanders (most notably Kutuzov) portrayed as simple instruments of the august will; the events of the Decembrist Revolt also weighed heavily on the historian's mind, forcing him to shift the focus away from implicated individuals and towards those who had proved their loyalty to the 'crown and sceptre.' Still, many praised the historian's ability to craft an accessible narrative that was based on a wide range of documents and combined description of military operations and battles with eyewitness testimonies that Mikhailovsky-Danilevsky had studiously gathered by personally interviewing participants; one of indisputable merits of Mikhailovsky-Danilevsky's work was his attempt to preserve diverse historical voices for the subsequent generations of scholars to confer with. Despite the obvious

7 Mikhailovsky-Danilevsky was buried at the Tikhvin Cemetery at the Saint Alexander of Neva Monastery near St Petersburg. His gravesite, however, was destroyed in later years.

8 In 1834 he received from the emperor a diamond-encrusted snuffbox for the book on 1812 Campaign. He was also awarded the Orders of St Vladimir (2nd class, 1836), of St George (4th class, 1836), of the White Eagle (1838), of the Red Eagle of Prussia (1st class, 1839) and of Alexander of Neva (1843). In 1839, Mikhailovsky-Danilevsky became member of the Emperor's Council of War and, four years later, was appointed to the Imperial Academy of Science.

9 In the appendix to this epic novel, Leo Tolstoy commented on the challenges of writing historical fiction and bemoaned that 'in the historians of the epoch that interested me I encountered a particular inclination to high-flown speech, in which falsehood and distortion often touch not only the events, but also the understanding of the meaning of an event. Often, in studying the two main historical productions of that epoch, Thiers and Mikhailovsky-Danilevsky, I would become perplexed at how these books could be printed and read.'

limitations of official histories, his publications formed the very foundation upon which the Russian historiography of the Napoleonic Wars was built and remain a crucial source for anyone seeking to understand the Russian involvement in the struggle against the Napoleonic Wars. One can only hope that alongside this new translation of Mikhailovsky-Danilevsky's campaign history, the reader will be soon able to enjoy the historian's less-known private journals and memoirs that contain a treasure-trove of personal insights and experiences of the Napoleonic era.

Alexander Mikaberidze
Shreveport, Louisiana

Translator's Introduction

During my professional career as an intelligence analyst, the vast majority of the Human Intelligence reports that I read or, indeed, produced, bore the caveat 'the source of this report may be seeking to influence rather than to inform.' I have always found this to be an extremely useful reminder when reading histories; what has motivated the author to write what they have written? How much have the author's conclusions been influenced by their own subconscious bias? What external editorial factors have played a role in the presentation of this work? More on this later...

I chose to translate Alexander Mikhailovsky-Danilevsky's history of the war of 1805 after retiring from a working lifetime of studying (among other things) the contemporary Russian military machine. When I began my intelligence training in 1985, towards the end of the Cold War, my knowledge of this subject was extremely limited, but in learning the Russian language, my colleagues and I were exposed for the first time to a rich and varied story. Our self-study periods included reading original Russian publications, such as *Voenny Vestnik*, or *Krasnaya Zvezda*, obtained for us by the British Defence Attaché's office in Moscow, who had paid subscriptions! We had all heard of Mikhail Kutuzov from the BBC's 1970s serialisation of Tolstoy's *War and Peace*, but were now exposed to Russian heroes from the Napoleonic period we had never heard of before; Alexander Suvorov and Prince Bagration in particular. I was astonished to learn that the British Army had fought alongside the Russians in North Holland in 1799, and now I was firmly down that rabbit hole of wanting to find out more, but upon scanning the bibliographies and sources of English language works covering campaigns in which Russia was directly involved, it was somewhat irritating to discover that so few used any original Russian sources - many relied on memoirs by French, German and British officers in Russian service, others covered the subject only from the British, French, Prussian or Austrian point of view. A welcome few used German translations of the works of Mikhailovsky-Danilevsky, Milyutin and Bogdanovich. After the collapse of the Soviet Union and easier access for western historians, thankfully, more historians published works in English, but the standard works of these nineteenth-century Russian authors remained unavailable in English, until now.

So who was Mikhailovsky-Danilevsky, how accurate and reliable is his history and how much of it is information (history) or influence (propaganda)?

Bogdanovich describes his fellow military historians as 'priests of Truth,' and Mikhailovsky-Danilevsky claims a similar dedication to the truth in this work, however, there are points that need to be born in mind regarding his accuracy, precision and reliability. The work was commissioned by the Tsar and was published on condition that the Tsar had editorial control, that he could, and did, censor the manuscript. Criticism of strategic decision making or of Alexander I's behaviour is, thus, almost entirely absent. Indeed, double standards are much in evidence when Napoleon is criticised for violating sovereign and neutral territories, but conveniently overlooks the fact that Russia was siding with the aggressor following Austria's invasion of Bavaria. Many of the reverses and failures in this campaign are blamed almost entirely on Austrian incompetence, which is clearly unjust, and incidents that could have been more thoroughly assessed are glossed over; such as the factors contributing to the startling collapse of Kolowrat's and Miloradovich's Fourth Column at Austerlitz. The court-martial and scapegoating of General Przhibyshevsky following the destruction of his Third Column at Austerlitz also receives no criticism (although this is very mild when compared with Fortescue's biting character assassinations in his History of the British Army). There is also no criticism of Alexander I's continued adherence to Tsar Paul's outdated tactical doctrine, based upon a misinterpretation of Frederick the Great's own, and God forbid that any mention be made of Alexander's involvement in the botched coup that resulted in his father's death and his own accession to the throne! There is a theme in all of Mikhailovsky-Danilevsky's histories, of Alexander I being elevated into a crusading, almost saintly being in pursuit of his foreign policy objectives, and 1805 is no exception. How much of this was down to Nicholas I's direct intervention and how much was self-censorship is difficult to discern. In an ideal world, I would have preferred to have translated Mikhailovsky-Danilevsky's uncensored manuscript (if it were available).

Notwithstanding the assistance of his researchers, Mikhailovsky-Danilevsky's histories are, in general, quite sparse. Bogdanovich was commissioned to re-write the official histories of 1812-13 and to add 1814, and was critical of Mikhailovsky-Danilevsky for omitting so many archival sources that Bogdanovich thought were essential to understanding these conflicts. Mikhailovsky-Danilevsky was also less than meticulous in spotting and correcting errors of fact, for instance in the 1805 work, in the order of battle for Austerlitz, he assigns the 5th Jäger Regiment to General Dokhturov's First Column, when they were in fact part of General Bagration's force on the opposite side of the battlefield. He also had a tendency to repeat errors made by other historians when borrowing from their works; in his history of the war in Finland, when writing about the British General Sir John Moore, he describes his death as occurring at the battle of Ferrol, rather than the battle of Corunna (as every British schoolboy of a certain age knows). Colonel Milyutin took over the drafting of the history of the 1799 campaigns upon Mikhailovsky-Danilevsky's death in 1848 and the level of detail, in comparison, is stunning, Milyutin producing an eight-part masterpiece to cover a single year of campaigning, which has an extensive annex on the sources used, including a candid assessment of their relative value - if only all military histories of this period were so painstaking!

Mikhailovsky-Danilevsky was essentially writing for the approval of the Tsar; he was not driven by the need to score commercial success through book sales, and therefore avoided the pitfall of being put under editorial pressure to sensationalise or draw controversial conclusions in order to produce a page-turner. Having not been present in 1805, he was also not seeking to justify his own actions or embellish his own feats – a common problem with personal memoirs. He was also going to be peer-reviewed in the sense that many of the participants were still alive and could take him to task over errors and omissions.

In conclusion, this history of the war of 1805 is flawed (as is, no doubt, my translation of it), but nonetheless valuable for the detail it provides that is unavailable elsewhere. In no particular order; the story of Kutuzov's masterful retreat from Braunau to Olmütz is a gripping read and shows how well the Russians could fight in spite of self-imposed disadvantages and Austrian obstacles; the peripheral campaigns are also covered; the Anglo-Russian invasion of Hanover, and a similar Anglo-Russian expedition to Naples.

In this translation, anything that I have added is shown in squared brackets, including dates using the Gregorian calendar, full names of personalities (wherever I could positively identify them), modern place names etcetera. Any errors in these additions are entirely my own.

Peter G.A. Phillips
2022

Author's Preface

Fulfilling the sacred will of the Monarch, I have composed, and now present to my compatriots, my history of the first war between Emperor Alexander and Napoleon, in 1805. Forty years have passed since Alexander first tested his strength against Napoleon, and false traditions about this first struggle of His pass from one generation to another in a distorted and perverse form. Everyone knows about the events, but who knows what actually happened? Russians until now have written almost nothing about this era, which is no less memorable than any other in our History. Perhaps avoiding sad memories of a time of humiliation for Germany, the Germans also published very few descriptions of the war of 1805, and the French exaggerate the already great successes at that time for Napoleon in their writings. Thus, Europe did not have a description where the bloody beginning of the ten-year-long contest between Emperor Alexander and Napoleon was reliably depicted.

The History I am presenting now makes up for this important shortcoming. It is based on the most rigorous truth – and how else could it be in the matter entrusted to me by the command of the Monarch – on original military and diplomatic documents, and the testimonies of the few surviving witnesses and participants from the war of 1805. The description is divided into three parts. The first sets out the reasons for mobilisation, the movement of armies to the theatre of war, the political actions of Emperor Alexander, and the destruction of the Austrian army near Ulm, presented briefly, as the Austrian Government has not yet [1844] published official information about it. The second period is a brighter page in the annals of the Russian military: the four hundred *verst* [420 km or 267 miles] withdrawal by Kutuzov [Mikhail Illarionovich Golenishchev-Kutuzov] from the Bavarian border to Moravia, and his first encounters with Napoleon, for whom fate later prepared enormous encounters with Kutuzov at Borodino, Maloyaroslavets and Krasny. The third period includes the offensive movements of the Allies, the Battle of Austerlitz [Slavkov u Brna] and its consequences. In order to connect and expand on events, the actions of the Austrians in Italy and Tyrol are briefly described, and the movements of the detached corps in Hanover and Italy are presented. Thus, the war of 1805 appears in full, the first desire of Emperor Alexander to complete the work entrusted to Him by Providence – to be the saviour of a Europe enslaved by Napoleon. The world is full of loud speculation about the fortunate wars of Emperor Alexander – let them hear from the most unbiased Russian news of that time, when, by coincidence, hitherto kept secret, and for the first time now announced by us, the fortunate change in Alexander's armed forces.

1

Causes of the War

The situation in Europe on the accession of Emperor Alexander. – The impossibility of maintaining peace. – The French war with Britain. – Napoleon's violations. – The death of the *Duc d'Enghien*. – The efforts of Emperor Alexander to form an alliance against Napoleon. The treaty between Russia and Britain. – Emperor Alexander's discussions with Austria. – Emperor Alexander's concept of operations. – The resumption and termination of negotiations with Napoleon. – Austrian mobilisation. – The new concept of operations. – The offer of armed mediation.

In the first year of the nineteenth century, the year of Emperor Alexander's accession to the Throne, the wars generated by the French Revolution had subsided. Russia was at peace with all the European Powers, except Britain, which had recently been broken during the reign of Emperor Paul. Emperor Alexander repaired this breach, and at the same time continued friendly relations with Napoleon, the first Consul of the French Republic at that time, begun under Emperor Paul, but not yet ratified by formal treaty. In September 1801, an agreement was signed restoring the friendship between Russia and France which had been interrupted since 1792.

The following year, 1802, passed quietly. But there was no calm, and it could not last, being incompatible with the nature of the sovereign of France at the time. He already ranked among the leading commanders of all time, had tamed the revolution, issued wise decrees, reconciled France with Europe. But Napoleon had a few laurels reaped by him in Italy and Egypt, a few honours as a legislator. He was consumed with a passion for stirring up trouble, a thirst to drink the cup of military glory to the dregs, and insatiable lust for power. And wherever turned his gaze, beyond the Rhine, the Alps, the Pyrenees, everywhere he appeared to pursue his plans, everywhere he saw the neighbours of France humbled by his armed forces. Only one thing had escaped Napoleon's eagle eye, or, more correctly, only one thing that Providence prevented him from knowing – the greatness of the soul of the 24-year-old Monarch with whom God blessed our Fatherland at that time. Napoleon did not see that he would meet an adversary in the young Russian Monarch, convinced that Heaven would give the Russian Autocrat tremendous strength, as much to protect her, as much to maintain common peace in Europe and the security of other kingdoms. Thus, at the onset of the nineteenth century there were: in the West, Napoleon, obsessed with intentions of hegemony, in the North, Alexander, as a protective force. Under these conditions, a clash between Napoleon and Alexander was inevitable; a stubborn struggle between them would be kindled, as the matter was not about smoothing the frontiers, not about petty settlements, but a solution of the following question: should the European Powers submit to a new conquering power, or continue their existence based on the sanctity of legitimate Rule and the inviolability of territories approved by treaty? This was the key to the wars between Alexander and Napoleon, of which the first, in 1805, we present this description. Without explaining the above circumstances, it is impossible to understand the reasons for the fierce, ten-year struggle between Alexander and Napoleon, which took place first in 1805, in the depths of Germany, the following year between the Vistula and the Neman, in 1812 in Russia, in 1813 in the lands from the Neman to the Rhine, and finally, in 1814 in the heart of France, where Alexander approved the principles for which he stood to arms for ten years, began to establish the general peace of Europe, which constituted the permanent aim of His foreign policy.

No sooner had 1802 ended, than war broke out between France and Britain again, as early as May 1803. The efforts of Emperor Alexander to prevent a breach were in vain. In preparing to deliver a decisive blow to Britain by landing on its shores, Napoleon wished to secure himself against the Powers of continental Europe, and he chose the trusted instrument of intending to sow discord amongst them. He managed to arouse mutual distrust to such an extent that each European State began to follow its private agenda, and all agreed on only one thing: the impossibility of relying upon each other. By keeping the governments inactive, taking advantage of their disagreements, Napoleon strengthened his influence on France's neighbours, forced Switzerland to recognise him as Mediator of its Union, contrary to treaties and under various pretexts, sent troops to Italy and the Netherlands and, finally, occupied Hanover, whose independence was guaranteed by treaty between Russia and France. Violation of treaty agreements prompted our Government to insist on compliance, but in moderate terms. Receiving evasive responses from Napoleon, Emperor Alexander urged Prussia to liberate Hanover, but they would not agree to accept the Sovereign's challenge. To the Emperor's question to the Viennese Court, asking what they intend to do about the apparent destruction of the political balance in Europe, Austria responded with their need for peace, having disrupted finances, and not having recovered from unsuccessful campaigns. In a word, Prussia and Austria avoided war, and did not heed Alexander, pointing out to them the danger of giving one power advantages harmful to the others. So ended 1803.

At the beginning of next year, Napoleon completed an act unworthy of the nineteenth century that destroyed all the rights of a State: a detachment of French troops abducted the Duc d'Enghien [Louis Antoine de Bourbon] from the territory of Baden to France for his execution. Europe shuddered, but the fear inspired by Napoleon was already so great that not a single State raised its voice, except Russia and Sweden. Considering it inconsistent with his dignity to be silent when the rights of the people are violated and that silence against such lawless acts will encourage further violations of the rights of the state, Emperor Alexander ordered the filing of protests against the assassination of the Duc d'Enghien and a period of mourning for him. Napoleon's objections to our Court were impertinent, and served as a catalyst, in the first half of 1804, for the withdrawal of embassies, the Russian from Paris and the French from St Petersburg; diplomatic relations between our Government and Napoleon had ceased, while he placed an imperial crown upon his head.

Recognising the old great necessity to unite the Powers, and not content with the actions of His embassies, Emperor Alexander entered into personal correspondence with the Monarchs. He wrote to Kaiser Franz; 'The fear that it has inspired has strengthened the French Government more than its actual power. It is trying to benefit from the fact that the major Powers each follow their own particular policies. The sad events of Ettenheim sufficiently prove what we should have realised a long time ago, that Bonaparte is solely guided in his actions by an unquenchable thirst for power and the desire for world domination.'[1] Sharing the mindset of the Russian Tsar, Kaiser Franz replied: 'In the current state of affairs, I regard the combination of our strengths, our sincere unity as the only hope for securing the future of Europe.'[2] He proposed concluding a defensive treaty of alliance; this treaty was signed on 13 [25] October, 1804, with the obligation for Russia to send 115,000 men to assist Austria should she come under attack. In the same year, as a result of correspondence between Emperor Alexander and the King of Prussia [Friedrich Wilhem III], already personal friends from the time they met in Memel [Klaipėda] in 1802, a treaty was concluded by which Russia and Prussia were obliged to ensure the common peace of northern Germany, and prevent Napoleon from making appropriations there. The kings of Sweden [Gustav IV Adolf] and Naples [Ferdinand IV] expressed their readiness to act in unison with Emperor Alexander against Napoleon. Thus, by the end of 1804, after two years of effort, Emperor Alexander finally managed to induce Austria and Prussia to take defensive measures, and found advocates for his opinions in the Kings of Sweden and Naples.

He did not stop there. Convinced that Napoleon could only be stopped by force, He concluded a treaty with Britain in March 1805, aimed at forcing Napoleon to withdraw troops from Hanover and Italy, recognize the independence of the Netherlands and Switzerland, reinstate the King of Sardinia-Piedmont [Victor Emmanuel I], in a word, destroy French dominion established by her in various lands. To enforce the treaty, Russia pledged to mobilise 180,000 men, and Britain to operate ashore and to pay subsidies to the States which would be acting for the common cause. Moreover, they trusted: on a successful conclusion to the war, not to interfere in the internal affairs of France, leaving them to elect a government as they wish, and not to appropriate territory by conquest, rather to distribute them after the war, at a general congress. We intend to cite this article of the treaty as evidence that Emperor Alexander thought in the same way preparing for his first war with Napoleon as he did in the final struggle with him in 1814, for the principles beginning here were the very ones by which he was guided after his triumph over

1 *Le gouvernement françois, plus fort encore de la crainte qu'il s su inspirer que de ses propres moyens, est soigneux de mettre à son profit l'isolement dans lequel les grandes puissances continuent à rester, et l'évènement affligeant d'Ettenheim prouve suffisamment si l'on ne devoit pas être persuadé depuis longtems, que Bonaparte n'a pour guide dans sa conduite qu'une soif insatiable de pouvoir et le désir de la domination universelle.*

2 *Dans l'état actuel des choses, je considère notre union, notre concert intime comme l'unique espoir qui reste à la sûreté future de l'Europe.*

Napoleon at the signing of the peace in Paris; opposed to conquest and unbiased. But we find a remarkable difference in the fact that in 1805, Alexander would leave Napoleon to rule in France, merely setting boundaries to his plunder. He did not think so when ten years of experience convinced Him of the impossibility of peace while Napoleon remained on the Throne. So, with the disinterestedness of victory hardened by complete success, Alexander laid the first condition – the demise of Napoleon.

Informing Austria of our treaty with Britain, Emperor Alexander invited them to conclude an alliance against Napoleon, who at that time, as if in support of our arguments regarding his greed for acquisitions, annexed the Kingdom of Italy to France. Aware of the justice of Emperor Alexander's demands, Austria spoke, however, of the great difficulties of fighting Napoleon, the need to profoundly ponder the risks of war, and the impossibility of triumphing over Napoleon without the assistance of Prussia[3], meanwhile, Prussia did not want to take up arms under any circumstances. Setting only the defence of northern Germany as its aim, they decided to remain at peace with Napoleon, whatever happened in the world, confident that all the benefits of war would fall to Napoleon[4]. It was all the more difficult for Emperor Alexander to persuade Prussia to join the alliance, because a cooling of the relationship between Him and the King of Prussia took place, when, on the occasion of a dispute with Sweden, the King of Prussia sent his troops into Swedish Pomerania. Firm in protecting the rights of everyone, the Emperor ordered that the Berlin Court be informed that under the terms of the Gatchina Treaty, He would go to the aid of Sweden should they request it.[5] Having exhausted meek and friendly persuasion, Emperor Alexander wrote to his ambassador in Vienna, Count Razumovsky [Andrey Kirillovich Razumovsky]:

> Does Austria really want to calmly wait for Bonaparte to appear in the centre of her Realm and sign a humiliating peace, without preparing for war, without taking security measures? Is the fear instilled in her by an ambitious man stronger than the hope of My assistance? Announce to the Viennese Court that instead of the 115,000 troops promised by Me, I will give them 180,000. The honour of My State does not allow Me to view the silence of My neighbours with indifference, through which they contribute to the enslavement of lands adjacent to France. It appears that in starting a war, the benefits of which are turning in favour of My allies rather than Me, I have acquired the right to be their proxy. Without seeing any evidence of this, I decided to increase the number of My supporting troops voluntarily and without external pressure. But in preparation for the defence of

3 Count Razumovsky's report from Vienna, dated 1 [13] May.

4 Alopaeus' report from Berlin, dated 1 [13] July.

5 *Déclarez au ministère Prussien, que Mon exactitude à remplir Mes engagemens est telle, que Je ne pois sous aucun prétexte me refuser à satisfaire à la première requisition que me fera le Roi de Suède de marcher à son secours.* Rescript to Adjutant-General Baron Wintzingerode in Berlin.

oppressed States, having set out soon to decide the fate of Europe, I have issued My assumptions and statements in the plan attached herewith.

This plan, which outlines the foundation of the campaign of 1805, was as follows:

Austria will provide 250,000 men and Russia 180,000, deployed as follows:

A. To protect Austria's hereditary lands, two armies will march from Russia:	
1st from Radsywyliw [Radziwiłłów] to Galicia	50,000 men.
2nd from Brest to Bohemia	50,000 men.
B. 3rd will deploy along the Prussian border	40,000 men.
C. Deploying by sea:	
To Stralsund	16,000 men.
From Corfu to Naples	25,000 men.
Russian Total:	181,000 men.

Upon the arrival of 50,000 in the Austrian hereditary lands, 50,000 in Bohemia, 16,000 in Swedish Pomerania and 40,000 on the Prussian border, Emperor Alexander wanted, together with Austria, to demand assistance from the Berlin Court and free passage to northern Germany through Prussian territory for the 40,000 waiting on the border. Emperor Alexander did not doubt the success of the common Russian and Austrian demands on Berlin and the accession of Prussia to us, but then, following her example, that of Denmark, Saxony, Hesse-Kassel, Mecklenburg and Brunswick [Braunschweig], after which they believed they would have in the theatre of war:

Russians	180,000
Austrians	150,000
Prussians	100,000
Swedes	16,000
Danes	16,000
Various German States	35,000
Neapolitans	20,000
British (from Malta)	5,000
Total:	622,000

In the event of our success, we also hoped for the participation of Bavaria, Württemberg, Baden and the King of Sardinia. Emperor Alexander planned to deploy all these forces into five fronts, as follows, starting from the left wing:

1. 25,000 Russians sailing from Corfu to Naples, joining 20,000 Neapolitans and 5,000 Austrians, driving the French out of southern Italy and turning their attention on Lombardy.

2. The main Austrian force waging an offensive war in northern Italy and Tyrol.
3. 100,000 Russians, together with troops from Austria, Bavaria, Baden and Württemberg, begin to campaign in Swabia, and then go beyond the Rhine.
4. 100,000 Prussians besiege Mainz, and operate along the Middle Rhine.
5. Two armies will be formed in the north:

First Army

Russians (from Stralsund)	16,000
Swedes	16,000
Danes	16,000
Mecklenburg	3,000
Total:	51,000

Second Army

Russians (advancing across Prussia)	40,000
Saxons, Hesse-Kassel, Brunswick	32,000
Total:	72,000

Both northern armies were to converge on the Netherlands. Cutting off their communications with France, they were not to march on France, but were to form new Dutch and Hanoverian forces. Thus, acting in various theatres of war, and moreover, reinforced by amphibious operations promised by Britain, they hoped to force Napoleon to a just peace in two campaigns.[6]

Adjutant-General Wintzingerode [Ferdinand Karl Friedrich Wintzingerode] was sent to Vienna with this plan in early [mid] May 1805. The Viennese Court reiterated to him their awareness of the need for convergence between Austria and Russia as the only way to put an end to the scourge of Europe, but they did not give decisive consent to their accession to the alliance and responded with a lack of preparedness for war, not even declaring their intentions. Assuming that Austria would not dare to fight in isolation without Russian troops, and since they were concerned about being subjected to rapid attacks by Napoleon, Emperor Alexander proposed that his army enter their territories under the pretext that the Russians had crossed the Austrian border by force.[7]

Meanwhile, Napoleon had learned about the Russian alliance with Britain and our negotiations in Vienna and Berlin. He proposed peace with Britain, which included a request for Emperor Alexander to be a mediator. Agreeing to this proposal, for the reason that, with a clear reluctance for war from Austria and Prussia, negotiations remained the only way to achieve peace, the Emperor sent Privy Councillor Novosiltsov [Nikolai Nikolaevich Novosiltsov] to Paris. But this was the final attempt for peace. On 15 [27] June, just as Novosiltsov arrived in Berlin he learned that Napoleon, contrary to the Treaty of Lunéville, had annexed the Republic of Genoa to France. With this obvious violation, he clearly contradicted his expressed desire to

6 Instructions for Count Razumovsky in Vienna, dated 24 April [6 May].
7 Instructions for Count Razumovsky, dated 2 [14] July.

make peace, because without even waiting for the start of negotiations, he continued to encroach on the independence of his neighbours. Emperor Alexander ordered Novosiltsov to return to St Petersburg from Berlin, and decided not to enter into relations with Napoleon any more: it was necessary to resolve this dispute by force.[8]

The unlawful occupation of Genoa had even exhausted the limits of patience of cautious Kaiser Franz. He ordered the negotiation of an alliance with Russia and Britain, began large scale mobilisation, and appointed meetings to agree on the operational plan sent to Adjutant-General Wintzingerode from St Petersburg, under the direction of Archduke Charles [Karl Ludwig Johann Joseph Lorenz von Österreich, Herzog von Teschen], Generals Prince Schwarzenberg [Karl Philipp Schwarzenberg] and Mack [Karl Mack], and Privy Councillor Baron Kulmbach. They concluded:

1. In accordance with Emperor Alexander's suggestion, to assemble a 50,000 man Russian Corps at Radsywyliw and, according to Austrian requests, march to join with their forces.
2. The other 50,000 promised to help Austria, and the 40,000 man corps, which were intended to be set up on the Prussian border, were to demand free passage from Prussia through this domain, threatening, upon refusal, to enter its borders by force.
3. Send a corps from Kronstadt to Stralsund, and direct it initially to threaten Prussia from the north, since the Viennese Court shared the opinion of Emperor Alexander concerning the possibility of fear pushing the Berlin Court to mobilise themselves against Napoleon.
4. Of the 90,000 Russians who were allocated to entering Prussia, 50,000 would be sent through Silesia to Bohemia, and 40,000 would join the 16,000 in Stralsund. There would be 16,000 Swedes added to these 56,000 Russian troops.

Austria hoped that the King of Prussia would probably send at least 60,000 to them, following which the army in the north would increase to 132,000, at the same time that 100,000 Russians would join 220,000 Austrians, and 25,000 Russians would concentrate in Naples, along with 5,000 British and 15,000 Neapolitans.

Thus, according to the calculations of the Viennese Court, the following would be available:

1st Russians, Swedes and Prussians in northern Germany	132,000
2nd Russians and Austrians in southern Germany and Italy	320,000
3rd Russians, British and Neapolitans in Naples	45,000
Total:	497,000

To these armed forces, the Viennese Court soon decided to add 100,000 Austrians and the troops of various German rulers. On 4 [16] July, these conditions of the

8 *Nous ne voulons plus traiter avec un homme, qui tout en protestant de son désir de la paix, continue ses envahissemens.* Supreme instructions for Novosiltsov.

operational plan, called the 'Military Convention,' were signed. The Plenipotentiaries of the Viennese Court expressed their desire to subordinate the Commander-in-Chief of the Russian troops, when acting jointly with the Austrians, to the Austrian General to whom the Kaiser Franz entrusted his army. Having no authority on this subject, Wintzingerode did not agree to the proposal, so they agreed: our Commander-in-Chief would be subordinate to the Austrians only when the army is led by Kaiser Franz, or one of the Archdukes.

Sending the Convention to St Petersburg, for the approval of the Sovereign, Kaiser Franz expressed to His Majesty the desire not to start the war immediately, but first to offer Napoleon his mediation in the reconciliation with Britain and Russia, at the same time, however, that the Russian and Austrian troops would be moving towards the borders of France. The Viennese Court prompted this act, in their desire to prove, especially to their subjects, that even without resorting to force, they had tried to exhaust all means of reconciliation, and by the need to gain time for the completion of their mobilisation and the unification of Russian troops with their army. Emperor Alexander agreed to the Military Convention sent to him from Vienna, and to the proposals of the Viennese Court, which aimed 'to combine the strength of force with peace talks so that during negotiations, or after curtailing them, it would be possible to protect Austria and neighbouring areas from any attack by France.' Moreover, Emperor Alexander announced that 'in negotiations He will display a most friendly disposition, and will pull His army back only when peace is firmly established.[9]

9 Supreme instructions to Count Razumovsky in Vienna.

2

Mobilisation

The state of the armed forces of Russia. – The formation of the operational army. – Moreau's invitation into Russian service. – The state of the armed forces of Austria. – Deployment of the Austrian army. – Their march into Bavaria. – Emperor Alexander's orders to the troops deploying abroad. – The state of the armed forces of France. Napoleon's refusal of armed mediation.

Bringing this description to the time when Emperor Alexander agreed with the Austrian Court to engage in armed mediation, and, consequently, to order his troops go abroad, we will present the calculations and the initial movements of the armies of the three main powers, Russia, Austria and France. By 1 [13] January, 1805, the land forces of Russia comprised:

Field Force

3 regiments and 1 battalion of Guards Infantry	6,882
13 regiments of Grenadiers	24,016
77 regiments of Musketeers	144,055
20 regiments of Jägers	26,975
2 battalions of Greeks	690
4 regiments and 1 *Sotnia* [about 100 men] of Guards Cavalry	3,051
6 regiments of Cuirassiers	4,941
26 regiments of Dragoons	22,038
1 regiment of Ulans (His Highness the Tsarevich's)	1,634
9 regiments of Hussars	14,042
Chuguev Cossacks	1,398
Tatar Horse	665
Lithuania Horse	698
Poland Horse	1,137
1 battalion of Guards Artillery	1,036
9 regiments of Foot Artillery and 2 battalions of Horse Artillery	19,362
1 regiment of Pontoniers	445
2 regiments of Pioneers	2,582
Engineers	385
Field Force Total:	276,032

Garrison Troops

19 regiments and 57 battalions	67,967
65 invalid companies and 51 invalid platoons	10,825
11 artillery companies and 62 artillery platoons	8,399
Garrison Total:	87,200

Cossack forces	110,215
Recruits in training	26,097
Non-combatants	50,952
Grand Total:	550,496

The Russian forces were not increased in the first six months of 1805, but in August, when war was anticipated, new regiments were ordered to be formed: the Zhitomir and Livland Dragoons; Mogilev, Kostroma, Kaluga, Vilna, Penza, Estland and Odessa Musketeers; 21st and 22nd Jägers, and two artillery regiments. Then orders were issued to procure a supply of muskets and rifles in Tula and Systerbäck [Sestroretsk] for the complete re-equipping of the ground forces, with the exception of the garrisons.

For the implementation of the armed mediation, and in accordance with the Military Convention concluded in Vienna on 4 [16] July, Emperor Alexander ordered:

1. To generate an army of 90,000 men from the troops located on the western border, under the command of Mikhelson [Ivan Ivanovich Mikhelson], divided into corps under Bennigsen [Leonty Leontyevich Bennigsen], of 40,000, Count Buxhoeveden [Fëdor Fëdorovich Buxhoeveden] and Essen [Ivan Nikolaevich Essen] of 50,000 men; including the guard.
2. Count Tolstoy [Pëtr Alexandrovich Tolstoy] was to assemble a corps in St Petersburg and Reval [Tallinn] for departure to Stralsund.
3. Anrep [Roman Karlovich Anrep], commander of the troops in Corfu was to be ready to sail to Naples.
4. The 50,000 man army concentrated in advance at Radsywyliw, to deploy abroad on the request of Kaiser Franz. Kutuzov – later Prince of Smolensk – was appointed Commander-in-Chief of the army, and so he was fated to be the first of the Russian generals to engage Napoleon.

During these preparations, at the command of the Emperor, negotiations were held in Stockholm and Naples about the assumptions for the campaign. He ordered His ambassadors in Copenhagen, Tsaregrad [Constantinople], Madrid and Lisbon to persuade Denmark, the [Ottoman] Porte, Spain and Portugal to join the alliance. Raising up all over Europe, Emperor Alexander in this great operation undertaken by Him, wished to take the advice of that commander in whom general opinion recognized talents equal to Napoleon's. We are referring to Moreau [Jean-Victor-Marie Moreau]. Exiled from France, he was living in America. The Tsar sent the

Chamberlain Count Pahlen [Friedrich Alexander Pahlen] to him, with an invitation to join the Russian service as a full General, or come to our army as a private individual, and it was ordered to assure him that no matter what turn events might take, he and his family would find a safe haven in Russia. Count Pahlen went to America, but returned from his journey on receiving news of the Battle of Austerlitz and the cessation of hostilities. In summoning Moreau to Russia, Emperor Alexander was doing the same as Peter the Great when he invited Marlborough [John Churchill, 1 Duke of Marlborough] to join him before starting the campaign in Russia against Charles XII.

Austria mobilised as vigorously as they had previously shown sloth. Their land forces consisted of the following:

Infantry

63 Line regiments	193,537
Grenadiers	14,364
Jägers	2,140
17 Grenzer regiments	53,000
Tyrolean forces	20,000
Garrisons	7,000
Invalids	1,780
Infantry Total:	291,821

Cavalry

8 Cuirassier, 6 Dragoon, 6 Light, 9 Hussar, 3 Ulan, 3 Staff-Dragoon regiments	50,800
Artillery	18,534
Field Engineers, Drivers, reserves	12,000
German and Hungarian Guards	280
Grand Total:	373,435

After years of unsuccessful wars with the French, followed by four years of peace, the Austrian army, for all their reforming measures, could not quickly be put on a proper military footing. As the regiments were formed for the campaign, they went to three assembly places: the river Traun near the Bavarian border, to Italy and Tyrol. Every day, the *Hofkriegsrat* gathered in Vienna, where Archdukes Charles, John [Johann Baptist Joseph Fabian Sebastian von Österreich] and Ferdinand [Ferdinand Karl Joseph von Österreich-Este], and the Quartermasters-General Mack, Meyer and Saxe, appointed to chair the armies, met. They eagerly awaited Emperor Alexander's decision on the 4 [16] July Convention and armed mediation, and when they received His consent to the Convention in Vienna and to the intention of the Austrians to move troops to the borders of France, Kaiser Franz immediately sent a proposal for mediation to Napoleon, and ordered: Firstly, send the request to Kutuzov in Radsywyliw to move to the Bavarian border. Secondly, advance the 80,000 man army concentrated along the banks of the Traun, into

Bavaria, and pause at Ulm to await Kutuzov. This army was assigned to the 24-year-old Archduke Ferdinand,[1] and appointed Mack to him as Quartermaster-General or, more accurately, as his Chief-of-Operations, equipped with *carte blanche* by Kaiser Franz, so that he could act at his discretion, not constrained by anyone. With such trust in Mack, it might have been easier to entrust him alone with supreme command, but they didn't do this, avoiding a difference of opinion, because after joining the Austrians, Kutuzov, on the basis of the Convention of 4 [16] July, could not serve under Mack's command, as Kutuzov was the more senior. Not wanting to entrust the army to Kutuzov, they appointed the Archduke as Commander-in-Chief, so that Mack could conduct deployments and operations, acting in the name of His Highness. Thirdly, Archduke Charles with 80,000 men was to take up positions on the borders of the Kingdom of Italy. Fourth, Archduke John, with 30,000 men located in Tyrol, was to maintain communications between the armies in Germany and Italy, and reinforcing whichever one needs support. Fifth, Prince Schwarzenberg was to go to Munich, to explain the Austrian entry into the territory to the Elector of Bavaria [Maximilian IV Joseph] and to persuade him to join the alliance, which had already been negotiated. Sixth, General Graf Merveldt [Maximilian Friedrich Merveldt] was to rush to Berlin, to explain to the Prussian King the reasons for the Austrian entry into Bavaria, and together with the Russian, Austrian and British envoys, again persuade him to join with us.

The commanders of the Austrian armies went immediately to their posts. On 28 August [9 September], Archduke Ferdinand crossed the Inn, not doubting the accession of the Bavarian troops, relying on the promise made by the Bavarian Elector to the Viennese Court to act in unison with us. But as soon as the Austrians crossed the border, the Elector, having already made a secret alliance with Napoleon, left for Würzburg at night, where his army hastily followed, including 18,000 men. This was the first Allied failure of the campaign. Firmly confident of the support of the Bavarians, they realised that the Elector's corps had turned to reinforce Napoleon. On 5 [17] September, the Austrians settled near Ulm, intending to unite with Kutuzov before Napoleon appeared on the scene. This calculation, approved in advance in Vienna, was based on the fact that Kutuzov, setting off on campaign before Napoleon had received the offer of military mediation, had time to reach Ulm before the outbreak of hostilities. The Austrian calculations for the union with Kutuzov turned out to be as erroneous as their hopes for the support of the Bavarians.

As the Austrians were crossing the Inn, Emperor Alexander ordered:

1. Mikhelson will advance with Count Buxhoeveden's corps from Brest, and stop on the banks of the Pilica, which marks the border between Galicia and Prussia;
2. Essen's corps is to form the reserve for Count Buxhoeveden;
3. Bennigsen is to concentrate his force at Grodno;
4. Count Tolstoy is to be ready to sail to Pomerania;
5. Issue a recruitment decree, four men per 500 souls.

1 Brother of the Duke of Modena, now [1844] Governor General of Galicia.

A Manifesto, published on the occasion of the recruitment, set out for the first time Emperor Alexander's intentions about the army's deployment abroad, as negotiations and concentrations of troops had not been announced until then. The Manifesto stated:

> Among the events so shocking to the peace of Europe, We could not look with indifference at the danger threatening it. The security of Our Empire, its dignity, the sanctity of alliances and the desire, the only and indispensable aim of our constitution, to establish peace in Europe on solid foundations, We have now decided to move some of Our troops abroad and make renewed efforts to achieve this aim.

When the troops were marching, it was prescribed to the regimental Colonels-in-Chief to observe the strictest discipline, they should not allow men to straggle along the road, but to march in ranks and files, in parade order, trying to keep in step as much as possible, maintain proper spacing between platoons, half-platoons and squads, always ready to go forwards; officers must be at their posts, and if they are given permission from their commander to ride, then in this event are not to leave their platoons.

Let us turn to Napoleon. His land forces consisted of the following:

90 regiments of Line Infantry.
27 regiments of Light Infantry.
2 regiments of Carabiniers.
12 regiments of Cuirassiers.
30 regiments of Dragoons.
10 regiments of Hussars.
24 regiments of *Chasseurs à Cheval.*

Artillery

8 regiments of Light Foot Artillery.
6 regiments of Light Horse Artillery.
16 battalions of Heavy Artillery.
15 wagon companies.
2 battalions of Pontoniers.
5 battalions of Sappers.
9 companies of Miners.
28 platoons of Horse and Foot *Gendårmes.*
10 regiments of Veterans.

In total these troops comprised 593,588 men.

Having travelled to Milan for his coronation as King of Italy, the summer of 1805 was spent by Napoleon in camp at Boulogne, busy with the gigantic idea of an amphibious landing in Britain. When the mediation accepted by Emperor Alexander for the reconciliation of Britain with France ended unsuccessfully in

June, and Austria began to place their forces under martial law, Napoleon demanded an explanation from Austria, asking them about the reasons for mobilisation. A correspondence began between the courts of Vienna and Tuileries. Both sides spoke of their love of peace, their desire to strengthen peace in Europe and to avoid bloodshed, meanwhile, they were preparing for war. Napoleon increased his forces in Italy, made up reserve corps, secretly made orders for a swift campaign by the main army from Boulogne onto German soil. In August, having received Austria's offer of armed mediation, Napoleon agreed to mediate if Austria returned their army to a peaceful footing and pulled their troops back from the border to their original garrisons. He said that he couldn't allow a situation in the middle between a state of war and of peace and, knowing about the Russian mobilisation, he had no expectation as long as the Russians were allied with the Austrians. Soon afterwards, Napoleon was informed of the Austrian entry into Bavaria. He ordered the following note to be submitted to the German [Perpetual] Diet of Regensburg:

> The time for explanations has passed: the time has come for action. Emperor Napoleon has one objective: to repel this most unjust attack and restore the independence of the German Union violated by the Austrian crossing of the Inn. He will not lay down his arms until Austria ceases to encroach on the security of Germany.

Considering the Austrian advance into Bavaria to be an act of war, Napoleon severed diplomatic relations with the Viennese Court, and directed his troops towards the middle Rhine and Main by forced marches. Thus, the die for Alexander's first war with Napoleon was cast.

3

Kutuzov's March From Russia to Braunau

The appointment of Kutuzov. – The entry into Austrian territory. – Forced marches. – Kutuzov's stay in Vienna. – Departure for Braunau. – Rumours about the Austrian defeat. – Archduke Ferdinand's letter to Kutuzov.

Having entrusted Kutuzov with the army concentrated at Radsywyliw, Emperor Alexander gave him the following orders: Firstly, to be at the disposal of Kaiser Franz, to go wherever ordered by him, even to Italy, and come under the command of the Archduke appointed to lead the Austrian army. Secondly, to impress upon everyone everywhere that Emperor Alexander does not seek to conquer, or to favour any one Power, but wishes to limit Napoleon's lust for power, restore peace to Europe, based on the specific security and independence of every nation and government. Thirdly, to reassure the French, Italians, and others, with the guarantee that Emperor Alexander will not allow anyone to deprive them of property acquired during the revolution, especially those who bought national estate, and will not force the choice of one Government over another; if France wishes to invite anyone from the house of Bourbon to the throne, then Emperor Alexander promises His support in order to adopt and preserve the rule of law, whichever proposals might be made to Him by the people. Fourth, with the exception of the Crown Princes, with all others including Austrian Generals and those of other nations, observe seniority of rank, extending this rule to the officers. Fifth, if you happen to be in the territory of an Imperial Prince who is not a belligerent in the war with France, then in accordance with earlier agreements with the Austrian Court, or Commander-in-Chief, invite and even coerce such a prince into the war. Sixth, to establish relations with the discontented in France, as when the purpose with which we are waging the war becomes known there, then most of the inhabitants are likely to join us to overthrow the Napoleonic government. Kutuzov was also given authority to conclude treaties and acts with the Princes of the German Empire and other Governments, who will join us to restore general peace and safeguard the future integrity of the sovereignty and independence of each Government on a sound basis.

Ready to advance, Kutuzov was waiting in Radsywyliw for orders from Kaiser Franz. On 9 [21] August, he received orders from Vienna to proceed through Teschen [Cieszyn], Brünn [Brno], Krems and Braunau, to join the Austrians in Bavaria, and to come under the command of Archduke Ferdinand there. On 13 [25] August, Kutuzov set off on the march. There were 46,405 men of all ranks in his army, excluding service support troops. They were divided into six columns: Prince Bagration's [Pëtr Ivanovich Bagration], Essen 2's [Pëtr Kirillovich Essen], Dokhturov's [Dmitry Sergeevich Dokhturov], Shepelev's [Vasiliy Fëdorovich Shepelev], Baron Maltitz's [Leonty Fëdorovich Maltitz] and Baron Rosen's [Ivan Karlovich Rosen]; Quartermaster-General was Gerard [Loggin Ivanovich Gerard], Duty General was Inzov [Ivan Nikitich Inzov].[1] The Cossacks were initially placed with the columns, but at the request of the Austrian Government, Kutuzov formed them into a separate detachment following the army, and so that the columns, upon their arrival at the theatre of war, in anticipation of the Cossacks not being needed by the light troops, the Austrians promised to send three light-horse regiments to Kutuzov.

The Austrian General Strauch [Gottfried Strauch] met Kutuzov in Brody, with instructions from his Court to accompany our troops across Austrian territory, and to take care of rations and supplying them with everything they need. The columns were on the march alternately. A few days later Kutuzov received an order from Emperor Alexander to return the sixth or rearmost column to the Podolsk Governorate, prompted by intelligence that the Porte had begun to mobilise, leaning toward the machinations of Napoleon who wanted to preoccupy Russia in a war with the Turks. Alarmed by this order, the Viennese Court asked the Emperor not to change the previous assignment of the column, promising to use all means to placate the Turks. Kutuzov reassured the Austrian Government in every possible way, and wrote to Vienna that the separation of one column from his army did not constitute a significant reduction, that the strength of the army is not measured in numbers of troops, but in their courage.[2] The eloquence of Kutuzov did not convince the Austrians, and they requested that Emperor Alexander return the sixth column to its original destination, vouching for the success of their negotiations in Constantinople [Istanbul]. Yielding to the wishes of Kaiser Franz, and commanding Tormasov [Alexander Petrovich Tormasov] to concentrate an army in the south, the Tsar ordered the column to rejoin Kutuzov; they set off on the march, but did not rejoin Kutuzov until he was already withdrawing from the Bavarian border, as we shall see below.

Meanwhile, the five columns continued to move calmly and unhurriedly along the agreed march route, welcomed warmly everywhere. But then, around 10 [22] September, as they were approaching Teschen, the Viennese Court learned of Napoleon's unusually swift movements from Boulogne towards the Middle Rhine. Concluding that his intention was to direct his main effort towards Germany, they successfully convinced Kutuzov to speed up the march, putting a great number of carts at his disposal, provided for each stage. Kutuzov ordered the swiftest troop movements. Forced marches began from Teschen. The infantry covered 45 to 60 *versts* [47-63 km or 30-40 miles] a day; they covered half of the distance on foot, the other half carried on carts, perched on top of backpacks, greatcoats, cavalry valises and bridles. Officers rode in *poste-chaises*; the cavalry added to their forage. Kutuzov ordered the dragoon regiments that were with the army to dismount and march

1 See Appendix
2 Kutuzov's report to the Russian ambassador in Vienna, dated 12 [24] September.

alongside the infantry, donating their horses to the cavalry, and forming a battalion from each regiment. The artillery was drawn by lead-horses, and our artillery horses were given a double forage ration, which was issued on the orders of Kaiser Franz at Austrian expense. Despite the speed of the march, the Viennese Court did not stop asking Kutuzov to accelerate his movements, marching later from four days to five days without a break. Kutuzov did not agree to this request, for fear of exhausting the army in the coming autumnal rainy season. He granted rest days at his discretion, considering the men's fatigue.[3]

Continuing the marches, Kutuzov travelled to Vienna wanting to discuss various subjects with the Austrian Government relating to the welfare of the service.[4] During his absence from the army, he entrusted the command of the infantry to Essen 2, the cavalry to Shepelev and the artillery to Meller-Zakomelsky [Pëtr Ivanovich Meller-Zakomelsky]. Kutuzov arrived in Vienna on 24 September [6 October]. The Court and all classes received him respectfully, but not with the same enthusiasm as was shown to Suvorov [Alexander Vasilevich Suvorov] six years earlier. Kaiser Franz thanked Kutuzov for the speed and orderly nature of his march, inspected the troops, enquired in detail about the needs of our corps, expressed complete readiness to help with anything, and granted our officers 60,000 silver guilders in the form of mess funds.[5] Kutuzov visited his old, short friend, the Prime Minister, Graf von Cobenzl [Ludwig von Cobenzl], who had once been the ambassador in St Petersburg and an interlocutor at Empress Catherine's Hermitage evenings. Graf von Cobenzl introduced him to the members of the *Hofkriegsrat*, which had a strong influence on military affairs at the time. At first, the members were afraid that they would find Kutuzov as stubborn and persistent as Suvorov had been on the way to Italy, but from the first meeting they saw in Kutuzov a readiness to agree with them on everything and even to be guided by their opinions. Possessing the rare ability to dominate minds and bind hearts to himself, Kutuzov completed the work requiring his presence in Vienna in a few days, in terms of rations, the delivery of ammunition and cartridges from the Austrian artillery department to us, sending Austrian officers from their General Staff, doctors, and topographic maps to our army. Moreover, Kutuzov eagerly accepted the proposal made to him by the *Hofkriegsrat* to consult with the Austrian generals appointed to be at his headquarters, especially with Schmitt [Johann Heinrich von Schmitt] who was assigned to him as Quartermaster-General.

Having confirmed his complete unanimity with the Viennese Cabinet, putting himself in the most friendly relations with them, Kutuzov left for Braunau on 27 September [9 October], the assembly area for the Russian force. He was absolutely sure of his impending union with the Austrians in Bavaria, having received in Vienna the most reassuring news from Ulm. Mack reported to his Court: 'Never has an army been posted in a manner more suited to assuring its superiority over the enemy, and I have only one regret, that of not seeing the Emperor being an eye

3 Report to the Tsar, dated 23 September [5 October].

4 Kutuzov's report to the Chief of the Ministry of Foreign Affairs, dated 23 September [5 October].

5 Kutuzov's report, dated 26 September [8 October].

witness to the triumph of His armies.'[6] These words from Mack would have removed even the slightest suspicion from Kutuzov concerning the threat to the Austrians. But as soon as he arrived in Braunau, the Russian envoy to Bavaria, Baron Bühler [Karl Yakovlevich Bühler], came and informed him that the French had occupied Munich, which had led to him leaving. Although Bühler and the Austrian officials quizzed by Kutuzov in Braunau did not know anything positive about what was happening at Ulm, it was already obvious that the French were astride Kutuzov's route through Bavaria, cutting his communications with Ulm. Kutuzov ordered Prince Bagration, who had arrived with his first column in Braunau, to form the vanguard of the army, placing outposts on the Inn, and to collect intelligence on the French. For this purpose scouts were sent in all directions, as were patrols from the Austrian cavalry regiment located in Braunau.

Three days after his arrival in Braunau, Kutuzov received the following letter from Archduke Ferdinand:

> The *Kaiserlich und Königlich* Army has previously had the important advantage of being master of the Iller, Ulm and Memmingen in order to keep our forces together and not have to weaken itself through protecting Tyrol. The enemy is not inclined to attack this position frontally. He wishes to outflank us and thereby prevent our union with the Imperial Russian Army; which Bonaparte made possible by the breakthrough of one of his armies through Prussian-Ansbach, because he earlier brought about the unification of his two armies. So our union with the Russian Imperial Army should really be postponed for the moment, or, since two enemy armies are already united and are masters of Donauwörth, it would be dangerous to seek them out immediately – or allow the Imperial Russian columns to advance immediately from the Inn in the order in which they arrive. In the meantime, we must survive in the region from the Lech to deep in Swabia for as long a period of time as is necessary for the Imperial Russian Army on the Inn to be supplied with everything and become operational.
>
> We have fully concentrated forces close to 70,000 men to attack and strike the enemy should they cross the Lech. Since we are masters of Ulm, we cannot lose the advantage of remaining masters of both banks of the Danube. Hence, at any moment if the enemy does not cross the Lech, we could cross the Danube, throw ourselves on his lines of communication, recross the Danube downstream and, if he wishes to turn against our faithful allies with all his might, immediately thwart his intentions. Thus, we will fearlessly wait for the time when the Imperial Russian Army will be ready, and then we will easily find together the opportunity to prepare that fate for the enemy which they deserve.
>
> Accordingly, it would be necessary for the Imperial Russian columns to exercise caution, and if at all possible not to concentrate at Braunau, but at

6 *Jamais armée n'a été postée d'une manière plus propre à assurer sa supériorité sur l'ennemi, et je n'ai qu'un seul regret, celui de ne pas voi l'Empereur être temoin Luimême du triomphe de Ses armées.* Report by the Russian ambassador to Vienna, dated 8 [20] October.

> Mühldorf behind the Inn, with the Austrian cavalry and artillery, which could join them, and equip themselves with the pontoons still at the rear – where they would soon be able to operate with the *Kaiserlich und Königlich* Cavalry and Artillery. Incidentally, the *Kaiserlich und Königlich* Army is in the best possible state and mood, and with full confidence we can hope for the same thing from the Imperial Russian to achieve the desired union soon, as nothing will be too difficult or impossible.[7]

Although the Archduke's letter testified to the excellent condition of his army, it was littered with obscure expressions, it did not explain to Kutuzov the Archduke's actual decisions. Speaking about the possibility of the French march on the Lech, should he understand the movements of the French to be on the left bank of this river, or on the right? Mentioning his intention to cross to the left bank of the Danube, and then again switch to the right bank, 'downstream,' he left in the unknown exactly where he would make this second crossing. Another day passed, filled with doubt for Kutuzov. The next morning, he received a report from the Austrian General Graf Crenneville [Ludwig Karl Graf Folliot de Crenneville] about the Archduke's victory

7 *Die Königliche-Kaiserlichen Armee hatte sich bisher den wichtigen Vorteil verschafft, Meister von der Iller, von Ulm und Memmingen zu sein, um zusammengehaltene Kräfte zu behalten, und sich nicht durch die Deckung Tyrols schwächen zu müssen. Der Feind findet nicht für gut diese Stellung mit offener Stirne anzugreifen. Er will sie tourniren, und hierdurch unsere Vereinigung mit der Russische-Kaiserlichen Armee verhindern; wozu Bonaparte durch den Durchbruch der einen seiner Armeen durch das Preussisch-Anspachsche sich die Möglichkeit verschafft hat, weil er die Vereinigung seiner beiden Armeen früher bewirkte. Wirklich dürfte also unsere Vereinigung mit den Russisch-Kaiserlichen Armeen für den Augenblick verhindert, oder, da die beiden feindlichen Armeen bereits vereinigt und Meister von Donauwerth sind, gefährlich werden, solche alsogleich aufzusuchen – oder die Kaiserlich-Russischen Colonnen in der Verfassung, wie sie ankommen, gleich augenblicklich vom Inn vorrücken zu lassen. Indessen haben wir in dem Lande vom Lech bis tief in Schwaben auf längere Zeit zu leben, als es uns nötig sein kann, bis die Kaiserlich-Russische Armee am Inn mit Allem versehen, und tätig zu werden vermögend sein wird.*

Wir haben vollkommen zusammengehaltene Kräfte nahe an 70,000 Mann, um den Feind, wenn er den Lech passirte, angreifen und schlagen zu können. Wir können da wir Meister von Ulm sind, den Vorteil, auch von beiden Ufern der Donau Meister zu bleiben, nicht verlieren. Mithin auch jeden Augenblick, wenn der Feind den Lech nicht passirte, die Donau übersetzen, uns auf seine Kommunikations Linie werfen, die Donau unterhalb repassiren und dem Feinde, wenn er sich gegen unsere treue Allirte mit ganzer Macht wenden wollte, seine Absicht alsobald vereiteln. Wir werden auf solche Weise dem Zeitpunkt, wo die Kaiserlich-Russische Armee ausgerüstet sein wird, mutig entgegen harren, und sodann leicht gemeinschaftlich die Möglichkeit finden, dem Feinde das Schicksal zuzubereiten, so es verdient.

Diesemnach wäre es notwendig, das die Kaiserlich-Russische Colonne die Vorsicht brauchte, jedoch wo möglich nicht die Braunau, sondern Mühldorf hinter dem Inn sich zu sammeln, mit der Östereichischen Cavallerie und Artillerie, die zu ihnen stoßen kann, und mit den noch rückwärts befindlichen Pontons sich ausrüsteten – wo sie dann, versehen mit Königliche-Kaiserlichen Cavallerie und Artillerie, sehr bald werden tätig werden können. Übrigens ist die Königliche-Kaiserlichen Armee in der möglichst besten Fassung und Stimmung, und mit voller Zuversicht können wir eben dasselbe von der Kaiserlich-Russischen hoffen, so wie uns, um die erwünschte Vereinigung bald zu erlangen, nichts schwehr und unmöglich sein wird.

Günßburg, den 8 October 1805.

E.H. Ferdinand.

over the French, but in short words and ambiguously. Congratulating the Archduke on his success,[8] Kutuzov remained perplexed by the present state of affairs, and meanwhile, things were in a most distressing state – the Austrian army no longer existed.

8 *Après avoir rendu compte à V.A.R. de tout ce qui regarde mon armée, je m'empresse de vous témoigner la joie très vive que j'éprouve dans ce moment en apprenant vos victoires. Elles sont les fruits des mesures sages, prises par V.A.R. et par conséquent une justice rendue à sa valeur militaire.* Kutuzov's letter to Archduke Ferdinand, dated 5 [17] October.

4

The Austrian Defeat at Ulm

Napoleon's advance to the Middle Rhine and Main. – Austrian dispositions. – Napoleon's advance from the Rhine to the Danube. – Napoleon's crossing of the Danube. – The initial failures of the Austrians. – Their offensive from Ulm. – Their return to Ulm and the disagreements of the commanders. – Napoleon's operations after crossing the Danube. – The investment of Ulm. – Continuing failures of the Austrians. – The capitulation of Ulm.

At the first news of the Austrian crossing of the Bavarian border, Napoleon ordered his troops to advance. The main French army was at Boulogne, Marmont's [Auguste Frédéric Louis Viesse de Marmont] corps was in the Netherlands while Bernadotte's [Jean Baptiste Jules Bernadotte] corps was in Hanover. Napoleon's movements were made with amazing speed and precision! By 13 [25] September, his troops, 180,000 men, including the Bavarians, were already in the following assembly areas:

Near Würzburg: Bernadotte's 1er Corps and Marmont's 2e Corps.

Between Strasbourg and Mannheim: Davout's [Louis-Nicolas Davout] 3e Corps, Soult's [Jean-de-Dieu Soult] 4e Corps, Lannes' [Jean Lannes] 5e Corps, Ney's [Michel Ney] 6e Corps, Murat's [Joachim Murat] *Réserve de cavalerie* and the *Garde impériale*.

Of the independent corps, Augereau's [Charles Pierre François Augereau] 7e Corps was assigned to Tyrol and Massena's [André Massena] 8e Corps was concentrating around Verona. Having stationed the main force, 120,000 men, between Strasbourg and Mannheim and two corps of 60,000 men at Würzburg, Napoleon intended to fall upon Mack before Kutuzov could catch up with him, to engulf the Austrian army, which had settled with its left wing on the Iller, cut their line of retreat and communications with the Russians, and ordered Massena to operate on the defensive in Italy, until he received news of success on the Danube. At that time, the Austrian army was stationed behind the Iller, with the right wing at Ulm, the left at Memmingen, having been ordered not to move forward before Kutuzov's arrival, and to hold their positions, believed to be extremely strong by the Austrians, should they be attacked in the meantime. Their front was protected by a river, the right wing was protected by neutral Prussian territory, the left was in communications with Archduke John's army in Tyrol. Not fearing for his flanks, Mack expected a frontal attack, but just in case, to secure his right wing, he had Kienmayer's [Michael von Kienmayer] independent corps between Donauwörth and Neuburg [-an der Donau], and Graf Nostitz's [Johann von Nostitz] detachment at Regensburg. The vanguard of the army was stationed in the Black Forest [Schwarzwald].

Napoleon's offensive advance began on 13–14 [25–26] September. He crossed the Rhine near Strasbourg with the corps of Lannes, Murat and the *Garde*, and moved towards Stuttgart. Giving the appearance and spreading rumours that he intended to attack the Austrians frontally, he left one cavalry division to occupy the Black Forest exits along the roads from Strasbourg to Ulm and Memmingen, and to move up the Rhine to Offenburg and Freiburg [-im Breisgau]. At the same time Ney crossed the Rhine at Karlsruhe, Soult at Speyer, Davout at Mannheim, thereafter Ney moved towards Stuttgart in order to link up with Napoleon, Soult towards Donauwörth via Heilbronn and Nördlingen, Davout to Oettingen and on to Neuburg, Bernadotte, Marmont and the Bavarians from Würzburg to Ingolstadt, across the Prussian territory of Ansbach, violating her neutrality, ignoring the representations of the Prussian officials located in Ansbach. This violent act, disrespecting the neutrality of Prussia, almost changed the course of the war, almost caused a rift between the Prussian King and Napoleon, as we shall see below. During these movements, Napoleon entered into alliances with the Elector of Württemberg [Friedrich Wilhelm Karl] and uncle of Emperor Alexander, and the Elector of Baden [Karl Friedrich] and grandfather of Empress Elizabeth Alekseevna, and the Duke of [Hesse] Darmstadt [Ludwig X] and the Duke of Nassau [Friedrich August]. Like the Bavarian Elector, they pledged to send their troops to join the French army. So the Austrian hope, before the outbreak of the war, of support from the rulers of southern Germany, evaporated.

On 24 September [6 October], ten days after the French crossed the Rhine, they arrived on the Danube. Leaving Ney's corps and some of the *Réserve de cavalerie* on the left bank of this river at Albeck, opposite Ulm, Napoleon ordered the army to cross: Bernadotte and the Bavarians at Ingolstadt, Marmont and Davout at Neuburg, Soult, Lannes, Murat and the *Garde* at Donauwörth. Archduke Ferdinand and Mack, deceived by the feints of enemy units from the Black Forest and Napoleon's crossing at Strasbourg, calmly remained in Ulm. At first they believed the French march to the Danube was Napoleon's attempt to distract them with threats to their communications, and force them to retreat from Ulm, and the concentration of Bernadotte and Marmont in Würzburg was accepted as Napoleon's wish to establish an army to monitor Prussia, confident that Napoleon would not violate the neutrality of Prussian territory. This delusion lasted a long time, until the very moment that Napoleon began to cross the Danube.

Kienmayer was the first to be struck by Napoleon, stationed between Donauwörth and Neuburg. Seeing the French corps approaching these towns, Kienmayer wanted to protect the entire Danube between them. He did not have time to complete his orders before Soult cut him off from Ulm through a quick crossing at Donauwörth and moving towards Augsburg, Bernadotte had turned his right wing by crossing at Ingolstadt, and Davout, crossing the Danube at Neuburg, threatened him head on. Threatened on all sides, Kienmayer retreated to Munich, was overtaken by the French, and having lost some 5,000 men, he hastened to join Kutuzov in Braunau.

Graf Nostitz also went there from his position at Regensburg. In reaction to Kienmayer's initial reports of the appearance of a large enemy force on the banks of the Danube, Mack sent General Auffenberg [Franz Xaver Freiherr von Auffenberg] with 6,000 men to reinforce him. Not taking due care on the march, Auffenberg soon found himself in the midst of the French columns and was completely and utterly routed [7 October, new style].

When confirmed intelligence was received in Ulm about the appearance of Napoleon to the rear of the Austrians, Archduke Ferdinand and Mack set out to meet him. Leaving a 7,000 man garrison in Memmingen, they moved down the right bank of the Danube in the direction of Günzburg, where the bridge was guarded by the 8,000 man detachment under General d'Aspré [Konstantin Ghilian Karl Freiherr d'Aspré]. The march was completed safely, but as soon as the army passed the high ground at Günzburg, Ney attacked General d'Aspré, who was carelessly isolated on the left bank of the Danube in front of the bridge, breaking and capturing him [9 October, new style]. The news of this failure, which betrayed the crossings at Günzburg to the French, prompted the Archduke and Mack to hastily return to Ulm. Seeing that their line of retreat on the right bank of the Danube was cut, they wanted to withdraw to Tyrol, and sent Jelačić's [Franz Jelačić] 6,000 man detachment on the route there to guard the crossings over the Iller. Thus, in the first six days of the campaign, the Austrian army was significantly weakened: Kienmayer's corps and Graf Nostitz's detachment were cut off from the army, Auffenberg's and d'Aspré's detachments were completely destroyed, and Jelačić's detachment departed for Tyrol. Meanwhile, time was spent in Ulm in fruitless meetings: appreciations were made and discarded; the troops were discouraged, food was scarce, the surrounding villages were looted, and the rains came.

Quite the opposite was happening in Napoleon's camp. Upon crossing the Danube, between 24 – 26 September [6 – 8 October], he divided the army into two parts: in the first, Bernadotte, Davout and the Bavarians were to pin down Kutuzov should he move from Braunau into Bavaria; in the second, Napoleon would turn on Ulm with the corps of Soult, Lannes, Murat, Marmont and the *Garde*. Murat was on the right wing, and had established links with Ney via the bridge at Günzburg. Soult formed the left wing, and was directed towards Memmingen. When he arrived, the local garrison under General Spangen [Karl Joseph Graf Spangen von Uyternesse] surrendered without a fight [14 October, new style], after which Soult cut the road leading from Ulm to Tyrol, and cut off Jelačić's detachment sent up the Iller by Mack. Napoleon slowly advanced on Ulm himself, with Lannes, Murat, Marmont and the *Garde*, waiting for Kutuzov to move. During these operations, the Austrians had a successful action against Dupont's [Pierre Antoine Dupont de l'Étang] division from Ney's Corps [11 October, new style]. Dupont approached Ulm from Albeck, intending to more closely invest this city, encountered the leading forces and was defeated, having lost 17 guns and 800 prisoners.

The success over Dupont could not restore matters. Two days later, having received a report from Bernadotte in Munich that all Kutuzov's troops had not yet arrived, and he would probably not advance from Braunau immediately, Napoleon moved forward, and invested Ulm on 1 [13] October, overwhelmed by disagreements among the main commanders. The Archduke stressed the need to leave Ulm, break through Ney's corps, and march to Bohemia. Mack disagreed with him, announcing a firm decision to stay in Ulm and wait for Kutuzov, saying that, according to accurate intelligence from his leading spy, riots had broken out in Paris, and Napoleon must hurry to his capital. To explain this circumstance, one needs to know that the spy was turned by Napoleon, and gave Mack false information. The arguments presented by various generals to Mack about the need to overwhelm the French right wing at Albeck and turn towards Bohemia were useless. Seeing Mack's intransigence, the Archduke decided to separate from him, and on 2 [14] October, he left Ulm with 18,000 men. Informed of this movement, Napoleon sent Murat and Ney to cut across his route. They overtook the Austrian infantry, and its commander, General Werneck [Franz von Werneck], who laid down their weapons without resistance. Taking 14 squadrons with him the Archduke continued the march, closely pursued by the French, and reached Bohemia with only four squadrons. The next day, 3 [15] October, Napoleon took the high ground close to Ulm in battle, began to bombard the city and threatened an assault. Mack entered into negotiations, and signed a capitulation, pledging to surrender if the Russians did not come to his aid within eight days. After the acceptance of this condition, Napoleon invited Mack to visit him, explained to him the locations of the French corps, and convinced him of the impossibility of expecting help from Kutuzov. Having no bread for the troops' rations for the agreed eight days, Mack concluded his reckless operations with an immediate surrender. On 8 [20] October he marched out of Ulm with 23,800 men and laid down his weapons. Napoleon marched on Munich having dealt with the Austrians and completely destroyed their army. For the Allies, this concluded the first disastrous period of the war of 1805, and since Russian troops did not participate in these military operations, they have been briefly described by us merely to clarify subsequent events. We will now turn to a detailed description of the second period, where Alexander's army came into combat with Napoleon.

5

Kutuzov's Stay in Braunau

Contradictory reports from the Austrian army at Ulm. – The arrival of Austrian and Russian troops with Kutuzov. – Kutuzov's decision to wait in Braunau. – His encounter with Mack. – Mack's fate. – The decisions of the *Hofkriegsrat* in Vienna. – Kutuzov's orders in Braunau.

At the time of the Austrian army's defeat, Kutuzov was in Braunau waiting for the arrival of his columns, devoid of information on events at Ulm. He had received only one letter, which we have mentioned previously, from Archduke Ferdinand, dated 28 September [10 October], in which he informed Kutuzov that the Austrian army was united and filled with courage. A day later, Graf Crenneville reported on the victory won by the Austrians – then they learned that it was the defeat of Dupont's division. After this, Kutuzov did not receive any letters, neither from the Archduke, nor from Mack, meanwhile, conflicting evidence was brought to him daily. According to one report, the Archduke had withdrawn to Tyrol, in another he had crossed to the left bank of the Danube, but all the news was consistent in asserting that some sort of disaster had happened at Ulm.[1] The Austrian cavalry sent into Bavaria could not capture a single Frenchman, and were captured by the enemy themselves. The intelligence reports were accurate, but Kutuzov thought them to be exaggerations. Having had the brilliant state of the army described by the Archduke and Mack so recently, he considered the destruction of this numerous force to be incredible, and he intended to begin an offensive once all his troops were concentrated.

Unexpected reinforcements soon began to arrive with Kutusov. General Kienmayer had been driven back from Donauwörth by Napoleon, with 24 battalions and 60 squadrons, a total of some 18,000 men. Following him, also cut off from Ulm, Graf Nostitz arrived with three battalions of Croats and the Prince of Hesse-Homburg's Hussars, currently [1844] the Heir Apparent, Tsarevich Alexander Nikolayevich's Regiment. Kienmayer and Graf Nostitz couldn't give any details about events in Ulm, not having been there. Kutuzov placed Kienmayer in Salzburg, and Graf Nostitz in Passau, entrusting both to the overall command of Graf Merveldt, to whom Kaiser Franz ordered the subordination of all Austrian troops joining Kutuzov on the way to Ulm. Meanwhile, the rearmost Russian columns, cavalry and artillery arrived in Braunau, exhausted by forced marches in inclement weather. With their shoes worn

1 Kutuzov's report to the Tsar, dated 7 [19] October.

out, some soldiers even went barefoot. The total of sick *en route* stayed at some 6,000. Upon arrival in Braunau, the strength of all five of our columns was no more than 32,000, and with the inclusion of Kienmayer's corps and Graf Nostitz's detachment, Kutuzov had over 50,000 men under arms.

The Austrian generals who were in Braunau, with whom, at the insistence of the Viennese Court, Kutuzov had to consult about his operations, tried to persuade him that he should advance, occupy Munich, and establish communications with Archduke Ferdinand at all costs.[2] Kutuzov would not budge. The senior Austrian General, Graf Merveldt, finally presented him with the written thoughts of the Viennese Court, almost in the form of a demand, stating the need to force open lines of communication with Ulm.[3] This submission was unsuccessful. Before initiating operations, Kutuzov was waiting until events in the main theatre of war, buried in utter obscurity, became clearer. Wishing to hold out until then, he sought the approval of Kaiser Franz,[4] and informed the Tsar:

> Having now become, so to speak, Vienna's last line of defence, if I advance, I could be cut off by an enemy that is three times stronger than me; and remaining here, I would equally expect to be attacked, and might easily find myself forced to retire to Vienna itself. I will consider the enemy's movements and any information that I might receive about the Archduke's army in order to make a decision about movements that I may need to make.[5]

Finally, the truth was revealed in all its terrifying nakedness. On 11 [23] October, Mack arrived in Braunau, returning from Ulm to Vienna. He told Kutuzov; 'Of the 70,000 man army, only the 10 battalions sent to Tyrol and the 14 squadrons that had gone with Archduke Ferdinand to Bohemia had been saved; the rest of the force, the artillery and transport had all gone to the enemy.'[6] Mack did not yet know that of the 14 squadrons he referred to, only four survived, and General Jelačić's ten battalions sent to Tyrol had laid down their weapons. At the end of the story of his disaster, Mack said that Napoleon's entire army was concentrating near Munich, preparing to advance soon, and begged Kutuzov to advance to meet Napoleon. Although the idea of undertaking an offensive was far from Kutuzov mind, but wishing in any case to show due respect to the Austrian generals, he asked Mack and Graf Merveldt for advice concerning his operations. They suggested that he cross to the left bank of the Danube, and join Count Buxhoeveden's corps that had been marching towards Bohemia. Agreeing to the need to concentrate our forces, Kutuzov replied that there were no troops other than his army on the route from Braunau to Vienna, and therefore, without the permission of Kaiser Franz, he could not leave Vienna as prey to

2 *Je ne pouvois pas avoir de nouvelles directes de l'armée autrichienne. Celles qui nous arrivoint étoient tristes, mais paroissoient exagérées. Dans ces entrefaites j'avois encore à lutter contre l'opinion de quelques généraux, qui croyoient devoir marcher en avant, attaquer Munich, et risquer tout pour se joindre à l'armée autrichienne.*

3 Graf Merveldt's letter to Kutuzov, dated 8 [20] October.

4 Kutuzov's request to the Russian Ambassador in Vienna, dated 9 [21] October.

5 Reports dated 7 and 10 [19 and 22] October.

6 Kutuzov's report to the Tsar, dated 11 [23] October.

the enemy, would wait for the orders of the Monarch and retreat to Lambach, and from there to Linz or Enns, depending on the direction taken by Napoleon's army. Bending Mack and Graf Merveldt to his opinion, and informing Kaiser Franz of the decisions made with them, Kutuzov added that without the approval of His Majesty he would not move his troops away from the route to Vienna, and would not abandon the city to the power of the French. Kutuzov concluded his report as follows: 'Sire, let me, the zealous servant of the common cause, with all my heart devoted to you, report my frank opinion to you on the present state of affairs. Of course, the failure of your Majesty's army at Ulm is very painful, but not to the extent that one could not make amends for it through the resolution and courage of the allied armies.'[7] In these words, we recognize the voice of the commander who, taking upon himself the terrible responsibility for the fall of the ancient capital of the Russian State, said to Alexander: 'the loss of Moscow does not mean the fall of Russia.'

After the meeting with Kutuzov, Mack left for Vienna. Officials were waiting for him at the gates, announced that he was forbidden from entering the capital, interrogated him, and escorted him to Brünn, where he was put on trial and sentenced to death. Kaiser Franz commuted the sentence: He commanded that Mack be deprived of his rank and imprisoned for life in a fortress. Two years later, his freedom was restored as was his rank.

Mack's testimony was the first accurate information received in Vienna about the fate of the army. Before his arrival, they had not heard from them because Napoleon had been across their lines of communication. They received incoherent intelligence only via roundabout routes. Our ambassador in Vienna reported; 'The disorder and confusion in the army were such that there's not even a description of the events that preceded the capitulation, or that prompted its conclusion. All the reports, incomplete and contradictory, bear the mark of confusion upon themselves, which were the hallmark of the last days of the existence of Mack's army.'[8] Having been reliably apprised of the disaster that had befallen the Monarchy, Vienna was numb with horror. Kaiser Franz immediately convened a council of war. They set up a militia in Hungary, and ordered Archdukes Charles and John to fall back, the first from Italy, the second from Tyrol, striving to race to the heart of the Monarchy, and joining up with Kutuzov, if possible, constituting the only stronghold of the Austrian State in the direction of Germany. Realizing the importance of the task ahead of Kutuzov, Kaiser Franz considered it necessary to confer with him personally, and set off to his army, having forewarned Kutuzov and concluded a letter to him with the following lines in his own hand: 'It is in critical moments like this that firmness is especially necessary; I count on yours, on your goodwill, you may also count on my eternal gratitude.'[9] Meanwhile, Kutuzov, cautiously and without haste, remained

---

7 Kutuzov's report to the Tsar, dated 11 [23] October

8 Count Razumovsky's report, dated 16 [28] October.

9 *Mon cher Général en chef Kutusoff! Vous savez le malheur de l'armée commandée par mon cousin l'Archiduc Ferdinand. L'importance, dont me devient dans se moment si la position de la votre, ma confiance dans vos talens et dans votre bonne volonté, m'engagent à me rendre en personne auprès de vous, afin de juger de ce qu'il y a à faire pour la cause qui m'est commune avec votre souverain. Je pars demain matin, vais sans m'arrêter, et désire beaucoup de vous trouver encore dans la position de l'Inn. Vienne, ce 26 Octobre 1805. N.B. (Autographe). C'est*

in Braunau, waiting for the development of Napoleon's operations. He ordered the evacuation of the sick, Austrian parks and artillery from Braunau, and the building of bridges along the Inn, on the left bank of which he left observation detachments. He also tried to revive the fallen morale of the inhabitants and the Austrian military and civilian authorities, stunned by Napoleon's successes. Unchanging in failure or success, Kutuzov maintained his usual composure. Amidst the general despondency of our Allies, his headquarters in Braunau was the focus of mirth, recalling the festive, magnificent era of Catherine. Kutuzov was its last representative. The Russian army being led by him impatiently wanted to fight Napoleon, full of the glorious memories of victories over the French won six years previously in Italy.

dans des moments critiques comme celuici, que la fermeté est surtout nécessaire; je compte sur la votre, sur vos bons sentiments, comptez aussi sur mon éternelle reconnaissance. Votre affectionné
François.

6

The Actions of Emperor Alexander

Prussia's refusal to allow the passage of Russian troops across Prussian territory. – The reasons for Emperor Alexander's departure abroad. – Orders before departing St Petersburg. – The journey. – The Emperor's intention to declare war on Prussia. – Correspondence with the Austrian Kaiser. – Prussia's changing relationship with Napoleon. – The Emperor's meeting with Graf Kalckreuth. – The Emperor's excursion to Berlin. – The Treaty of Potsdam. – The Emperor's letter to Kutuzov. – The Emperor's relations with Britain and Sweden. – Excursion from Potsdam to Weimar and Dresden. – The King of Prussia's letter. – Arrival in Olmütz.

Leaving the main theatre of war with Napoleon marching from Ulm to Munich, and Kutuzov waiting in Braunau, we turn to Emperor Alexander, for his first appearance on a battlefield. The reasons for His departure from St Petersburg to the expeditionary army were the following: According to the war plans approved between Russia and Austria, Mikhelson was appointed to enter Prussian territory in early September, with the corps under Bennigsen, Count Buxhoeveden and Essen, and march to northern Germany with Bennigsen's Corps, sending Count Buxhoeveden and Essen to join Kutuzov. The Russian envoy in Berlin, Alopeus [Maksim Maksimovich Alopeus], was ordered to proceed with the request for permission from the King of Prussia for the passage of Russian troops through his territory. In the event of a refusal, Mikhelson was to enter Prussia by force, and treat the Prussians as enemies should he meet resistance.[1]

The proposal made by Alopeus on this subject to the Berlin Court, supported by the Austrian envoy Graf Metternich [Klemens Wenzel Lothar von Metternich], now the State Chancellor, was rejected. The Prussian Minister of Foreign Affairs, Baron Hardenberg [Karl August von Hardenberg], repeated to them Prussia's firm, unchanging decision to maintain strict neutrality and defend it with force of arms against anyone. He added; 'Relying on the friendship of Emperor Alexander, the King is sure that without the consent of Prussia, Russian troops will not come within its borders, but if forcible entry follows on your part, he will make an extreme stand at any cost for the honour and independence of his State, and probably unite with Napoleon.' Baron Hardenberg concluded saying; 'For God's sake, do not make

1 Supreme instructions to Mikhelson.

us increase Napoleon's army by 200,000 men.'[2] Reporting on the comments of the Berlin Court, Alopeus wrote that in the end the only means to succeed with our intentions was a personal meeting between Emperor Alexander and the Prussian King, and it must happen before the entry of our troops into Prussia, so that this measure would appear to the Prussians to be the execution of a previously mutually agreed decision by the Monarchs.[3] As these negotiations were proceeding, Napoleon sent his favourite, Duroc [Géraud Hubert Christophe de Michel Duroc], to Berlin, offering Prussia greater rewards if they were to act with him in concert.[4] Duroc and the French envoy in Berlin, Laforêt [Antoine René Charles Mathurin de Laforêt], tried every possible means to succeed with their intentions; furthermore, knowing the Queen's [Luise von Mecklenburg-Strelitz] position on the alliance between Russia with Prussia, they attempted to settle the disagreement between her and her husband.[5]

Weighing the importance of circumstances, Emperor Alexander decided to go abroad and meet the King, as the issue was regarding persuading Prussia of an alliance and preventing them from joining Napoleon. He had previously sent Adjutant-General Prince Dolgorukov [Mikhail Petrovich Dolgorukov] to Berlin to invite the King to a meeting. In order to disguise the real purpose of Prince Dolgorukov's visit, he was ordered to announce that he was going to Berlin to attend manoeuvres. Before leaving St Petersburg, the Emperor ordered:

1. Mikhelson is not to enter Prussia, and station Count Buxhoeveden's and Essen's corps along the border between Prussia and Galicia, along the river Pilica, and Bennigsen's in Grodno.[6]
2. Count Tolstoy's corps will go by sea from Kronstadt and Revel to Stralsund, and come under the command of the Swedish King, to whom the Emperor wrote: 'Your feelings, Sire, are a sure guarantee to Me, that by directing or commanding the Russian and Swedish troops yourself, one will not prevail in affection over the other, as I guarantee that their devotion for your person will be equal. It is therefore to Your Majesty that I entrust the honour and conservation of My troops.'[7]

---

2 Alopeus' report, dated 16 [28] March.

3 *C'est dans l'entrevue de l'Empereur et du roi que je fonde tout mon espoir. Je voudrais qu'elle put précéder l'entrée de nos troupes. Alors les esprits eront moins exaspérés par cette marche, parcequ'on la regardera comme une suite d'un arrangement pris entre les souverains. Cela entendu, je la regarde comme le seul et dernier moyen de déterminer le roi: tout autre manquerait son effet, et il serait defficile de répondre que ce prince ne tourna du côté de la France.* Alopeus' report, dated 25 August [6 September].

4 *Mr Hardenberg m'avoua que Duroc a été chargé de faire l'offre d'avantages très considérables à la Prusse, si le roi voulait se joindre à Bonaparte, mais il n'a pas voulu s'expliquer sur la nature de ces avantages, assurant que le roi était fort loin d'y prêter attention.* Alopeus' report, dated 24 August [5 September].

5 Alopeus' report, dated 2 [14] November.

6 Mikhelson's orders, dated 6 [18] September.

7 *Vos sentimens, Sire, Me sont un sûr garant, qu'en dirigeant ou en commandant vous-même les troupes russes et suédoises, les unes ne l'emporteront pas d'affection sur les autres, comme Je*

3. The Russian Ambassador to London, Count Vorontsov [Semën Romanovich Vorontsov], was to insist that the British, upon the departure of Napoleon's army from the Boulogne camp, do not concern themselves with a French amphibious assault, and act offensively at sea, harassing the coast of France, and hurry to send the promised troops to Germany, to the mouth of the Weser, or Elbe, where they should link up with the Russians and Swedes.[8]
4. The Committee of Ministers would be guided by a special decree determining its actions during the Sovereign's absence.

The Emperor left St Petersburg on 9 [21] September. He was accompanied by *Ober-Hofmarshal* Count Tolstoy [Nikolai Alexandrovich Tolstoy], Adjutants-General Count Lieven [Khristofor Andreevich Lieven] and Prince Volkonsky [Pëtr Mikhailovich Volkonsky], Head of the Ministry of Foreign Affairs Prince Chartorysky [Adam Adamovich Chartorysky], and Privy Councillors Count Stroganov [Pavel Alexandrovich Stroganov] and Novosiltsov. The departure of Emperor Alexander to the army was considered an extraordinary event, because for the 80 years that had elapsed since the death of Peter the Great, Russian Monarchs had not appeared at the front. The Emperor travelled via Orsha, Minsk and Brest, and on 17 [29] September arrived in Puławy, near Kozienice, the assembly area for Count Buxhoeveden's corps. The Commander-in-Chief, Mikhelson, had already made all preparations for the movement into Prussia, and he sent the generals detailed instructions on military actions to take should the Prussians oppose our entry.

Not knowing what the answer from Berlin might be to the letter sent with Prince Dolgorukov, the Sovereign decided: if Prussia would not agree to the passage of our troops across their territory, to declare war on them, so that it could not be said that the Russian Emperor came to the banks of the Pilica with an army, and was forced to withdraw at the behest of the King of Prussia. No matter how harmful this war might be, putting honour above all else, they did not want to compromise the dignity of Russia at the very outset of the campaign.[9] Meanwhile, the Emperor inspected his troops, and ordered the formation of a reserve army of 56 battalions, 70 squadrons and 15 Cossack regiments under the command of General Rimsky-Korsakov [Alexander Mikhailovich Rimsky-Korsakov], to be stationed between Polangen [Palanga] and Proskurow [Khmelnytskyi].[10] Then the Emperor received a most compelling invitation from Kaiser Franz to attend a meeting with him in Krakow. He wrote to the Tsar: 'I count in anticipation as being among the happiest

---

garantis que leur dévouement pour votre personne sera égal. C'est donc à Votre Majesté que Je confie l'honneur et la conservation de Mes troupes.

8 Supreme instructions to Count Vorontsov, dated 3 and 4 [15 and 16] September.

9 *L'Empereur Alexandre ne se dissimule pas tous les désavantages qu'offre dans ce moment une guerre avec la Prusse, mais l'honneur va avant tout, et nous perdrions la plus grande partie de notre force, s'il était compromis à ce point dès le début de la campagne. Il ne faut pas que l'Europe dise, que l'Empereur de Russie a fait avancer une armée, s'y est rendu en personne, et a fini par reculer devant la volonté du roi Prusse.* Instructions from the Minister of Foreign Affairs to Count Razumovsky in Vienna, dated 20 September [2 October].

10 Supreme rescript to Rimsky-Korsakov, dated 6 [18] October.

of my life, the day when I will be able to press to my heart the benevolent and loyal sovereign who first gave life to our great and fortunate undertaking.'[11] Responding to Kaiser Franz with a sincere desire to meet and personally get to know him, the Tsar wrote to him about the impossibility of coming to Krakow without first concluding affairs with Prussia.

The Prussian King accepted the offer of Emperor Alexander, and was about to go to him when an unexpected report was received in Berlin about the passage of French troops through Ansbach, and, consequently, a violation of Prussian neutrality, the maintenance of which dominated their constant efforts. All of Berlin was in a state of excitement. The unanimous desire of the Court, the army and the people was bloody revenge for the offended honour of the Prussian Monarchy. In the first outburst of indignation, the King ordered the expulsion of the French envoy and Duroc from Berlin, but he cancelled the order, and commanded the five chief State dignitaries to submit to him written opinions on the measures that could be taken against Napoleon. They unanimously declared the French act treacherous, demanding satisfaction. The King agreed with their thoughts, and replied to Napoleon's letter justifying the passage of troops through Ansbach quoting examples from previous wars, that these examples could not be applied to the present case, that Napoleon had been reminded several times of Prussia's firm intention to maintain neutrality, and since he did not respect their intent, the King saw himself compelled to consider all the treaties and ties with France that were hitherto honoured to be destroyed and take active measures to protect his territories, while cultivating a sincere desire to contribute to the restoration of peace. Thus, Napoleon himself prompted Prussia to change its humble posture in relation to France. The Prussian corps, assigned to go to the Russian border and to the Pilica, received counter orders, and were directed to the Elbe and the Weser. The formation of four armies was ordered, in Hanover, in Westphalia, in Bayreuth, and a reserve in Berlin. Councils of war were held daily. The heart of these meetings was Field Marshal the Duke of Brunswick [Friedrich Wilhelm von Braunschweig], and the drafters of the plans were Colonels Scharnhorst [Gerhard Johann David Scharnhorst] and Phull [Karl Ludwig August Friedrich von Phull], who later entered Russian service. The Elector of Saxony [Friedrich August III], the King of Denmark [Christian VII], Landgrave of Hesse-Kassel [Wilhelm I] and the Dukes of Mecklenburg [Friedrich Franz I and Karl II] were invited to join Prussia, military cliques sprang up from one side to the other. Not restricting themselves to mobilisation, Baron Hardenberg announced to our Ambassador the King's consent for Russian troops to pass through Prussian territory, assuming that in the unsettled circumstances the King could not leave Berlin and go to meet Emperor Alexander, he laid down instead that General Graf Kalckreuth [Friedrich Adolf von Kalckreuth] would have full powers of negotiation.[12] On 4 [16] October, Graf Kalckreuth arrived in Kozienice, Mikhelson's headquarters. The Tsar arrived there from Puławy, and after consultations with Graf Kalckreuth, he ordered: Firstly,

11 *Je compte d'avance parmi les jours les plus heureux de ma vie celui où je pourrai serrer contre mon coeur le souverain bienfaisant et loyal qui a donné le premier le mouvement à tout ce qui va s'entreprendre de grand et d'heureux.* Letter from Kaiser Franz, dated 4 [16] September.

12 The Russian Ambassador's report from Berlin, dated 28 September [10 October].

Count Buxhoeveden's and subsequently Essen's corps were to go from the vicinity of Puławy through Prussian territory via Troppau [Opava], Olmütz [Olomouc] and Krems in order to link up with Kutuzov. Secondly, Bennigsen was to advance from Grodno via Warsaw and Novomesto to Breslau [Wrocław] and onwards, as circumstances demanded,[13] since, at that time the Sovereign did not know about the Austrian disaster at Ulm, where Mack had concluded the capitulation at the same time as the Tsar was in Kozienice. During the negotiations held here with Graf Kalckreuth, the Emperor informed the Swedish King about the favourable change in Prussian policy, writing to him that we had nothing to fear from Prussia, and as Count Tolstoy's corps had already arrived in Pomerania, asked the King to hasten their advance in order to prevent the French from occupying Hanover again.[14]

Meanwhile, irritation with Napoleon increased daily in Berlin, and the intention of the King of Prussia to enter into an alliance became apparent. Wishing to support this advantageous change of policy and to persuade the King to immediately declare war on Napoleon through his personal presence,[15] Emperor Alexander arrived in Berlin on 8 [20] October, notifying Kaiser Franz of His desire, upon returning from Berlin, to see him as soon as possible in Prague, Vienna or any other place. A *Meile* [8 kilometres] from Berlin, in Friedrichsfelde, the Tsar was met by the King's brothers. He sat in a carriage with the elder, Prince Heinrich, and drove into Berlin to a cannon salute. The entire garrison stood to arms. The monarchs observed the troops performing a ceremonial march, and in the evening went to Potsdam. Here, on 22 October [3 November], an agreement was signed, in which Prussia pledged to join the alliance of Russia, Austria and Britain, if Napoleon did not agree to the following proposal:

1. Assign secure military borders to Austria;
2. Compensate the King of Sardinia;
3. Withdraw troops from Germany, the Netherlands and Switzerland;
4. Separate the crown of France from the crown of the Kingdom of Italy.

The Prussian Minister Graf Haugwitz [Christian August Heinrich Kurt Haugwitz] was to go to Napoleon with these proposals, and if Napoleon did not accept them, declare war on him. Although Emperor Alexander was confident of Napoleon's refusal of our terms,[16] however, He viewed the indecision of Prussia to immediately begin hostilities with extreme displeasure, and their desire initially to appear merely as an armed mediator. Vainly reminding them of their own words, often

13 Emperor Alexander's letter to Kaiser Franz, dated 8 [20] October.

14 Letter to the King of Sweden, dated 7 [19] October.

15 *L'Empereur part pour Berlin afin de profiter des dispositions, manifestées par le roi pour presser l'acte d'adhésion de la Prusse avec l'Autriche et l'Angleterre, et pour l'engager à agir immédiatement de manière à éloigner les français de la position qu'ils ont prise et qui ménace les états héréditaires de l'Autriche.* Instructions to Prince Chartorysky, Russian Ambassador to Vienna, dated 4 [16] October.

16 *Nous n'avons souscrit au voeu du roi de Prusse que parceque Bonaparte n'acceptera jamais nos propositions.* Supreme instructions to Count Vorontsov in London, dated 24 October [5 November].

repeated to our and Austrian envoys, that they would immediately draw swords should any Power violate their neutrality, they fruitlessly presented the need to move troops quickly to stop Napoleon, as news had already come to Berlin about his great successes over the Austrians. All our arguments could not gain the upper hand over the implacable will of the Berlin Court to enter into preliminarily negotiations with Napoleon, to which Prussia was partly driven by a desire to win a month of time in order to allow the deployment of troops into locations where it would be more advantageous for them to operate. However, the King promised to declare war on Napoleon if he did not give a satisfactory answer within a month. Agreeing properly to the postponement that Prussia desired: otherwise, they would not join the alliance.[17]

Equally it was necessary to accept another of Prussia's demands, which Emperor Alexander found highly regrettable: 'To use His influence such that Britain would cede Hanover to Prussia, and in return receive Prussian territory in Westphalia.' This demand, which constituted a separate, secret article of the Potsdam Treaty, was so persistent that negotiations with Prussia nearly collapsed when our commissioners tried to persuade the Prussian Ministers to abandon the acquisition of Hanover.[18] In commanding His ambassador in London, Count Vorontsov, to persuade the King of England [George III] to cede this territory, Emperor Alexander told him: 'I know how painful it will be for the King to lose an ancient hereditary territory, but the sacrifice is necessary for success in the common cause: without the assistance of Prussia, Napoleon cannot be defeated, and Austria will have to sign a shameful peace.'

At the conclusion of the Potsdam Treaty, Archduke Anton [Anton Viktor Joseph Johann Raimund von Österreich] arrived in Berlin from Vienna, with news of Mack's defeat and his request to the King of Prussia to fully participate in the war. He handed the Emperor a letter from Kaiser Franz, who wrote *inter alia*: 'Despite all the unfortunate things that have happened to me, my unlimited confidence in your Majesty's sentiments has unswervingly supported my courage and my hopes. Nothing shall disturb the indescribable joy and happiness that I will experience when I embrace the intimate and faithful ally, to whom I will be eternally attached by the closest ties that any friendship, admiration and recognition could have.'[19]

Having learned from Archduke Anton all the details of events, Emperor Alexander wrote to Kutuzov: 'Following the Austrian army's disaster, you could be in a most awkward predicament. This remains your best guide: **always keep in mind that you**

17 *Sa Majesté l'Empereur n'a consenti à ce que la Prusse traite avec Bonaparte, que parceque sans cela il aurait été impossible de se procurer la coopération de la cour de Berlin.* Instructions to Prince Chartorysky from Alopeus in Potsdam, dated 24 October [5 November].

18 *La demande du Hanovre tient tellement au coeur du roi de Prusse, que nous avons plus d'une fois vu la négociation prêt à se rompre par notre éloignement à y souscrire.* Supreme instructions to Count Vorontsov in London, dated 24 October [5 November].

19 *Malgré tout ce qu'il m'arrive de malheureux, ma confiance illimitée dans les sentimens de Votre Majesté soutient inébranlablement mon courage et mes espérances. Rien ne troublera la joie et le bonheur indicible que j'éprouverai au moment d'embrasser l'intime et fidèle allié, auquel je serai éternellement attaché par tout ce que l'amitié, l'admiration et la reconnaissance ont de liens les plus étroits.* Kaiser Franz's letter, dated 14 [26] October.

are leading a Russian army. I place all my authority with you and on the courage of my troops. I also hope for your conviction that you must choose measures yourself to preserve the honour of My arms and save the common cause. I know that nothing should now be left to chance, and it is necessary to gain time, until Buxhoeveden's corps arrives in the theatre of war, and the Prussians have yet to begin hostilities. However, if you cannot avoid a battle, then I believe that according to your initial thoughts, you should advance to attack the enemy, and should not wait for him in a position. You must maintain good relations with the Austrian generals, but ensure from the experience of General Mack's inability, you should not rely on his advice. Only when I discover that you have decided to take on yourself the supreme responsibility of protecting Vienna will I remain calm. You have My authority for the army and the Allies. Prove to the enemy your worthiness for that authority.'

The regrettable news brought by Archduke Anton preoccupied the Prussian Court, on the one hand, alarmed by Napoleon's latest exploits, who had long been terrifying to them, on the other, the association of the Potsdam Treaty with the Allies.[20] Emperor Alexander persuaded the King of Prussia not to lose hope for a favourable change of situation, saying that the Russian troops assigned to operate in various theatres of war had not yet fired a shot; that the aims of the Austrian army in Italy and Tyrol, the Swedes were embarking on campaign, the British were equipped for amphibious landings, Denmark, Saxony, Mecklenburg and Hesse-Kassel were ready to follow Prussia's lead, and that with such forces remaining at the disposal of the Allies, 'it would be possible to push the French back over the Rhine, and meanwhile the army of the King of Sweden would occupy the Netherlands.'[21]

Encouraging Prussia towards the alliance, Emperor Alexander again turned to Britain, insisting on the swift dispatch of the promised troops to German soil, where they were to come under the command of the King of Sweden and conquer the Netherlands, currently stripped of the French.[22] He also begged the Swedish King not to hesitate to set off on campaign, and tried in every way to end his quarrels with Prussia, which had arisen in the months immediately before the war, and threatened a breach but for the mediation of the Emperor. The Sovereign summoned Count Tolstoy from Stralsund to Berlin, and personally ordered him to speed up operations in the north. Sending him back, the Emperor wrote to the Swedish King: 'It is more than probable that Bonaparte will not accept our proposals, and it will certainly not have escaped Your Majesty, that the condescension which I have made to subscribe to the wishes of the king of Prussia to start negotiations, is a continuation of the natural need for cooperation, which the Austrian disasters have made even more pressing. I beg you to believe, whatever the outcome of this negotiation, which in

20 *Les difficultés de tout temps, lorsque nous avons proposé à la Prusse un concours énergique, se sont bien accrues depuis la certitude de la défaite complète des Autrichiens.* Supreme instructions to Count Vorontsov in London, dated 24 October [5 November].

21 Original text from a letter from the Head of the Ministry of Foreign Affairs in Potsdam to Alopeus in Berlin, dated 24 October [5 November].

22 Supreme instructions to Count Vorontsov in London, dated 24 October [5 November].

any event should not extend beyond a few weeks, that I will not abandon your interests. I implore Your Majesty to advance promptly.'[23]

Such were the activities of Emperor Alexander in Potsdam, from where He initially travelled to Berlin, where he visited members of the Royal Household, Princess Holstein-Beck [Katharina von Holstein-Beck], Field Marshal Möllendorf [Wichard Joachim Heinrich von Möllendorf] and Graf Schulenburg-Kehnert [Friedrich Wilhelm von der Schulenburg-Kehnert]. On the day appointed for His departure from Potsdam, 24 October [5 November], the Emperor went with the King and Queen to the tomb of Frederick II, and standing near the remains of the great man, the monarchs said goodbye, vowing eternal friendship. They kept the vow unbroken until the ends of their lives, through the fearful upheavals of fate, in happiness and misfortune. To commemorate Emperor Alexander's stay in Berlin, the King ordered the Sandgasse, located in the [Königs] Vorstadt, to be renamed Kaiser Strasse, and a square in the same area, Alexander Platz. The Sovereign granted the St Andrew's sash to the Duke of Brunswick, Field Marshal Möllendorf and the Minister of Foreign Affairs Baron Hardenberg.

Having concluded his business with Prussia, the Emperor went from Potsdam to Weimar to Grand Duchess Maria Pavlovna, having not seen her since her marriage, which had taken place two years previously. The Emperor spent three days with the Grand Duchess, and on 29 October [10 November] he set off from Weimar for Dresden. Having strengthened friendly relations with the Elector of Saxony, he went to Olmütz to meet with Kaiser Franz. He had intended to go via Prague, but at the first station from Dresden, learning of the appearance of French cavalry patrols in Pilsen, from where they could quickly reach Prague, he turned left towards Breslau. On his entry into Silesia, the Emperor stopped in the border town of Schmidefeld and wrote to the King of Prussia with the reasons that prompted him to proceed through Prussian territory. Having received the news, during His sojourn in Weimar and Dresden, of Napoleon's rapid pursuit of Kutuzov, and seeing the despondency prevailing in Germany caused by Napoleon's successes, the Sovereign added in the same letter to the King: 'Things are in a much worse state than we expected them to be on My departure from Berlin. Every minute is precious. The fate of Europe is in your hands. I'm starting to be worried for Kutuzov. Every day his troops fight bravely, but fighting alone against superior forces, they will have to give way to the crowd. I lay all My hope on Your Majesty, on your friendship and resolve.'[24]

The Emperor sent the letter with Adjutant-General Prince Dolgorukov, ordering him to find out about the situation in Berlin, and to encourage Prussia to take part in the war as soon as possible. Prince Dolgorukov also carried an Order of St Catherine 1 class sent by the Emperor for the wife of Prince Ferdinand [Anna Elisabeth Luise

23 *Il est plus que probable que Bonaparte n'acceptera pas nos propositions, et il n'échappera certainement pas à Votre Majesté, que la condescendance que j'ai mise à souscrire au voeu du roi de Prusse d'entamer une négociation, est une suite naturelle du besoin de sa coopération, que les désastres de l'Autriche ont rendu encore plus pressante. Je la prie de croire, quelle que soit l'issue de cette négociation, qui dans aucun cas ne doit s'étendre audelà de quelques semaines, que je n'abandonnerai point ses intérès. Je conjure Votre Majesté de se porter promptement en avant.* Letter dated 24 October [5 November].

24 The Sovereign's letter to the King of Prussia from Schmidefeld, dated 2 [14] November.

von Brandenburg-Schwedt]. From Schmidefeld, His Majesty rode quickly through Silesia, hurrying to Moravia, the assembly area of the main Russian army. At the last station before Olmütz, Kaiser Franz met our Monarch, squeezed him in his arms, could not find words to express his gratitude, and greeted him with joyful news – a detailed account of the courage that marked every step of the Russian army's withdrawal from Braunau.

7

Kutuzov's Withdrawal From Braunau to Krems

Napoleon's plans. – Fragmented Allied forces. – Kutuzov's relations with the Austrians. – Kutuzov's withdrawal to Wels. – Council of war. – Negotiations with Napoleon. – Action at Lambach. – Withdrawal to Enns. – Napoleon's orders. – Action at Amstetten. – Napoleon's intention to encircle Kutuzov. – Kutuzov's withdrawal to the Danube.

After the capitulation at Ulm, Napoleon detached Augereau's and Ney's corps to Tyrol, to operate against the Austrian troops there and to quell the popular uprising, thereby securing his right wing, and went to Munich, the assembly area of the French army. On 15 [27] October he began the offensive towards the river Inn, with the immediate objective of defeating Kutuzov. Receiving news of Prussia's indignation at the violation of their neutrality, and knowing about their mobilisation, Napoleon foresaw the likelihood of a war with this Power, and wanted to deal with Kutuzov before a breach with Prussia, and before troops coming from Russia could join Kutuzov's corps or any troops that Austria could send as reinforcements.

At that time, the combined forces of Russia and Austria covered a vast area. The Archdukes Charles and John had not yet received orders dispatched from Vienna to withdraw from Italy and Tyrol; Count Buxhoeveden was on the march from Troppau to Olmütz, Bennigsen was near Warsaw; the Lifeguard had just set off from Brest. Waiting at Braunau, Kutuzov was the focus of the disparate allied armies, who were supposed to gather in the heart of the Austrian Monarchy, and the first to face Napoleon's offensive. The burden of battle fell to Kutuzov. In general, his career was marked by the fact that he was always leading an army when all the advantages were on the enemy's side. In 1805, he was supposed to hold Napoleon with 50,000 men; in 1811, he fought against the Turks, following five years of unsuccessful campaigning by his predecessors; in 1812, he took command of the army when Napoleon was within 150 *versts* [157 km or 100 miles] of Moscow. And Kutuzov always justified Alexander's choice, entrusting him with the honour and glory of the Russian army in difficult circumstances.

Coming under the direction of the Viennese Court, Kutuzov received the following orders: 'Avoid defeat, keep the force secure and intact, do not engage in battle with Napoleon, but challenge him at every turn, gaining time for Archdukes Charles and John to reach the theatre of war, and the corps underway from Russia.'

Kutuzov replied to Kaiser Franz: 'Encouraged by the trust with which Your Majesty honours me, and recalling the moment when I had the good fortune to introduce myself to you in Vienna, to speak frankly with Your Majesty, I dare to report that I am convinced of the need to follow the operational plan sent to me but, with all due respect, I foresee great difficulties. If I challenge the enemy at every turn I will have to withstand their attacks, and when some of the troops go into action there will be a need to support them, from which a general battle may ensue followed by defeat. I would neglect my duties if I did not present to you, Sovereign, this opinion inspired by the zeal of a faithful servant for the benefit of the sincere ally of my Monarch.'

This was the situation on 15 [27] October, when Napoleon departed from Munich, dividing his army into two formations. The first, led by him personally, consisted of the corps under Lannes, Davout, Soult and the *Garde*, and was directed on Braunau; in the second were the corps under Bernadotte, Marmont and the Bavarians, directed on Salzburg, to outflank Kutuzov's left.

The vanguard was commanded by Murat. Having learned about these movements, and the appearance of French leading troops on the banks of the Inn, Kutuzov ordered a withdrawal on 17 [29] October;

1. The Russians from Braunau to Lambach.
2. Kienmayer from Salzburg, keeping level with the Russians, covering our left flank, and having a detachment to liaise with us.
3. Graf Nostitz from Passau to Linz.

Kutuzov assigned the Russian rearguard to Prince Bagration, having appointed command of his cavalry to Count Wittgenstein [Pëtr Khristianovich Wittgenstein] and the artillery to Lieutenant-Colonel Yermolov [Alexei Petrovich Yermolov]; a half-march from the rearguard a separate reserve detachment was set up under Miloradovich [Mikhail Andreevich Miloradovich]. With this first step by Kutuzov, we see his great gift in selecting subordinates. Who were these men? Bagration, Miloradovich, Wittgenstein, Yermolov. By entrusting them with the protection of the army, Kutuzov could indulge in the considerations of fighting his famous adversary without distracting concerns.

On 19 [31] October Kutuzov arrived in Lambach, and settled down behind the river Traun, in the vicinity of Wels, where he waited for two days, waiting for Kienmayer, who had not yet had time to draw level with us. Napoleon could also not follow quickly, delayed on the way by bridges destroyed on Kutuzov's orders over the rivers Inn and Salzach. Kaiser Franz soon arrived in Wels, a council of war was assembled, which, apart from Kutuzov, consisted of Austrian generals. Asked by the Kaiser for his thoughts regarding future operations, Kutuzov replied that he considered it necessary to propose a serious measure, but one that could restore the situation: not to persist in holding Vienna, to give it to the French, only operating without haste. According to Kutuzov, it was first necessary to strongly protect the crossing at Enns; then cross over to the left bank of the Danube, preventing the enemy from following, restricting them to the right bank, and meanwhile linking up all the disparate parts of the allied armies on the left bank, and having gathered strength, begin, as it were, a new campaign. Kaiser Franz expressed his readiness to sacrifice the capital, but His Majesty and the Austrian generals wished that Kutuzov remain on the right bank of the Danube as long as possible, first holding on the river Enns, and then in the bridgehead fortifications at Krems, which the Austrians had just begun to build. They wanted Kutuzov to defend himself in these fortifications, while Count Buxhoeveden came up to him, and the Archdukes Charles and John approached, to whom they sent a second order after the council of war to hurry to join Kutuzov, and if they found the direct route to him was blocked, divert to Vienna, or Pressburg [Bratislava], and try to cross the Danube there.

Before returning from Wels to Vienna, Kaiser Franz wanted to know the future intentions of Napoleon, and sent Graf Gyulay [Ignac Gyulay] to him with a proposal for a truce. The victor replied: 'Let the Russians return from Austria to Russia, before concluding peace give me back Venice and Tyrol, and forbid the Hungarians from mobilising the militia. If you agree, then we may begin negotiations.' Such conditions were not acceptable. Kaiser Franz ordered the publication of Napoleon's response, wanting to clarify the necessity of continuing the war,[1] and placed all means of defence of the Austrian Monarchy in opposition to him. These means were insignificant, not because they were lacking in the State but because of the complete breakdown of all elements of the government after the horror caused by the defeat of the army almost without a fight. Grumbling about the continuation of the war combined with the general loss of hope for success and the desire to achieve peace as soon as possible led to the fact that all the measures prescribed and confirmed by the Government were carried out sluggishly and without goodwill. No one thought to help their fatherland by the power of the means that existed in the Monarchy.

Soon after the departure of Kaiser Franz from Wels, the first fighting began. Four Austrian battalions, marching between Kutuzov and Kienmayer, were overtaken by Murat, and came under heavy pressure. Going into action, Graf Merveldt asked for help from Prince Bagration, who was waiting in Lambach. Prince Bagration sent him a squadron of Pavlograd Hussars, 6th Jäger and 8th Jäger Regiments, and a company of artillery. This was our first engagement with Napoleon's forces. The courage that animated the Russians and the French can be imagined: neither one nor the other had previously known defeat.

Together with the Austrians, we held up Murat for five hours.[2] Graf Merveldt testified to Kutuzov of the exemplary courage of the detachment sent to him by Prince Bagration.[3] Our jägers charged twice with fixed bayonets. Some of the 8th Jäger Regiment, having lost their commander, Count Golovkin [Gavriil Gavriilovich Golovkin], who was mortally wounded, were disordered for several minutes, but were rallied by *Flügel-Adjutant* [equerry] Count Tiesenhausen [Fedor Ivanovich Tiesenhausen].[4] Our casualties were 152 men and one gun was lost destroyed.

At the end of the action, Kutuzov ordered the bridges over the Traun to be destroyed, and went to Enns, sending Graf Merveldt, with Kienmayer's corps, to

1 *Publication à Brunn, le 1ere/13eme Novembre.*
2 Kutuzov's report to the Head of the Ministry of Foreign Affairs, dated 22 October [3 November].
3 Graf Merveldt's report to the *Hofkriegsrat*, dated 1 November.
4 [P.I.] Meller-Zakomelsky's report to Count Arakcheev, dated 10 [22] September 1806.

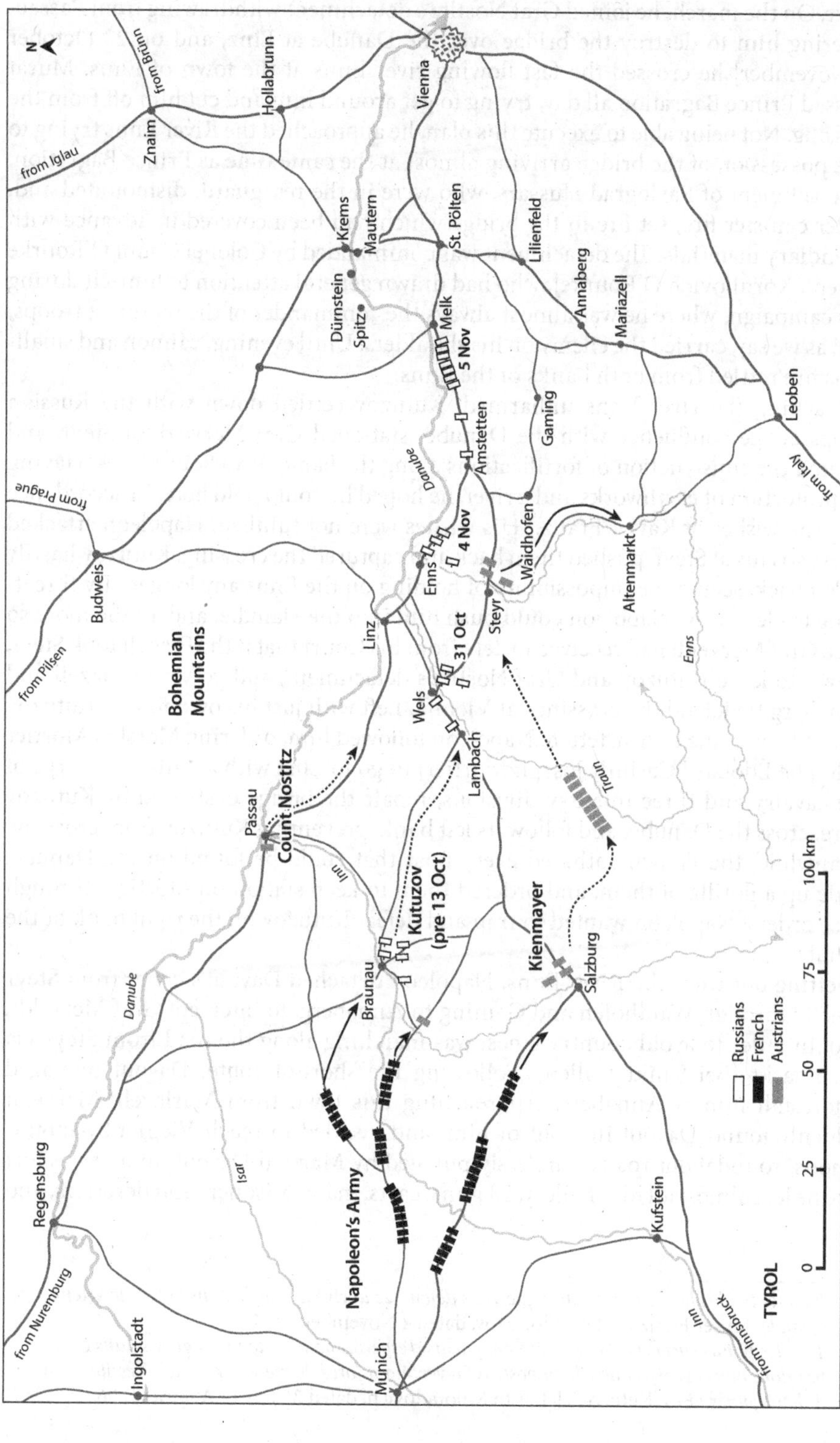

Map of Kutuzov's retreat from Braunau to Krems.

Steyr. On the march, he joined Graf Nostitz's detachment withdrawing from Passau, ordering him to destroy the bridge over the Danube at Linz, and on 23 October [4 November] he crossed the fast flowing river Enns at the town of Enns. Murat pressed Prince Bagration all day, trying to get around him and cut him off from the crossing. Not being able to execute this plan, he approached the River Enns trying to take possession of the bridge arriving almost at the same time as Prince Bagration. A detachment of Pavlograd Hussars, who were in the rearguard, dismounted and, under canister fire, set fire to the bridge which had been covered in advance with incendiary materials. The detachment was commanded by Colonel Count O'Rourke [Joseph Kornilovich O'Rourke], who had drawn general attention to himself during this campaign, where he was almost always the commander of the rearmost troops, and, as we say, carried the enemy on his shoulders. Until evening, cannon and small-arms fire rattled from both banks of the Enns.

Reaching the river Enns unharmed, Kutuzov settled down with the Russian troops at the confluence with the Danube, stationed Graf Merveldt at Steyr, and ordered the construction of fortifications along the bank, in various places. Having the protection of earthworks and a river, he hoped he could hold here, in accordance with the wishes of Kaiser Franz.[5] His wishes were not fulfilled. Napoleon attacked the Austrians at Steyr, pushed them back and captured the crossing. Kutuzov hastily pulled back, seeing the impossibility of holding on the Enns any longer.[6] By threatening his left wing, Napoleon could push him into the Danube, and all the more so since Graf Merveldt had received orders from his Court that if the French took Steyr, he was to leave Kutuzov and Graf Nostitz's detachment, and go via Mariazell and Annaberg to defend the crossings at Vienna. Left with just his own forces, Kutuzov moved from Enns to Amstetten. Napoleon followed him, ordering Marshal Mortier [Adolphe Édouard Casimir Joseph Mortier] to go to Linz with an all-arms corps of one cavalry and three infantry divisions, repair the bridge destroyed by Kutuzov there, cross the Danube, and follow its left bank, preventing Kutuzov from crossing. Meanwhile, the French gathered every boat that could be found on the Danube, made up a flotilla of them, and ordered them to keep station on Mortier. Through these orders, Napoleon wanted to trap and defeat Kutuzov on the right bank of the Danube.

Setting out from the River Enns, Napoleon detached Davout's corps from Steyr directly through Waidhofen and Gaming to Annaberg, to intercept Graf Merveldt, who, in order to avoid country lanes, was marching along the road from Steyr via Altenmarkt [bei Sankt Gallen]. Following the shortest route, Davout managed to forestall him at Annaberg. Approaching this town from Mariazell, Merveldt suddenly found Davout in front of him, and decided to reach Vienna by mountainous, roundabout roads. Tirelessly pursued by Marshal Davout, in a very short time he lost almost all his artillery, 24 guns, carts, many prisoners and deserters, and

5 *Il est de la plus haute importance que vous défendiez la rive droite de l'Ens le plus longtems possible.* Kaiser Franz's letter to Kutuzov, dated 4 November.

6 *Tous les points suspects sur l'Ens étoient garnis. J'espérois pouvoir tenir longtems dans cette position, mais le corps autrichien posté à Steyer, étant forcé, je me vis dans la nécessité d'abandonner l'Ens.* Kutuzov's letter to Miloradovich, dated 26 July [7 August] 1806.

made his way to Hungary with a small number of troops, where we will find him again after the battle of Austerlitz. Having scattered Graf Merveldt's corps, Davout went through Lilienfeld to Sankt Pölten by forced marches, to rejoin Napoleon.

The day after Kutuzov's departure from Enns, on 24 October [5 November], Murat caught up with our rearguard, under the command of Prince Bagration, with nine battalions, the Pavlograd Hussar Regiment, four battalions of Croats and several squadrons of the Hessen-Homburg Hussars at Amstetten. The attack was so powerful that, having personally visited the rearguard, he considered it impossible for Prince Bagration to resist, and ordered Miloradovich to go to his support with his independent detachment that made up the rear guard reserve, comprising the Malorussia Grenadiers, Apsheron Musketeers, Smolensk Musketeers, 8th Jägers and Mariupol Hussars.[7]

Miloradovich arrived on the battlefield as Prince Bagration was withdrawing. Passing them, he formed his detachment into two lines. Murat resumed his advance and attacked the right wing, where the Malorussia Grenadiers were. They repelled the attack. An attempt on the left flank, commanded by Count Wittgenstein, also ended unsuccessfully. The enemy advanced again. Miloradovich led the grenadier battalions of the Apsheron Musketeers and Smolensk Musketeers forward, forbidding them from loading their guns, and reminding them how Suvorov taught them to use their bayonets in Italy. They charged at Oudinot's [Nicholas Charles Oudinot] French grenadiers; a most stubborn battle took place, which had not been experienced before; fought the French to a standstill and crushed them; in general, the Amstetten action was marked by particular bitterness. The wounded, after treatment, were in a hurry to return to combat. The French claim that the Russians they captured threw themselves ferociously at their escorts.[8] By the end of the action, the French were pulling back in disorder, pursued by skirmishers.[9] From then on, Miloradovich remained the commander of the rearguard. Count Wittgenstein covered his movements, constantly exchanging fire with Murat. Meanwhile, Kutuzov retreated through Melk to Sankt Pölten. Murat caught up with Miloradovich at Melk. Here a fierce action again took place. Both sides claimed victory: ours because we were able to deliver a rebuff and withdraw in good order, the French because they were able to move forward.

Following Murat, Napoleon received intelligence from his spies that the second Russian army was passing through Moravia and was already several days' march from Krems. This was Kutuzov's sixth column from his departure from Russia, which had returned to the Podolsk Governorate on the occasion of the Turkish mobilisation, and then returned to Kutuzov. The spies had mistaken this column for Count Buxhoeveden's army. Napoleon believed them, and concluded that Kutuzov

---

7 Kutuzov's report to the Tsar, dated 25 October [6 November].

8 *Dans ce moment òn l'infanterie française et l'infanterie russe s'abordèrent corps à corps, les grenadiers d'Oudinot montrèrent la plus grande intrépidité, et les russes un courage féroce: blessés, mutilés, ils combattaient avec fureur, jusqu'a ce qu'on les eut désarmés; les prisonniers même attaquaient leur escorte. Dumas, Précis des évènements militaires. Tome XIII, p. 303.*

9 *Vous avez en la gloire de terminer cette journée bien sérieuse décidement à notre avantage. Plusieurs bataillons ennemis étaient en pleine déroute et se retirèrent bien loin.* Kutuzov's letter to Miloradovich, dated 26 July [7 August] 1806.

would probably await the arrival of this army before crossing the Danube at Krems, and would defend Vienna with it. The bitter fighting at Lambach, Amstetten and Melk confirmed his belief that Kutuzov wanted to gain time for the arrival of the second army. Based on these assumptions, and considering that Sankt Pölten was the only place that provided Kutuzov with the opportunity to link up with Count Buxhoeveden, Napoleon set out to prevent the junction and defeat Kutuzov in isolation. After passing Melk, he issued the following orders:

1. Lannes' corps, Oudinot's grenadier division and Murat's *Réserve de cavalerie*, are to attack Kutuzov's right wing;
2. Soult and the *Garde* are to strike the centre;
3. Bernadotte and Davout are to bypass our left wing, isolating Kutuzov from Vienna;
4. Mortier, with his all-arms corps, is to hurry to Krems on the left bank of the Danube, behind Kutuzov.

Marmont's corps had been sent to Leoben two days previously, to seek out Archduke Charles, and to try to block him if he took the direct route to Vienna.

During Napoleon's preparations, which threatened us with imminent defeat in the event of a delay, Kutuzov waited at Sankt Pölten, to where Miloradovich was falling back, fighting off Murat. He soon received intelligence of the appearance of Mortier on the left bank of the Danube. Reading the mind of his great adversary, to trap him against the Danube, Kutuzov immediately led the army from Sankt Pölten to Krems, crossed the Danube there and ordered Miloradovich to destroy the bridge, which was accomplished under fire from the French. Thus Kutuzov abandoned the right bank of the Danube, contrary to two instructions from Kaiser Franz, ordering him to defend the bridgehead at Krems at all costs, which, however, the Austrians had only just begun to build.[10] The officers sent in advance by Kutuzov examined the fortifications, and reported that construction had hardly been started; therefore, protecting it was out of the question. But even if it was ready, then by waiting in it Kutuzov would find himself in a trap, surrounded on both banks of the Danube by Napoleon, exactly the situation in which he had once placed the army of the Grand Vizier at Ruschuk [Ruse].

10 Kaiser Franz's instructions to Kutuzov:
1. dated 4 November: *Si des circonstances majeures vous imposent la dure nécessité d'abandonner la rive droite de l'Ens, il faut que votre retraite se fasse aussi lentement que possible. Vous la dirigerez vers Krems, où Je fais bâtir une tête de pont, qui quand même elle ne seroit pas achevée au moment où vous arriverez à Krems, devroit être soutenue coute qui coute, et dont je ferai continuer l'ouvrage jusqu'à ce qu'elle soit en état de défense parfaite.*
2. dated 5 November: *Si, comme Je vous retirer, cela ne devroiot être que pas à pas vers Krems, où il est du plus grand intérêt que vous attendiez les renforts qui vous arrivent, et que vous protégiez coute qui coute la construction de la tète du pont que je fais ériger devant Krems, et qui demande encore plusieurs semaines avant de pouvoir être abandonnée à une simple garnison. Je mets trop de confiance en votre intelligence pour entrer dans les détails sur l'importance que je mets d'abord à la défense de la rive droite de l'Ens, puis a celle de la retraite la plus lente vers Krems, enfin à la conservation d'une tête de pont en avant de cette place.*

Apologising to Kaiser Franz for his inability to comply with orders, Kutuzov informed His Majesty:

> The persistent pursuit of me by the enemy in recent days has given me reason to think that they want to attack us, or have particular intentions from the left bank of the Danube. In fact, I am not mistaken. Crossing to the left side of the river, we saw French marksmen in the vineyards, and assessed there to be up to 40. They all appeared to belong to the corps that crossed the Danube in Linz, and hurried to Krems, intending to place me between two fires. A singular circumstance, Sire, which seems to justify my retreat. As for the bridge fortifications, we found none; just the foundations of a battery, and no one was in it. In general, the local situation of the bridge fortifications is not convenient. I dare to assure Your Majesty that I have challenged the enemy at every step, in the full sense of the word. The evidence is bloody vanguard actions. But it was impossible for me to stop Napoleon for longer without entering into a general battle, which would be contrary to the orders given to me by Your Majesty.[11]

Kutuzov's crossing of the Danube deprived Napoleon of the achievement of the objective with which he had rushed against him from Munich, completely changed the state of affairs, and preoccupied Napoleon. With foresight, he immediately saw Mortier's dangerous position beyond the Danube, ordered a halt to the general offensive of the army, and Soult and Bernadotte to go to Dürnstein, crossing the Danube there in the flotilla to reinforce Mortier, who ordered that all precautions be taken. Napoleon himself settled in Sankt Pölten, awaiting the fulfilment of his instructions, but his orders had not yet been put into effect when Kutuzov repelled Marshal Mortier behind the Danube.

11 Report dated 30 October [11 November].

8

The Battle of Krems

Mortier's movements. – Kutuzov's orders. – The actions of Miloradovich's detachment. – Dokhturov's outflanking movement. – Mortier's withdrawal. – Dokhturov's operations. – The battle at Dürnstein. – The subsequent battle at Krems. – Kutuzov's awards.

Crossing to the left bank of the Danube on the evening of 28 October [9 November], Kutuzov made the collection of intelligence on the strength and movements of Marshal Mortier's force his first priority. Soon Miloradovich presented to him the Frenchmen captured in the vineyards, who had come ashore from the flotilla in order to go looting. They announced that Mortier was at Dürnstein, with Gazan's [Honoré Théodore Maxime Gazan] infantry division, on the march to Krems, and his other troops were further back. The next morning, scouts confirmed the testimony of the prisoners, adding that the other division, Dupont's, was at Spitz 12 *versts* [12.6 km or 8 miles] behind Mortier, a third, Dumonceau's [Jean-Baptiste Dumonceau], was on the march behind Dupont; which was most of the division. Relying on their claims, Kutuzov ordered Miloradovich to fix Marshal Mortier frontally, and Dokhturov to outflank him and cut off his line of retreat. In these features is the essence of Kutuzov's decisions for the fighting at Krems. The details of his orders were as follows:

1. Miloradovich, taking the Apsheron Musketeer Regiment and a battalion each from the Malorussia Grenadiers, Smolensk Musketeers and 8th Jägers, and two squadrons of the Mariupol Hussars, was to wait in front of Stein and fix the head of the French column.
2. Dokhturov, taking 6th Jäger Regiment, Moscow Musketeers, Yaroslavl Musketeers and Vyatka Musketeers, and two battalions each of Bryansk Musketeers and Narva Musketeers, a total of 16 battalions, and two squadrons of Mariupol Hussars, was to go via Egelsee to Scheibenhof and, leaving an observation detachment there, descend from the mountains to Dürnstein, behind Mortier.
3. Strich [Fëdor Borisovich Shtrik] was to follow Dohturov with the Butyrsk Musketeers and two battalions of 8th Jägers, and stopping at Egelsee, operate against the flank of the French.
4. Prince Bagration, with Her Majesty's Leib Cuirassiers, Chernigov Dragoons, Pavlograd Hussars, Kiev Grenadiers, Podolsk Musketeers and Azov Musketeers,

and two battalions of Narva Musketeers and Novgorod Musketeers was to depart from Krems along the road to Zwettl, guard our rear, and watch the roads leading to Krems.

5. Lieutenant-General Essen 2nd with the remaining troops, was to wait behind Stein in reserve.
6. Batteries were to be set up along the bank of the Danube to operate against the flotilla.

Secretly ordering the attack, Kutuzov worried only that Mortier, having learned of his arrival in Krems, would not stay in Dürnstein to wait for his troops to attack. Wanting to lure him out of there further into the defile, Kutuzov deceived Mortier through agents, that we were hurrying to Moravia, stopping in Krems only for the briefest rest for the troops, we were making preparations for the march with local authorities, and had posted Miloradovich at Stein to cover the withdrawal. Mortier believed the false intelligence,[1] and the next morning, without sending observation detachments into the mountains, he hurried from Dürnstein towards Krems, where Miloradovich was getting ready to meet him, Dokhturov made a flanking movement guided by the Austrian Quartermaster-General Schmitt and Strich followed him; he calculated that it would be possible to get behind enemy lines by seven o'clock in the morning. This was the situation on 30 October [11 November], as dawn broke on a cold and cloudy day; the ground was covered with snow.

At the beginning of the eighth hour, the French vanguard, having stayed overnight in Ober-Loiben and Unter-Loiben, set off for Stein. A firefight ensued between the outposts. An hour later, Mortier appeared with a brigade for the assault. Miloradovich advanced to engage him with two detachments: one followed the bank of the Danube, the other through the foothills. The combat began to intensify. Our left column burst into Unter-Loiben with fixed bayonets, but was driven out. Having received help from the reserve, Miloradovich again took possession of the village. Mortier's attack on our right wing in the hills was also unsuccessful; our men held their ground. Rallying Gazan's division, Mortier resumed the attack all along the line, persisting in the false belief that it was necessary to occupy Stein, the better to go from there after Kutuzov. Once more he pushed Miloradovich out of Unter-Loiben. Expecting Dokhturov's arrival at Dürnstein at any minute, Kutuzov ordered Miloradovich to slowly fall back. Mortier moved after us. Before reaching Stein, he was greeted with canister, and attacked in the left wing by the Butyrsk Musketeers descending from Egelsee in the hills. Realising then that he was dealing with superior forces, and not with a weak rearguard, Mortier saw the impossibility of capturing Stein with just one of his divisions, he stopped the assault, limiting himself to an exchange of fire, and sent orders to Dupont to speed up his march.

The day was slipping towards evening and still Dokhturov had not appeared. The guides had led him into impassable mountains, covered with forests, where two

1 *Le maréchal Mortier jugeant par l'incendie du pont de Krems, la nuit précédente, pa les avis qu'il avoit reçus, et par la position de l'ennemi, que Koutousoff marchoit vers la Moravie, et tenoit fortement Stein pour couvrir sa retraite, résolut de forcer ce poste.* Dumas, *Precis des évènements militaires, Tome XIV, p. 10.*

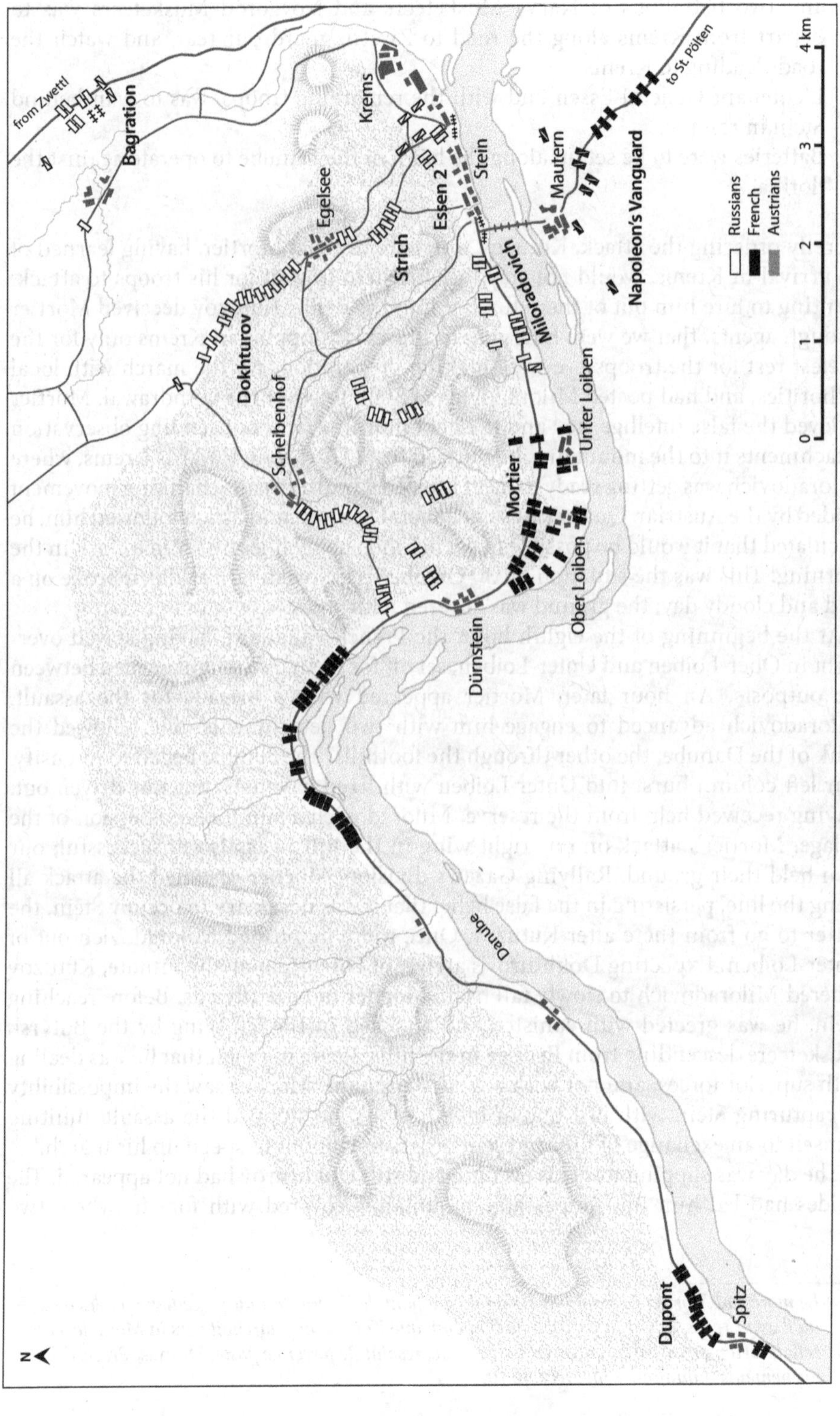

Plan of the Battle at Krems, 11 November 1805.

men could barely walk side by side, and encountering obstacles at every step. Rain increased the difficulty of the march. Hearing the cannon fire to the left, our men tore towards the fighting, but could barely move, stretched out over a wide area. Dokhturov finally left the artillery and cavalry in the defiles, and decided to press on with infantry alone. At five o'clock in the afternoon, instead of eight o'clock in the morning, his vanguard emerged from the mountains, under the command of Ulanius [Karl Karlovich Ulanius] and consisting of his 6th Jäger Regiment and the grenadier battalion of the Yaroslavl Musketeers. Ulanius occupied Dürnstein, having dispersed a small French detachment with three guns that had been defending the gates of the town. The guns were captured by us; one of them being taken by Captain Glebov [Andrei Savvich Glebov] of the 6th Jäger Regiment. Having captured Dürnstein, Ulanius deployed the detachment facing Krems. The Vyatka Musketeers emerged from the mountains behind him. Dokhturov put them on the other side of Dürnstein, facing towards Spitz, seeing the approach of the French from there. This was Dupont's division; they were in a hurry to join Mortier.

At the first news of the appearance of the Russians in his rear, Mortier hastily sent dragoons towards Dürnstein. They attacked Ulanius, but were thrown back. Upon learning from this that the route back through the defile was blocked to him, Mortier summoned his generals and colonels for a council of war. Considering captivity to be inevitable, they invited Mortier to escape by boat to the right bank of the Danube, considering it shameful if Russian trophies were increased with the capture of a Marshal of the French Empire. Mortier rejected the offer, believing his duty was to share the fate of his troops, formed a rearguard to hold Miloradovich, and went looking for a gap at Dürnstein. Noticing the withdrawal of the French, Miloradovich moved forward.

Dokhturov was already in a bloody battle. Even in the morning, hearing the cannonade from Gazan's division, Dupont quickened his march and approached Dürnstein at the same time as Dokhturov was occupying the town. Dupont decided to break through, trying to get in touch with his corps commander. He wrote; 'I still did not know what situation Marshal Mortier was in, but I realized the urgent need to link up with him.'[2] Dupont attacked the Vyatka Musketeer Regiment facing him on the road. Dokhturov reinforced the regiment with troops as they emerged from the mountains, which took place with increasing difficulty because of the encroaching darkness. In the darkness and rain it was impossible to distinguish between mountain paths. Dokhturov soon found himself between two fires. While Dupont was conducting an attack on him on the right, Mortier burst into Dürnstein on his left, having managed to overrun Ulanius, and was squeezed himself from the rear by Miloradovich, who had taken two French guns there. No less bloodshed took place on the slopes of the mountains, in the paths and gorges, where Dupont directed some of his troops to hold and prevent our men from emerging. The cramped nature of the place exacerbated the brutality of the battle. Round shot and canister, rumbling in the mountains, felled trees and crushed rocks. Men were struck with splinters and branches. When Mortier burst into Dürnstein, they cut

2 *Journal des sciences militaires, Tome V, p. 171.*

their way down the streets with bayonets and musket butts. Dupont, for his part, intensified the attack, Dokhturov was in a difficult position, without artillery, in the dark, deprived of the ability to deploy or to discern the actions of the enemy, with his line of retreat along barely passable defiles. Therefore, he was finally forced to clear a route and bypass Mortier. Dupont, one of Napoleon's best generals, describing the battle, said: 'The most lethal fire was blazing along the banks of the Danube and in the mountains. Where the ground only allowed, the troops threw themselves in with the bayonet. The resolve of the Russians was equal to the courage of the French. Both mingled in desperate close quarter combat.'[3]

The fighting around Dürnstein lasted until nine o'clock in the evening, so that for more than three hours they fought in the darkness, lit only by the flash of cannon and muskets firing. Mortier, surrounded several times himself, cut his way out with the sabre. There were moments when the French lost hope of salvation in Gazan's division, led by him, and indulged in fearful panic, which they – a rare case – confessed to themselves.[4] So General Graindorge [Jean-François Graindorge] and two colonels rushed into a boat to save themselves and were stranded in the shallows near the shore. Lieutenant Shklyarevich with several grenadiers from his Apsheron Musketeers rowed to them on a ferry and captured them. The French lost five guns, a colour, the Moscow Musketeer Regiment captured a colour, and 1,500 prisoners. Our batteries set up on the bank, shot at French boats which the enemy was loading with sick, wounded and artillery until late in the evening. Gazan's division was disrupted to the extent that it would no longer be committed to battle during this war. Our losses are not known. There is no official information about this, and they are shown only in a general total, when, after joining up with Count Buxhoeveden, Kutuzov reported on the total losses incurred on the withdrawal from Braunau. It is believed that approximately 2,000 men were lost to our service. Among those killed was Quartermaster-General Schmitt, struck by a bullet during Ulanius' descent from the mountains. His position was filled by the Austrian General Weyrother [Franz von Weyrother]. Mortier withdrew all night to Spitz and before dawn received Napoleon's orders to cross the entire corps to the right bank of the Danube as quickly as possible. Two days later, there was not a single Frenchman left on the left bank.

Such was the Battle of Krems, Napoleon rightly called it a 'massacre.'[5] If it did not end with the complete extermination of Gazan's division, the cause was Kutuzov's ignorance of the ground, because topographic maps of the vicinity of Krems did not exist then, and Kutuzov had to rely on our Allies, locals, who not only vouched for the feasibility of a flanking move, but also took it upon themselves to lead Dokhturov behind enemy lines. However, if the damage suffered by the French was great, the importance of the action was not rated by enemy losses and the trophies we took,

3 *Journal des sciences militaires, Tome V, p. 172.*

4 *Dans ce moment difficile, le général Graindorge céda subitement à une terreur panique, et se jeta sur une barque qui se trouvait sur les bords du Danube. Journal d l'armée, 1835, p. 140. Un général de brigade ayant lui même pris l'épouvante, se jeta dans un bateau pour gagner l'autre rive. Journal des sciences militaires. Tome III, p 92.*

5 *Cette journée a été une journée de massacre. 22me bulletin de la grande armée.*

but by the consequences of the battle. In forcing Napoleon to pull Marshal Mortier back to the right bank of the Danube, Kutuzov gained complete freedom of action, and by observing Napoleon's movements, he could stay in Krems and wait for Count Buxhoeveden, or go to meet him without fear of immediate pursuit, or turn towards Vienna. In any case, he had the means to defend the crossing of the Danube, in anticipation of fresh troops, and carry out operations according to the opinions set out by him at the council of war convened in Wels. In addition, the Battle of Krems had a great influence on morale in Europe. All the battles from Braunau to Krems were rearguard actions that proved Napoleon had finally exhausted the time of easy victories, and he met opponents leaving him the battlefield not from enemy action but by the will of the commander. But as all these actions were followed by our withdrawal, they were depicted by Napoleon as French victories. The Battle of Krems revealed for the first time a marked superiority over Napoleon's troops. Therefore, the news of this battle was greeted everywhere with indescribable joy and as a guarantee of future success. Kaiser Franz immediately sent Kutuzov the Order of Maria Theresa, first class. This is the highest award in Austria in honour of military exploits, and only two Russians had been recipients before Kutuzov: Tsarevich Konstantin Pavlovich and Suvorov. At the same time, the Austrian Kaiser ordered Kutuzov to present him with a list of generals and officers who had distinguished themselves at Krems, and he intended to grant the lower ranks a cash reward.[6] Emperor Alexander honoured Kutuzov with the following rescript:

> The battle of Krems is a new crown of glory for the Russian army, and for the man who led it. My words cannot suffice to express to you and to the whole corps under your command, the pleasure and appreciation that I feel from receiving this pleasant news. I look forward to your reports on those who have distinguished themselves, both in this action and in the preceding ones. I also entrust you to announce to the whole corps the sentiments I have expressed in this rescript.

6 *Lieber General en Chef Kutusoff! Ich habe aus Ihren Berichten vom 12ten dieses mit Vergnügen dasjenige ersehen, was Ich von Ihren Einsichten, Geschicklichkeit und Eifer, der thätigsten Mitwirkung Ihrer Generale, Stabs- und Ober-Officiere und den Muth und der Standhaftigkeit der ganzen, Ihrem Commando anvertrauten braven Armee, welche sogleich hievon zu verständigen ist, erwartete. Ich glaube meine Erkentlichkeit nicht besser an Tag legen zu können, als wenn ich Ihnen, als deren Chef, das Militair-Theresienordens-Großkreuz hiemit, zur stäten Erinnerung an Mich und den glücklichen Sieg, verleihe, hoffend, daß der Kaiser von Rußland, Ihr Herr, dessen Tragung zu bewilligen keinen Anstand nehmen wird. Ferner wollen Sie Mir sobald als möglich, die Generale, Stab- und Ober-Officiere bekannt machen, die sich bei dieser Gelegenheit ausgezeichnet haben, damit Ich auch diesen Beweise Meiner Erkentlichkeit geben kann; dabei behalte Ich Mir vor, für die Mannschaft, vom Felwebel und Wachtmeister abwärts, ehestens einige Gratification anzuweisen.*

Brünn, den 14 November, 1805
Franz.

9

Kutuzov's Withdrawal From Krems

Napoleon's decision to cut off Kutuzov's line of retreat. – The French capture of the bridge at Vienna. – Kutuzov's movements from Braunau to Znaim. – Prince Bagration's march to Hollabrunn. – Murat's vain attempt to deceive Kutuzov. – Action at Schöngrabern. – Kaiser Franz orders Kutuzov to attack. – Kutuzov's response. – The withdrawal ends.

The French describe Napoleon's wrath when he heard about the battle of Krems in vivid colours – the first failure that befell his armed forces in the midst of a most brilliant campaign, on the eve of the day when he hoped to surround and defeat Kutuzov. Instead of the victory expected by Napoleon over the Russians, Kutuzov forced him to be an inactive spectator of the defeat of Mortier. While in Sankt Pölten, Napoleon heard the cannonade near Krems, knew that Mortier's fatal position had been discovered, and could not help him. Having lost the chance to attack Kutuzov on the right bank of the Danube, Napoleon set out to strike him on the left, and at the same time drown out the talk of a momentary setback with a brilliant prize, the occupation of Vienna, adding new laurels to his crown of victory. He ordered Murat, with the corps under Lannes and Soult and Oudinot's grenadier division, to hurry towards Vienna, to seize a bridge over the Danube there, by whatever means, by force or by cunning, then go to the Znaim [Znojmo] road day and night, to get behind Kutuzov on the route connecting him with the troops marching from Russia. He hoped that Kutuzov, who had been secured from attacks from the front by the Danube, would not be in a hurry to pull back from Krems. Indeed, Kutuzov wanted to stay in Krems for some time, and Napoleon guessed his intention. The corps under Bernadotte and Mortier stood at Mautern, opposite Krems, with orders to quickly prepare materials for the construction of a bridge, and at the first news of Kutuzov withdrawing, to cross the Danube in a flotilla and pressure him from behind, placing him between their corps and the troops assigned to Murat. Napoleon himself, with Davout's corps and the *Garde*, marched from Sankt Pölten to Vienna, where since time immemorial enemy flags had not flown.

On the day when these actions were taking place in the French army, on 31 October [12 November], the Russian troops, gathered at Krems after the battle, no longer threatened by an attack and rested calmly for the first time in two weeks of continuous marches and battles. Whereupon the sixth column of Kutuzov's army arrived, which had stopped for a short time in Podolsk Governorate after they left Russia, on the occasion of the mobilisation by the Porte. Kutuzov waited at Krems watching out for further operations by Napoleon, who only had the bridge at Vienna for crossing the Danube. Kutuzov was sure that, according to his thoughts approved by Kaiser Franz in the council of war in Wels, the crossing of Vienna would be stubbornly defended by the Austrians. The expectations of our commander were not realised.

Murat and Lannes arrived in Vienna on 1 [13] November, where there were no Austrian troops at all. Without stopping for a moment in the city, they turned directly towards the bridge, in view of which, on the left bank of the Danube, the Vienna garrison was located, under the command of the Prince of Auersperg [Karl Joseph Franz von Auersperg], who had orders to blow up the bridge, and then defend the crossing point. Close to the bridge, which was covered with incendiary material, there was a cannon to give the signal shot to ignite the bridge; nearby was an officer with a smouldering slow-match. Having thus decided to complete the assignment entrusted to him, the Prince of Auersperg awaited the appearance of the French in order to blow up the bridge. Suddenly, Murat and Lannes appeared on the opposite bank of the Danube with several horsemen waving white handkerchiefs and rode up to the bridge, assuring the Prince of Auersperg that they had the honour of concluding a truce with Kaiser Franz. Having no further hostile intentions against the Austrians, they claimed they were going to look for the Russians, and demanded free passage across the bridge.

The Prince of Auersperg entered into a conversation with them, and without doubting the truth of the words and oaths of Murat and Lannes, asked them about the details of the alleged truce, and meanwhile French columns appeared, and rushed toward the bridge. Confused by the suddenness of their appearance, and trusting the honest words of the enemy about the conclusion of a truce, the Prince of Auersperg fell back from the bank of the Danube and turned onto the road to Brünn. Murat and Lannes immediately crossed the bridge and headed to Korneuburg, on the route to Znaim; Soult and Oudinot followed them.

Napoleon was two days from Vienna when he was informed of the lucky event that gifted this important crossing into his hands. Disguising himself, he immediately went to Vienna, straight to the bridge, gave thanks to his generals for the successful completion of this mission, and ordered the acceleration of the march to the location where the roads from Vienna and Krems join at Znaim, holding Kutuzov there until Bernadotte and Mortier could attack him from behind. Napoleon sent Margaron's cavalry division after the Prince of Auersperg, towards Wolkersdorf, and they captured many treasury and private carts fleeing from Vienna on the way. Having issued his orders, Napoleon left Caffarelli's [Marie François Auguste Caffarelli] division in Vienna, from Lannes' corps, and went to Schönbrunn, where the *Garde* and Davout's corps soon arrived. A myriad of all kinds of weapons, ammunition, colours, military armour were trophies of the French in the capital of Austria. The inhabitants remained quietly calm. The confidante of Kaiser Franz – particularly distinguished by Emperor Alexander after the campaign of 1813 – Count Wrbna [Rudolph von Wrbna], had previously been appointed to remain in Vienna during the French occupation, went to the victor, declaring his readiness to obey his orders, and begging for mercy for the capital. Alexander would not do that, watching Moscow fall prey to the enemy!

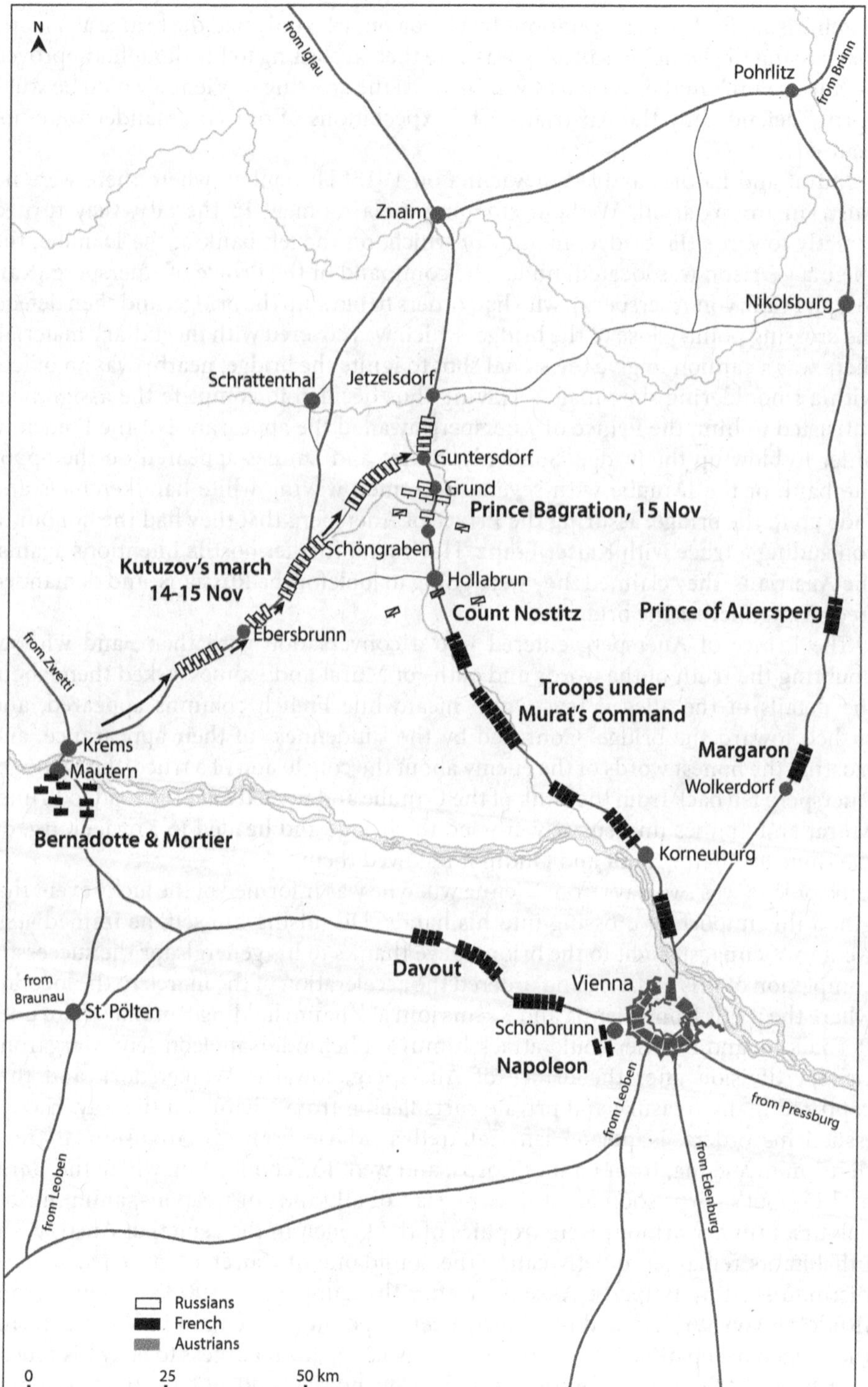

Map of Kutuzov's retreat from Krems.

Kutuzov paid his informants generously and was notified by them on the evening of the same day, 1 [13] November, about the French crossing the Danube in Vienna and their direction towards Korneuburg and Wolkersdorf. Based on these first-hand reports, he concluded that the French would go from Korneuburg to Hollabrunn to cut the road to Znaim, and from Wolkersdorf they would go towards Brünn, for a second chance to engage him there should he break through at Znaim. The conclusion about the march to Hollabrunn was fair, but the second, about the enemy movement towards Brünn, was not substantive, although it was believable, since the informants saw that the French were moving towards Brünn, but in what strength, and at what pace they could not know. From all appreciations, Kutuzov saw the impossibility of staying in Krems, and the need to rush to the road from Vienna to Brünn, his line of communications to Count Buxhoeveden.[1] He immediately ordered the withdrawal, sent the heavy equipment ahead, assigned the rearguard to Miloradovich, and during the night of 1 to 2 [13 to 14] November, he departed from Krems, leaving the sick and wounded in this city, out of concern that taking them with him would slow down the army, which had to move quickly along unpaved roads in late autumn.

Marching all night, Kutuzov arrived in Ebersbrunn on 2 [14] November, where he received official confirmation from Kaiser Franz of the enemy crossing over the Vienna Bridge. The Kaiser wrote to him:

> The most decisive moments are coming. The enemy's intent is obvious: to prevent the unification of the Russian armies, as one might expect. Napoleon's operations are complex, and he has divided the army into several corps, one of which, having crossed the Danube in Vienna is moving towards you. The best thing would be to smash his corps in detail, similar to how Mortier was defeated by your skill and courage. However, in this case, you must take into consideration the strength of the enemy facing you, and the possibility of him falling back on the supports coming after him, which is why I leave operations to your discretion and prudence, knowing in advance that you, together with General Weyrother, will take measures that are most advantageous for the common cause and glory of your army, and take advantage of the excellent morale of your troops.

Further, Kaiser Franz informed Kutuzov that he had dismissed the Prince of Auersperg from the service for frivolously allowing the French to cross the Vienna Bridge, and entrusted his detachment, formerly comprising the Vienna Garrison, to Prince Liechtenstein [Johann Baptist Josef Adam Liechtenstein], hoping Kutuzov was in communications with him, and directing Prince Liechtenstein, who was withdrawing on Wolkersdorf and Nikolsburg [Mikulov], on the French flank and rear.

1 *Le pont forcé près de Vienne, évènement auquel on ne devoit pas s'attendre, et la marche de l'ennemi sur Hollabrunn, me forcèrent de changer mon plan. Aulieu de défendre le passage du Danube et d'attendre tranquillement nos secours, je me vis forcé de précipiter ma marche et de dépasser Hollabrunn pour éviter un combat inégal avec des forces infiniment plus supérieures.* Kutuzov's letter to Miloradovich, dated 26 July [7 August] 1806.

The Kaiser concluded his letter with the words: 'The arrival of Emperor Alexander is eagerly anticipated. When I meet with him, my first priority will be to recommend His generosity to you and your army, and I offer my gratitude again to you and the army led by you, wishing you all good fortune in the coming important operations.'[2]

The letter from Kaiser Franz was an important directive, confirming the intelligence of Napoleon's intention to prevent the unification of our armies. Trying to disrupt Napoleon's plans, Kutuzov hastened to occupy the road from Vienna to Znaim, and immediately after arriving in Ebersbrunn, he sent Prince Bagration to Hollabrunn, ordering him to stay there until the army passed behind him as far as Jetzelsdorf on the Znaim road. Prince Bagration's detachment had just arrived at Ebersbrunn from Krems that night, and the soldiers had not yet had time to cook porridge when they received orders to depart. Despite the fatigue of the troops, Prince Bagration had already reached Hollabrunn by nine o'clock in the morning on 3 [15] November. Although from Ebersbrunn to this town is no more than twenty *versts* [21 km or 13 miles], the march was extremely difficult, in impenetrable darkness, along narrow lanes, vineyards and ravines. The army marched briskly, overcoming local obstacles under Bagration's guidance, who had studied these difficulties under Suvorov, not many generals understood the art of forced marches with the least exhaustion of the men. Having sent off Prince Bagration, and after a brief rest for the army in Ebersbrunn, Kutuzov went on the march on the evening of 2 [14] November, informing the Tsar: 'I will not deceive myself, but on this march I may lose, perhaps, up to 1,000 men, but the whole must be saved, if at all possible.' During the night march, from 2 to 3 [14 to 15] November, in the midst of rain and storm, Kutuzov received reassuring news from Miloradovich that Bernadotte's and

2 *Es scheint, daß dermalen die entscheidentsten Augenblicke begonnen, und die Absicht des Feindes ist klar am Tage, die weitere Vereinigung der Russisch-Kaiserlichen Armee zu verhindern, wie solches zu vermughen war. Die feindliche Operation ist combinirt, und er hat sich in mehrere Corps vertheilt, wovon eines bei Wien die Donau passirt und auf ihre Armee losgehet. Diese Corps en detail zu schlagen, wie es bereits durch die Geschicklichkeit und Bravour der Armee, der feindlichen Division Mortier's erging, wäre freilich das Entscheidentste; da aber hier die Stärke des auf sich zukommenden Feindes, die etwaige Möglichkeit sich dennoch auf die nachkommenden Verstärkungen zurückziehen zu können, das Nähere bestimmen müssen, so kann Ich es nur Ihrer Einsicht un Klugheit anheimstellen und weiß im voraus, daß Sie einvernehmlich mit dem Generalen Weyrother thun werden, was das Beste Unserer gemeinschaftlichen Sache und dem erworbenen Ruhm Ihrer Armee dienlich seyn kann, so wie Sie die gute Stimmung Ihrer ausgezeichneten Krieger zu benüßen wissen werden. Trachten Sie das Corps des Fürsten Lichtenstein (den Feldmarschall-Lieutenant Fürsten Auersberg sehe Ich Mich bemüßiget ablösen zu lassen) von allen Ihren Bewegungen und Absichten zu verständige, damit er nach Meiner Anweisung ihre Operationen mit Bedrohung der feindlichen Flanque un Rückens unterstüßen kann, und erhalten Mich in genauester Kenntniß jeder Ihrer Bewegungen und Vorhaben, wobei der thätige Feind, dessen Unternehmungen bisher das Glück jeder art begünstiget hatte, keine Zeit zu lassen ist. Ich erwarte mit Ungeduld den Kaiser Ihren Herrn, und Mein angelegentlichstes erstes Geschäft wird seyn, Sie an Ihre ganze Armee, wie Sie es insgesammt verdienen, anzuempfehlen, so wie Ich Meine obige Danksagung hier nochmals bei Ihnen insbesondere, als bei der ganzen Armee wiederhole, und Ihnen zu ferneren und vielleicht wichtig werdenden Unternehmungen Glück wünsche.*

Brünn, den 14 November, 1805. Franz.

Mortier's corps, sent after us by Napoleon, were held up crossing the Danube at Krems by the bad weather, they could not catch up with us soon, and only cavalry patrols were seen by our rearguard.

While Kutuzov and, following him, Miloradovich were knee-deep in mud, Prince Bagration, upon arriving in Hollabrunn, found the area unsuitable for defence, and pulled back a few *versts* behind Schöngrabern and beyond the stream. His detachment comprised; the Kiev Grenadiers, Podolsk Musketeers, Azov Musketeers and 6th Jägers, one battalion each of the Novgorod Musketeers and Narva Musketeers, the Pavlograd Hussars, Hessen-Homburg Hussars, Chernigov Dragoons and two Cossack Regiments and a company of heavy artillery. In the forward line Prince Bagration stationed the Kiev Grenadiers, Podolsk Musketeers, Azov Musketeers with the Chernigov Dragoons on the right wing and Pavlograd Hussars on the left, in reserve were a battalion each of Novgorod Musketeers and Narva Musketeers; the 6th Jägers occupied Schöngrabern; forwards in the centre, the heavy artillery company was deployed across the main highway. Graf Nostitz with two Cossack regiments and the Hessen-Homburg Hussars formed the vanguard in Hollabrunn. The village of Grund, to the rear, was hastily fortified; making loopholes in the houses. Preparing to fight to the last drop of blood, Prince Bagration, as usual, as he always did before a battle, gathered the generals and regimental commanders around himself, and talked with them about various events, how the powerful will show themselves while Kutuzov manages to lead the army along a safe route. During the conversation, where the military insights of Prince Bagration were in full splendour, he was informed of the approach of the French. The news of the appearance of the enemy was expected, and therefore it did not alarm anyone, but there was another surprise, later a report was received that Graf Nostitz, having talked with the French, was withdrawing from Hollabrunn. The circumstances of events were as follows:

Murat, unexpectedly meeting our troops on the Znaim road, where he had hoped to forestall us, and seeing the Hessen-Homburg Hussars on the front line, he sent for their commander, Graf Nostitz, saying that a separate peace had been concluded between the Austrians and Napoleon, and the unrestricted French passage across the Danube in Vienna was proof of this. Graf Nostitz believed Murat, and refused Prince Bagration's request to go into combat alongside him. Prince Bagration vainly tried to convince him of the implausibility of a truce, saying that the French assurances were a ruse of war. Graf Nostitz was adamant, and withdrew with his hussars.[3] Prince Bagration put the Cossacks from the vanguard along the flanks of the detachment, sent patrols to observe neighbouring roads, and ordered the army to prepare for battle. Taking advantage of the withdrawal of the Cossacks and the Austrian hussars, Murat immediately approached Schöngrabern, occupied by the 6th Jäger Regiment. Prince Bagration ordered the jägers to leave the village and join the right wing of the detachment. The French entered Schöngrabern, and advanced

3 *Le Général Nostitz, qui depuis qu'il se trouve auprès de moi, a servi avec distinction, trompé par les assurances de l'ennemi, que la paix étoit conclue entre Vous, Sire, et la France, a eu la faiblesse de se retirer, en lasissant aux françois le chemin libre pour tomber sur les russes.* Kutuzov's report to Kaiser Franz, dated 5 [17] November.

towards the forward battery. So both sides, filled with heroic spirit, stood alone in sight of each other at very close range. On the French side there were generals, famed for their glory, Murat, Lannes, Soult, Suchet, Vandamme, Oudinot; on the Russian side was – Bagration. At that moment, Kutuzov had just passed behind him with the army heading for Jetzelsdorf. He informed the Tsar: 'The annihilation of Prince Bagration's detachment was inevitable, as was the defeat of the army itself, because the proximity of the outposts denied us the means for a swift withdrawal, and the exhaustion of the soldiers from forced marches and bivouacs made them unable to resist even in battle. The good fortune which always accompanies Your Majesty's armed forces presented here too the means by which the army was saved.'[4]

Finding himself in the vicinity of Prince Bagration, and learning that Kutuzov was several *versts* away, Murat did not dare to attack, because his infantry had not yet arrived, and were half a day away. He intended to stop Kutuzov's movement by a ploy until the rearmost troops arrived and Bernadotte and Mortier appeared in our rear. As soon as the exchange of fire began on the front line, Murat sent a *parlementaire* to Prince Bagration with the offer of a truce, on condition that the armies remain in their positions, saying that it was useless to shed blood now that there was peace with Austria. Arranging a trap for Kutuzov, hoping to deceive him as easily as he had deceived the Prince of Auersperg and Graf Nostitz, Murat was mistaken in his calculations. Kutuzov turned the trick against Murat, and sent Adjutant-General Wintzingerode to him, with orders to enter into negotiations and conclude a truce. He reported to the Tsar; 'My intention was, above all, to gain time to seek the means to save the army and to have time to move away from the enemy.'[5]

Wintzingerode was met at the French outposts by the Chief-of-Staff of Murat's headquarters, Belliard [Augustin-Daniel Belliard], and signed a truce with him on condition that the Russian army return to Russia from Austria along the same route along which it arrived, and Murat was not to advance further towards Moravia. The conditions were to be submitted for ratification by Napoleon and Kutuzov, and until their approval, the armies of Kutuzov and Murat were to remain in their positions, and in the event of non-approval of the treaty, not to start hostilities without first granting each other four hours notice. This was on 3 [15] November.

The truce was sent to Kutuzov and to Napoleon in Vienna. Murat triumphed, confident of Napoleon's appreciation for his actions. It seemed to him that he had accomplished a great work, through the simple writings of his pen, first forcing the Russian army to stand still, and then return to Russia as if by capitulation, terminating Emperor Alexander's alliance with the Viennese Court, and leaving Austria under the protection of her own depleted forces. Instead of the expected gratitude, Murat received a most severe reprimand. After reading the armistice, Napoleon not only refused to approve the conditions, but reproached Murat in strong terms for ending hostilities, he said that Kutuzov was deceiving him, and ordered him to attack immediately. Fearing new blunders on the part of his generals at any point when he intended to decide the fate of the Russian army, Napoleon hastened to Murat from Vienna himself with the *Garde* and Caffarelli's division. His impatience

4 Kutuzov's report to the Tsar, dated 3 [15] November.
5 Kutuzov's report to the Tsar, dated 3 [15] November.

to make amends for the time lost by Murat was so great that after travelling several *versts* with the *Garde*, he got into his carriage and galloped to Hollabrunn at the full speed of the horses.

Murat was not the only one to feel the wrath of Napoleon: he raged at Bernadotte, who was supposed to pursue Kortuzov with Mortier from Krems. When he left Vienna for Hollabrunn, learning that Bernadotte had not yet crossed the Danube, Napoleon ordered Marshal Berthier [Louis-Alexandre Berthier] to write to him:

> The Emperor is angry with you. Prince Murat, Marshals Lannes and Soult have been fighting the Russians two days march from Vienna, and you have not crossed the Danube yet. Of course, your troops are sadly deprived of their part in the glory of the actual campaign. The Emperor expects to receive a report from you via the same officer sent to you, that you are pursuing Kutuzov, prodding Russians with the bayonet, *que vous leur serrez les bayonnetes dans les reins.*[6]

While what is being described here was taking place in Vienna, Kutuzov received the armistice document and, as he wrote to the Tsar; 'I never considered accepting the conditions. I delayed answering for 20 hours, and I continued meanwhile to pull back, and managed to move two days march away from the French.' Upon reaching the Znaim Road, Kutuzov was to forestall the French in Pohrlitz [Pohorelice], located on the shortest route from Vienna to Brünn. Wanting to hide his movement from Jetzelsdorf to Pohrlitz, he decided to sacrifice Prince Bagration's detachment and left him in sight of the enemy. Condemning Prince Bagration to a glorious fate, Kutuzov made the sign of the cross for him: the ultimate subject for the brush of a Russian artist – Kutuzov blesses Bagration!

On the next day, 4 [16] November, at five o'clock in the afternoon Murat received Napoleon's reprimand and orders to attack immediately. Murat sent a message to Prince Bagration that, having not received ratification from Kutuzov, he no longer agreed to a truce and even refused the agreed four-hour deadline before hostilities could resume. As soon as Bagration had heard Murat's messenger out, round shot and shells dropped on us. All the French troops assembled behind Schöngrabern during the cessation of hostilities began to move. Oudinot's grenadiers and the *Réserve de cavalerie* were to march on the centre; Soult was to envelope Prince Bagration's right wing, while Lannes enveloped the left. Experienced generals, they understood the need for swift movements to compensate for the time lost in negotiations, and to take advantage of what little remained of the autumn daylight. But in the heat of the offensive, some of the enemy troops suddenly stopped. Our gunners, responding to the first enemy shots, had set fire to Schöngrabern, the centre of Murat's position. The fire quickly spread; flames and smoke blew into the faces of the French; embers and sparks threatened to blow up ammunition caissons. The enemy began to evacuate them. The fire would slow down the movement of troops that were closest

6 Dumas, *Précis des événemens militaires, Tome XIV, p. 236.*

to Prince Bagration, that is, in the centre, on the main road, but Soult and Lannes, who went around the flanks, soon began to catch up with our troops.

Our right wing was first attacked by *Grenadiers à cheval*. The Kiev Grenadiers, 6th Jägers and Chernigov Dragoons were under Ulanius' command here. The Grenadiers and Jägers halted, let the *Grenadiers à cheval* close up, greeted them with battalion volleys and repulsed two attacks. The Chernigov Dragoons and Cossacks pursued the French. Under the protection of artillery, skirmishers and Cossacks, Ulanius continued to fall back. The French cavalry again caught up with him, but seeing an orderly march, did not attack this time. There was a stronger attack on the left wing, where Lannes managed to deploy more troops. After several attacks, he separated the Pavlograd Hussar Regiment from the infantry, the hussars were forced to find another route in order to rejoin the army. Then Lannes surrounded the Podolsk Musketeers and Azov Musketeers, who twice resorted to bayonet charges. Meanwhile, Murat and Oudinot, detained for some time by the fires in Schöngrabern, pushed along the highway following Prince Bagration, firing on him with artillery. Like grotesque clouds, the French swirled around us from different directions. Their cavalry took every opportunity to attack the centre and flanks. Our men fought back, maintaining their good order. Prince Bagration moved step by step from one regiment to another, encouraged by the bravery of the troops, and not encouraging anyone, for there was no need for encouragement. Death stalked around Bagration, but spared the hero as if saving him until the battle of Borodino, where a world event was combined with great sacrifice.

Falling back, our troops approached the village of Guntersdorf, where Prince Bagration had sent two battalions of infantry and the Cossacks in advance, ordering them to let the formation pass through and form a rearguard. Here the enemy pressure became stronger, because delays are inevitable during a passage through villages and surrounding gardens. Passing this obstacle gave the French the same problem. Guntersdorf was traversed in darkness. In the darkness of the November evening, coordination in the orders given by commanders disappeared. Their voices were drowned out by cannon and musket fire, the shouts of the attackers and defenders, the groans of the wounded, the screams of men trampled by horses. Each battalion and squadron commander acted as their personal courage dictated to them and in their own formation. The French and Russians were keen to fulfil their duties of service and honour. The enemy tried to surround and envelope; our troops burst through their ranks with their chests several times. Some Russian officers managed to save cut-off elements of the army by cunning: standing in the path of their columns, they shouted in French: 'What are you doing? Stop your retreating!' The pressure, which finally turned into a perfect pursuit, continued until midnight, when Napoleon, having galloped up to Murat, and seeing the futility of further assault, gave the order to cease firing. Prince Bagration hastened to withdraw, giving the army the shortest rest, and two days later, leading a captured colonel, two officers and 50 privates, and carrying a trophy; a French colour, taken at night in battle, restored communications with Kutuzov, who had meanwhile already arrived in Pohrlitz, the objective for this withdrawal. Not finding the French there, Kutuzov saw that there were no more obstacles preventing him from linking up with the troops coming from Russia, and he stopped to wait for Prince Bagration who was, in his own words; 'left facing certain death to save the army.'

When he was informed of the arrival of Prince Bagration, Kutuzov went to meet him, hugged him and said: 'I won't ask about the losses: you're alive – that's enough for me!' Our losses were more than 2,000 casualties. Congratulations for Prince Bagration poured in from everywhere; his troops scorched by battle were viewed with reverence. The name Bagration, already popular in Russia since the Italian campaign, was famous in all parts of the Empire. Kaiser Franz granted Prince Bagration the Commanders Cross of Maria Theresa, which no Russian had at that time. The Austrians, not generous with their praise, in their histories still call this detachment their 'company of heroes,' *Heldenschaar.* Emperor Alexander awarded St George standards to the Pavlograd Hussars and Chernigov Dragoons for the Schöngrabern action; St George colours to the Kiev Grenadiers, Sysoev 3rd's Cossacks and Khanzhenkov 1st's Cossacks and silver trumpets for the 6th Jägers.

Leaving Prince Bagration with the rearguard, Kutuzov marched from Pohrlitz to Brünn. On the march he received orders from the Austrian Kaiser to stop and give battle to Napoleon. Kutuzov replied: 'My loyalty to Your Majesty alone should be enough for the precise execution of your orders, even if the sacred duty did not compel me to do this and obey your will. I dare not, however, hide from you, Sire, how much I would have provided for the event, trusting the outcome of the war to one battle. It's all the more difficult for me to dare to fight, because the troops, although filled with zeal and an ardent desire to excel, are devoid of strength. Exhausted from forced marches and incessant bivouacs, they can barely move, having sometimes gone for days without food, because as soon as they start to cook it, the enemy have caught up with them, and they have to throw their food out of the cauldrons. I believe it necessary to withdraw until I have linked up with Count Buxhoeveden and the various Austrian detachments. Having reinforced with these troops, the enemy will hold us in awe, and we force them to give us several days rest, after which we can switch to the offensive. I hope that the mark of battle will be a harbinger for success for the allied army.'[7]

Sending the report to Kaiser Franz, Kutuzov arrived in Brünn on the same day, 6 [18] November. Prince Liechtenstein had arrived here with his command, the troops of the Vienna garrison. An hour later, Lieutenant Chernyshev [Alexander Ivanovich Chernyshev] of the Chevalier Guard Regiment, now [1844] the Minister of War, came to him with a report that the first column under Count Buxhoeveden was one and a half days march from Brünn. Thus, over the space of 400 *versts* [420 km or 265 miles], Kutuzov had avoided the traps prepared for him by Napoleon several times. Pursued and surrounded by a large army led by this great commander, he anticipated and forestalled his plans, he defeated the enemy at Krems, and carried out a withdrawal, regarded in military history as exemplary. But history still wouldn't fully appreciate Kutuzov's merits, since it was not known until now that on the withdrawal, during the daily struggles, over a three-week period against Napoleon, Kutuzov was often forced to disagree with the *Hofkriegsrat* in Vienna and

7 Kutuzov's report to the Austrian Kaiser from Snanowitz, dated 6 [18] November.

act contrary to the instructions sent to him from Vienna, the execution of which would have led to the certain deaths of the troops led by Kutuzov. Under such an obvious misalignment of thought with the Austrian Court, under whose command Kutuzov worked, he knew how to maintain the same relations with them as with an acquaintance. Honour to the skill and deep intelligence of the Commander, but praise must be given to the unit commanders and soldiers who made this feat possible! From Braunau to Brünn, our army repelled the French at every turn, never giving them the slightest advantage. The generals, officers, soldiers, all sought to retain their superiority in military operations, gained by Russians across a whole century of victories over all of Russia's enemies. Kutuzov's losses from Braunau to Brünn consisted of 5,840 killed and wounded. Performing the feat, Kutuzov, on the very day he entered Brünn, hurried to apply for awards for his two main assistants, Miloradovich and Prince Bagration. Following his recommendations, they were both promoted to Lieutenant-General. Kaiser Franz gave Kutuzov a cash grant of 10,000 silver guilders.

Kutuzov continued to withdraw from Brünn, and on 7 [19] November he linked up with Count Buxhoeveden in Wischau [Vyskov]. Napoleon halted his rapid pursuit, seeing that after the unification of our armies a new period of the campaign was beginning. He stopped, on 8 [20] November, in Brünn and began to concentrate his army there, which, like ours, needed a rest. His troops were stationed in winter quarters, ready to concentrate for the day of battle; the vanguard was at Raussnitz [Rousinov]; Strong French garrisons occupied Pressburg, Vienna and Krems. From these position, Napoleon indulged in the considerations for the third, distressing period of the war.

10

Operations in Italy and Tyrol

Austrian decisions regarding the war in Italy. – Changes to the plan of operations. – The French offensive. – Battle of Caldiero. – Archduke Charles's withdrawal from Italy. – The situation of the Austrians in Tyrol. – Their failures and withdrawal.

Having described operations in the main theatre of war until the time when the belligerent armies arrived in Moravia where, two weeks later, the turning point of the campaign would take place at the Battle of Austerlitz, it is necessary, for a general understanding of events, to briefly describe the operations of the Austrian armies in northern Italy and Tyrol.

The Viennese Court intended to wage an offensive war in Italy, initially to take possession of the fortresses of Mantua and Peschiera, and then advance across Switzerland to France. The command was entrusted to a hero of Austria adored by the army, Archduke Charles. His army consisted of 80,000 men and in September, when Mack marched on Ulm, he was located between Verona and Legnago, on the left bank of the Adige River, at the time the border between Austria and the Kingdom of Italy. They hoped to increase the army to 100,000 men by the end of October. Hiller's [Johann von Hiller] 10,000 man independent corps was in Trient [Trento] and Botzen [Bolzano] guarding communications with Tyrol. Massena commanded the French in Italy, with 56,000 men under arms, and had orders to operate on the defensive, while matters were resolving on the Danube, and to link up with Saint-Cyr's [Laurent de Gouvion Saint-Cyr] 17,000 man corps located in Naples.

The initial Austrian decisions soon changed. When Vienna learned about the alliance between the Bavarian Elector and Napoleon and then about the movement of Napoleon from Boulogne to central Germany, Archduke Charles was ordered to send 20,000 men to Ulm. Having been informed by Vienna of this order, Mack considered it unnecessary to strengthen the army entrusted to him, faithful in the hope of linking his own with Kutuzov's and sent orders to the troops on their way to Ulm from Archduke Charles to return to Italy. The courier found them on the march from Italy. They went back, but did not reach Archduke Charles in time for his battle with Massena and continued the campaign in useless marches. Soon afterwards, the Commander-in-Chief in Tyrol, Archduke John demanded half of Hiller's detachment in Trient.

Having lost the use of the 20,000 men sent to Mack and half of Hiller's detachment, Archduke Charles's strength dropped to almost equal with the enemy, and he had to consider a defensive war, especially since Saint-Cyr's corps was rushing to Massena from Naples. Thus, at the beginning of the campaign, the Archduke and Massena were condemned to inaction by circumstances. Meanwhile, news of French successes on the Danube came to both. On 16 [28] October, Massena received details from Napoleon about the defeat of the Austrians at Ulm, and ordered the offensive to be launched. Victory's favourite – as the French called him – began to prepare to cross the Adige. For his part, the Archduke, concluding from the state of affairs in Germany that an imminent withdrawal from Italy was likely, concentrated his troops in a strong position at Caldiero, between Verona and Vicenza. Stunned by the calamities of his fatherland, he decided to save the honour of Austrian arms, in Italy at least, and not leave this country without winning the victory he needed to secure his anticipated withdrawal. Therefore, knowing about Massena's preparations, he did not shy away from battle. Two days later, on 18 [30] October, crossing the Adige, the French attacked him at Caldiero. This most bitter battle lasted three days. Massena and his troops were keen not to let all the glory go to their comrades on the banks of the Danube; The Archduke and his army exhausted themselves in their efforts to wash the disgrace of Ulm from the name of Austria and repelled all Massena's attacks. On the last day of the battle, the Archduke was ordered by Vienna to leave a strong garrison in Venice, and to hurry to join Kutuzov. During the night of 20 to 21 October [1 to 2 November], he began to pull back. The French chased after him. Having kept them for 24 hours at Vicenza, he reached Treviso unharmed, sent 18 battalions to strengthen the Venetian garrison, and continued to Palmanova. Receiving news on the way of Kutuzov's withdrawal, and seeing the impossibility of linking up with him through Tarvis [Tarvisio] and Villach, the Archduke left Palmanova on 30 October [11 November], the day of the Battle of Krems, and turned towards Goritz [Goricia] and Laibach [Ljubljana], where he arrived on 8 [20] November, the day that Kutuzov and Count Buxhoeveden linked up. During his withdrawal, he put out rumours of the imminent arrival of Russian troops in Dalmatia, and his intention to join them. Believing the rumours, and knowing also that Russians and British were waiting hour by hour in Naples, Massena, who had at first followed the Archduke relentlessly, stopped on the banks of the Isonzo [Soča], wishing to consolidate in the territories he had captured, and not to strip out the army of Italy, threatened by Russian amphibious landings. Having halted on the Isonzo, he sent cavalry patrols to observe the movements of the Archduke, and ordered Saint-Cyr, who had meanwhile marched from Naples to Padua, to invest Venice. Freed from the French pursuit, Archduke Charles continued to withdraw, with the main objective of joining his brother, John, and then marching with him to Vienna.

Such were Archduke Charles's operations. Let us turn now to his brother John. At the opening of the campaign, he was in Tyrol, with 30,000 men divided into detachments to guard the entrances to this mountainous country. They were deployed as follows: having gone from Ulm to guard the Iller crossings and cut off from Mack by Soult, Jelačić was in Feldkirch; Prince Rohan [Victor Louis Mériadec Rohan] was in Füssen; Saint-Julien [Franz Xaver Joseph Herr von Guyard, Graf von Saint-Julien] was in Scharnitz; Tyrolean militia in Kufstein; Archduke John himself was with the reserve in Innsbruck, liaising with the army in Italy through Hiller's detachment in Trient and Botzen.

After the destruction of the Austrians at Ulm, wanting to secure his right wing for further operations against Kutuzov, Napoleon ordered Ney from Ulm, Deroy's [Bernhard Erasmus Deroy] Bavarian division from Salzburg and Marshal Augereau from Feldkirch to go to Tyrol. Ney advanced to Scharnitz, fortified by nature and skill. Despite the impregnability of the place, he attacked and took Scharnitz on 24 October [5 November], after which he turned to the main city of Innsbruck, from where, on Ney's approach, the Archduke pulled back to a strong position on the Brenner, having already received orders from Vienna to leave Tyrol and was in a hurry towards the centre of the Monarchy with Archduke Charles. He ordered Jelačić, who was at Feldkirch, and Prince Rohan, who was at Füssen, to join him via Botzen. Jelačić had not yet received the orders when Augereau managed to get around him and forced him to lay down his weapons without a fight. The same dreadful fate awaited Prince Rohan. On the march from Füssen to Botzen, he was forestalled by Ney, who had already taken the Brenner position, from where, in the meantime, Archduke John had marched to Klagenfurt, fearing to lose communications with Archduke Charles. Seeing Frenchmen on his route, and unable to link up with the Commander-in-Chief, Prince Rohan followed mountain paths to Italy, hoping to make his way behind Massena's army and take refuge in Venice. Notified of the appearance of Austrians in his rear, Saint-Cyr, observing Venice, came out against them, scattered Prince Rohan's detachment at Castelfranco [Castelfranco Veneto], taking him himself. The Tyrolean militia stationed at Kufstein also suffered misfortune. It was surrounded by Deroy's Bavarian division and surrendered. Thus, three formations of the Tyrolean army perished: Jelačić's, Prince Rohan's and the Militia. Pulling together the detachments under Saint-Julien and Hiller, as well as the troops, the messages at the beginning of the campaign from Italy to Ulm, and hence the appeal of Mack to return, Archduke John was hurrying through Villach and Klagenfurt to Windischgrätz [Slovenj Gradec], it was agreed to link up with the army of Italy, on 14 [26] November, the day when the Emperors Alexander and Franz in Olmütz decided to advance.

11

The Camp at Olmütz

The composition of Count Buxhoeveden's corps. – The march of the Lifeguard from St Petersburg to Olmütz. – The Olmütz position. – Napoleon's letter to Emperor Alexander. – The reply to Napoleon. – Austrian negotiations with Napoleon. – Emperor Alexander's orders. – Prussian mobilisation. – Reasons for abandoning the Olmütz position. – Political dealings. – the Austrians assume supreme command of the army. – Expressions of Supreme gratitude to the residents of St Petersburg.

On 8 [20] November, the day Napoleon entered Brünn, Kutuzov linked up with the first column of Count Buxhoeveden's corps at Wischau, and continued to retreat to Olmütz, where the rearmost troops of this corps were, consisting of 26,828 men.[1]

On 10 [22] November, Kutuzov entered Olmütz, where the Emperors Alexander and Franz were, and was appointed Commander-in-Chief of the Russian and Austrian forces concentrated in Moravia. Adjutant-General Prince Volkonsky, now [1844] Minister of the Supreme Court, was appointed Duty General of the army by Quartermaster-General Weyrother. The monarchs planned to remain in Olmütz, wanting to give the glorious but weary army that arrived with Kutuzov a rest, to link up with the Lifeguard and Essen's corps and wait for Bennigsen and Archduke Charles to approach the theatre of war, and await the final decision of the Berlin Court.

Two days later, the Lifeguard arrived in Olmütz, under the command of Tsarevich Konstantin Pavlovich, including 8,500 combatants.[2]

---

1 Count Buxhoeveden's corps consisted of: the Yelisavetgrad Hussars, His Highness the Tsarevich's Ulans and six Cossack Regiments; the Fanagoria Grenadiers, Ryazhsk Musketeers, Arkhangelogorod Musketeers, Pskov Musketeers, Perm Musketeers, Staroingermanland Musketeers, Vyborg Musketeers, Kursk Musketeers, 5th Jägers and 7th Jägers; nine Foot Artillery and two Horse Artillery Companies; two Pioneer and one Pontonier Companies.

2 The Lifeguard consisted of:
Preobrazhensky Regiment – 2 Bns
Semyenovsky Regiment – 2 Bns
Izmailovsky Regiment – 2 Bns
Lifeguard Jäger Regiment – 1 Bn
Leib Grenadier Regiment – 3 Bns
Total: 10 Bns

Full of confidence in victory, the Lifeguard had set out from St Petersburg on 10 [22] August, three days before Kutuzov's departure from the borders of Russia, and arrived in Brest two months later having been greeted joyfully all the way, while Kutuzov waited in Braunau, and Napoleon was in Munich. The peasants of the village of Beshkovichi in the Porkhov *uyezd* [district] distinguished themselves with particular hospitality, and were awarded a thousand roubles by the Tsar. In Brest the troops were granted five days of rest, the baggage transport was reduced and the manning of the Lifeguard was brought up to strength with soldiers from the Petrov and Tenguinsk Regiments. From Brest, the Lifeguard went to Krakow by forced marches, sometimes forty *versts* [42 km or 26½ miles] or more. From the border of Austrian territory lunches were prepared at the half-way point of each march for the officers, on the orders of Kaiser Franz; the soldiers' munitions were carried on carts. The Lifeguard entered Olmütz in full parade dress directly under the gaze of their Monarch, and his gaze found them brilliant. In the centre stood the troops that had carried out the withdrawal from Braunau; on the right wing were the Lifeguard and on the left were Count Buxhoeveden's corps. Emperor Alexander thanked all the troops, especially those who had fought the enemy every day. They were not remarkable for the smartness of their dress or polished weapons like the Lifeguard or Count Buxhoeveden's corps, but for their recent achievements, still fresh in their memories.

After the arrival of the Lifeguard, there were 104 battalions, 159 squadrons and eight Cossack regiments in the army concentrated at Olmütz, including the Austrians under the command of Prince Liechtenstein, 54 very weak squadrons and 20 battalions, for the most part newly formed and mobilised in a month. There were 68,500 Russians and 14,000 Austrians, a total of 82,500 men. The army was bivouacked on an elevated and dominant defensive battlefield, from where it was possible to survey the area for a distance of 7 *versts* [7.3 km or 4.6 miles]. To the rear were wide, deep valleys convenient for concealing the reserves. The batteries were in mutually supporting positions. The front was covered by a river and marshes. To the rear, bridges were laid over the river Morava in case of a withdrawal. The Russians formed the front line, the Austrians the reserve. Prince Bagration's vanguard occupied Prossnitz [Prostejov] and Kienmayer's detachment was in Tobitschau [Tovačov]. Archduke Ferdinand was in Bohemia, near Iglau [Jihlava], with just 10,000 men; the remnants of forces escaping with him from Ulm, various garrisons, commands and depots, maintaining communications with the army through constant movement.

The area between Olmütz and Brünn, a distance of 70 *versts* [73.5 km or 46½ miles], was shared with the enemy army. Despite Napoleon's great successes and conquests over Vienna, his situation was dangerous. Drawn far from France into the

---

Chevalier Guard Regiment – 5 Sqns
Lifeguard Horse Regiment – 5 Sqns
Lifeguard Hussar Regiment – 5 Sqns
Lifeguard Cossack Regiment – 2 Sqns
Artillery Battalion
The infantry were commanded by Malyutin, the cavalry by Kologrivov, the artillery by Kaspersky.

depths of Moravia, he stood within sight of a Russian army previously undefeated by anyone, and which had proved over a 400 *versts* [420 km or 265 miles] withdrawal that the upcoming battle would be bitter. Napoleon knew about reinforcements marching to the Russians and had received intelligence on Archduke Charles's progress, and confirmed through intercepted papers from an Austrian courier that Prussia had entered into an alliance against him. Seeing the allied forces gathering from everywhere, giving them a considerable superiority, Napoleon did not dare to attack the Russian army in their strong positions near Olmütz, not wishing to move even further from his line of communications. He set out to enter into negotiations, and sent the following letter to Emperor Alexander:

> I am sending my adjutant, General Savary [Anne Jean Marie René Savary], to congratulate Your Majesty on your arrival with the army, to pay all my respects to your person, and the desire to find evidence to prove to you how much I cherish the acquisition of your friendship. Deign to accept the message with your characteristic grace, and believe that more than anyone else, I would like to do as you wish. I pray to God that He will keep you under His Holy protection.

Emperor Alexander replied:

> I acknowledge receipt of the letter handed to me by General Savary, and I hasten to express all my gratitude to you. All My desires are for the restoration of general peace on a just basis. I would also like to have the opportunity to do something pleasant for you personally. Accept my assurance of this, as well as My complete respect.

The letter was addressed to the Head of the French Government: '*Au chef du gouvernement françois.*'

The response of Emperor Alexander deprived Napoleon of hope for reconciliation, for he knew for what objective the Tsar was waging war, and consequently, he knew under what conditions our Monarch intended to establish a lasting peace. Napoleon found Kaiser Franz better disposed to an approach. Since the Ulm disaster, wishing to end the war without even sparing sacrifices, Kaiser Franz believed that, given his own disadvantages in Moravia and the imminent war with Prussia, it would not at all be difficult for Napoleon to accept peace with Austria. He expressed his intention to send *parlementaires* to Napoleon to Emperor Alexander. No matter how disgusting such an offer was to the Tsar, seeing his Allies' absolute desire to begin negotiations, He left him to act at his discretion for the good and benefit of Austria, as he perceived it. As a consequence of this comment, Graf Stadion [Graf von Stadion-Warthausen] and Graf Gyulay were sent to Brünn. After hearing them, Napoleon sent them to Vienna to negotiate the conclusion of peace between France and Austria with the Foreign Minister Talleyrand [Charles-Maurice de Talleyrand-Périgord].

The Viennese Court's secret correspondence with Napoleon about peace had already begun earlier. Although this was kept secret from Emperor Alexander, since His determination not to enter into negotiations with Napoleon was well known, however, it did not escape Kutuzov's attention. At a meeting with Mack, when the unfortunate commander was travelling from Ulm to Vienna, Kutuzov found out from him about Napoleon's instructions to offer Austria peace, but he could not find out the details of the proposal, carefully hidden even to the extent that Graf Merveldt, who was present at Kutuzov's meeting with Mack, expressed displeasure when Mack mentioned the commission entrusted to him by Napoleon.[3] Another event confirmed Kutuzov's speculation about the existence of secret relations. When he arrived in Melk, a letter was brought to him from the French vanguard addressed to Graf Merveldt, who was separated from our army at the time following their movement from Steyr to Mariazell. In the room with Kutuzov were the Austrian Generals Strauch, Schmitt and Kienmayer. With their consent, Kutuzov opened the letter. It was from Marshal Berthier, who wrote to Graf Merveldt: 'I have received Kaiser Franz's letter addressed to Emperor Napoleon, and I transmit herewith the answer'. The content of the answer remained unknown to Kutuzov: the Austrian generals immediately asked him to hand them Napoleon's letter for forwarding to Vienna.[4]

Meanwhile, all Emperor Alexander's thoughts were directed towards the continuation of the war. And here we see our young Monarch the same as he ever was, constantly absorbed with the thought – to break Napoleon's sceptre with the sword, for allowing all kinds of violations of people's rights. Concluding from the state of the war that the troops sent by Russia from Corfu to Naples would not be able to influence the situation by remaining in Italy, and would be much more useful in the main theatre of war, He ordered General Lacy [Boris Petrovich Lacy] to embark Anrep's corps on ships and sail from Naples to Trieste and attempt to link up with Archduke Charles. Then the Emperor ordered Essen to quicken his march, Bennigsen to hurry through Breslau to Bohemia, to link up with Archduke Ferdinand, Rimsky-Korsakov to deploy 45 squadrons and 35 battalions from the troops in the border provinces between Brest and Brody, 'so that they can be sent into action at immediate notice.'[5] Mikhelson, who was with Bennigsen's corps, was entrusted with the command of this reserve. Having been ordered to return to Russia for a new appointment, Mikhelson, the saviour of Kazan, in a fit of unsuppressed rage and anger, fell into a chair and burst into tears. He saw himself denied the objective of his fiery desires – to fight Napoleon and crush him, as he had crushed Pugachev [Yemelyan Ivanovich Pugachev].

Good news concerning Archduke Charles was received in Olmütz. He wrote that he had left Massena far behind, established communications with Archduke John, and hoped to link up with him on 14 [26] November at Windischgrätz, 260 *versts* [273 km or 172 miles] from Vienna, after which he would rush to the Danube with 80,000 men. From Berlin they reported on the readiness of the King of Prussia to contribute to the wishes of the Emperor Alexander, portrayed the delight of the Guard on their departure from Potsdam, and the courage that energised the

3 Kutuzov's report to the Head of the Ministry of Foreign Affairs and Count Razumovsky, dated 12 [24] October.

4 Kutuzov's report to Prince Chartorysky, dated 24th October [5th November].

5 Supreme instructions to Rimsky-Korsakov, dated 8 [20] November.

Prussian troops. The following plan of operations was drafted in Berlin: as was usual with Prussian Monarchs, the King was determined to personally lead the main army. The right flank was entrusted to the Duke of Brunswick, the left to the Prince of Hohenlohe [Friedrich Ludwig], the reserve to Field Marshal Möllendorf. The army was supposed to march via Bayreuth and Bamberg cutting Napoleon's communications, and consisted of 103,235 Prussians, 16,000 Saxons and 1,000 from Weimar – 120,235 men.

Independent Corps
General Schmettau's [Friedrich Wilhelm Karl von Schmettau] 1st Corps, 50,000 troops from Prussia and Hesse-Kassel assigned to cut Napoleon's communications by advancing through Fulda.
General Kalckreuth's 2nd Corps, 15,235 troops assigned to march to Hanover and link up with Count Tolstoy.

Reserve Corps
Prince Eugene of Württemburg's 1st Reserve Corps, with 17,367 men in Magdeburg.
General Bila's 2nd Reserve Corps, with 14,579 men in Silesia.
General Grawert's [Julius August Reinhold von Grawert] 3rd Reserve Corps, with 25,278 men in Silesia.
Total: 242,694 men.[6]

All Prussian troops moved to the places from which they were supposed to operate. Just three circumstances were delaying a declaration of war by the Berlin Court: disagreement with the British regarding the amount of money in subsidies, debate with them about exchanging Hanover for Prussian possessions in Westphalia, and not having received a response from Graf Haugwitz sent to Napoleon with the requirements set forth in the Potsdam Treaty. Expecting, however, the imminent declaration of war by the Prussian King on Napoleon with the onset of the month, if he did not receive a satisfactory answer, it was not in doubt that Prussia would soon break with him, imagining that Napoleon would probably refuse the offered terms. Thus, everything favoured Emperor Alexander's views. The Allied forces were concentrating and 170,000 Prussians threatened Napoleon's communications. One had only to wait, and the advantages were apparently turning to our side. Winning time was more valuable than winning a battle. Threatened from many directions, Napoleon would be forced to fight with forces incomparably superior to his own. Victory over him seemed inevitable. The opposite happened.

A shortage of food was experienced in the Olmütz camp. Intending to operate in Swabia, the Austrians had not conceived that the war could quickly shift to Moravia, where no magazines were prepared. The transports were far away and moving slowly. The extremely strict regulations met secret resistance from the civilian authorities. Following the disaster at Ulm, the decline in the morale of the

6 Alopeus' report, dated 24 November [6 December].

population increased daily, the desire for peace grew stronger, peace at any price was all that could save the State from the French. In the area around Olmütz the peasants had dispersed; the villages were empty; it became necessary to use force to get bread. Hunger threatened a lengthy stay in Olmütz. A council of war was convened. Kutuzov recommended pulling back to be closer to the supplies. His views were not accepted and it was decided to advance, despite the fact that two or three days of aggressive marching would be needed to bring Napoleon to battle, which Kutuzov considered untimely.

There were other reasons for the decision to advance, which cannot be understood without explanation of the reasons for the battle of Austerlitz. Unknown to anyone before now [1844], they were: those who had influence in the Viennese Cabinet shared a common opinion in Austria regarding the impossibility of defeating Napoleon and thought that a continuation of the struggle against him would bring terrible catastrophe to the Monarchy, and their fatherland would be turned into the eternal theatre of war even with the assistance of Prussia. Rather, wanting to be rid of the misfortunes that weighed on the state, and those that were foreseen, they wanted peace. Emperor Alexander was an obstacle to achieving this objective. Therefore, they intended to bring His army into battle, from which their compatriots could gain little. In the camp at Olmütz there were only 14,000 Austrians, most of them recruits; the rest of the troops were Russian. The contribution from Austria was not great. The entire burden of battle fell upon the Russians. And victory or defeat led the champions of peace towards the one goal they longed for – peace.[7] It was thought that Napoleon would withdraw if defeated; if he won he would take the opportunity to offer peace. From the Russian side, almost everyone wanted to rush to engage Napoleon, confident in victory, and flushed with passion to fight in front of Alexander's eyes. In addition to lack of food, these were the reasons for the advance from Olmütz, at a time when there was no overall commander of the armies.

In describing Kutuzov's operations, we see that the Viennese Court repeatedly sent him orders regarding his operations, as they had to Suvorov in Italy. Suvorov strongly objected to the orders of the *Hofkriegsrat*, argued with them, and turned their very name into a mocking play on words. The irritation that arose from the frequent disagreements between Suvorov and the *Hofkriegsrat* led to the failed conclusion of the war of 1799 gloriously begun by this great commander. Kutuzov responded differently. Agreeing verbally and in writing with the *Hofkriegsrat*, endorsing the decisions of Austrian generals, he was not embarrassed by the opinions of outsiders and operated as he saw fit, and – a hallmark of all his wars – assumed the responsibility. The Austrians' distrust of Suvorov and Kutuzov did not come from any disrespect

7 Emperor Alexander's confidant, Prince Dolgorukov, informing the Prussian King about the whole truth of the Battle of Austerlitz, told the Tsar:

Je représentai au roi les derniers évènemens tels qu'ils étoient, sans y rien pallier. J'exposai la conduite du ministerè et des armées autrichiennes, sans charger le tableau, ni les ménager. J'éclaircis cette conduite incompréhensible par le désir ardent qu'ils avoient tous de forcer leur Souverain à la paix, quelle qu'elle fut, et qu'ils ne comptoient parvenir à cet abaissement que par la destruction de notre armée, qui seule pouvoit défendre et relever la monarchie autrichienne après l'anéantissement de la leur. Pour parvenir à leurs fins, ils travailloient de toute force.

of our generals or the Russian army. They have always valued the courage of our army more than other foreigners, and give them due respect still, but they have a particular outlook on war. They have their own doctrine and regulations, revered as immutable. They believed the Russians were discontented with their development of strategic military thought. We saw a similar thing later on, in 1813 and 1814 years, when it was rare for a day to pass without Emperor Alexander disagreeing with them. Praising Kutuzov's operations from Braunau to Brünn, they considered it necessary, when linking up with him in Olmütz, to guide his further movements directly. Emperor Alexander, still unfamiliar with war, did not trust Himself – this continued until the year 1812 – and believed that the Austrians after many years of campaigns against the French were thoroughly versed in the methods of warfare against them. Being simply an ally of Kaiser Franz, who had came to his assistance, He gave his main orders to the generals. Their spirit was embodied in Quartermaster-General Weyrother, held in high esteem by the Monarchs, and Adjutants-General Prince Dolgorukov and Wintzingerode, who were advocates for his opinions, both taking advantage of the particular presence of Emperor Alexander. Due to the combination of these reasons, in the last period of this campaign, which included the Allied offensive and the Battle of Austerlitz, Kutuzov ceased to be influential, bearing the title of Commander-in-Chief, but finding himself without any command authority, he submitted to circumstances, issued to the army any orders given to him, and remained a mere spectator of events.

Concluding the description of Emperor Alexander's stay in Olmütz, we will describe the following occurrence in St Petersburg, unaccustomed to the absence of the Monarch, there was concern for the health and welfare of Emperor Alexander; news from the army was eagerly awaited; the churches were full of prayers for the Tsar's comfort. Touched by the expressions of love for Him and the zeal of his subjects, the Emperor honoured the Commander-in-Chief of St Petersburg, Vyazmitinov [Sergey Kuzmich Vyazmitinov], with the following rescript, published for general dissemination:

> From all sides the news reaches me about the repeated expressions of affection for me by the public of St Petersburg, and in general all the inhabitants of this city so dear to Me. I am unable to describe quite how flattering this feeling is for Me. Express to them on My behalf My sincere and heartfelt gratitude. I have never been happier that I am honoured to be the head of such a respectable and excellent nation. Express equally to all that My one desire is to deserve the title that I bear, not for Myself, and that all My efforts are addressed to this one objective.

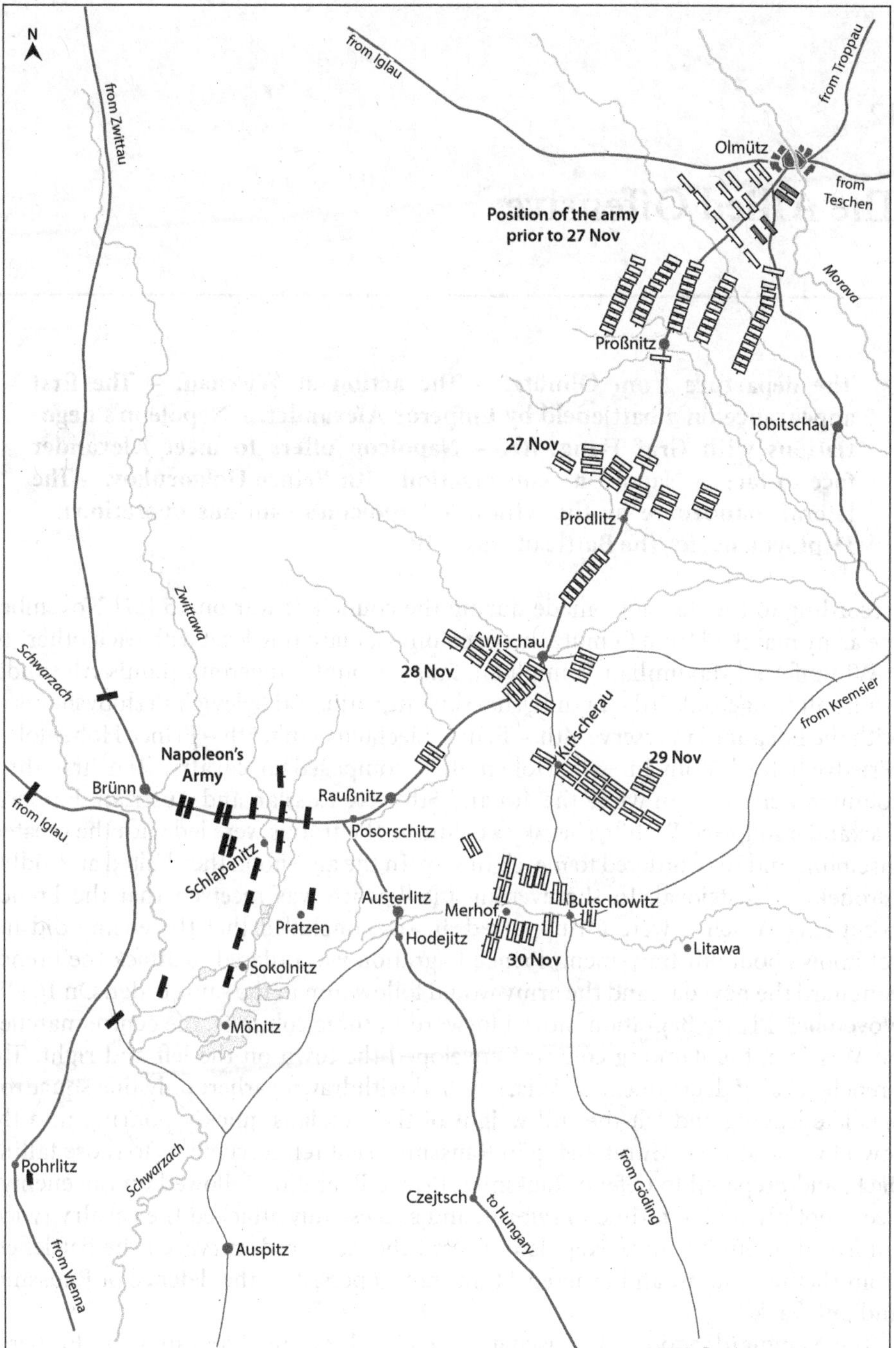

Map of the advance on Austerlitz.

12

The Allied Offensive

The departure from Olmütz. – The action at Wischau. – The first appearance on a battlefield by Emperor Alexander. – Napoleon's negotiations with Graf Haugwitz. – Napoleon offers to meet Alexander face-to-face. – Napoleon's conversation with Prince Dolgorukov. – The lateral manoeuvre by the Allies. – Napoleon's cautious operations. – Deployments for the Battle of Austerlitz.

According to the decisions made during the council of war on 15 [27] November, the army marched from Olmütz in five columns, marching level with each other: 1st – Wimpffen's [Maximilian Wimpffen], 2nd – Count Langeron's [Louis Alexander Andrault Langeron], 3rd – Przhibyshevsky's [Ignatius Yakovlevich Przhibyshevsky], with the Lifeguard in reserve, 4th – Prince Liechtenstein's, 5th – Prince Hohenlohe's [Friedrich Karl Wilhelm von Hohenlohe], composed of cavalry. The first three columns were Russian while the 4th and 5th were Russian and Austrian. Emperor Alexander followed Przhibyshevsky's column. The troops were led with the greatest discipline and were ordered to march in step. In the afternoon they halted at Prödlitz [Brodek u Prostejova]. In the evening intelligence was received that the French occupying Wischau were unsupported, it was concluded that the enemy did not yet know about our movement; Prince Bagration was ordered to attack the French vanguard the next day, and the army would follow him in the same order. On 16 [28] November, Prince Bagration moved forward in three columns, the centre marched on Wischau, the flanking columns enveloped the town on the left and right. The French cavalry detachment in Wischau had withdrawn earlier; only one squadron was late leaving and felt the full weight of the Russians quickly pouring into the town by side streets. Murat, being in Raussnitz, sent reinforcements to those falling back, and prepared to defend Raussnitz. Prince Bagration followed on the enemy's heels, not giving them time to reform, and successfully attacked the cavalry twice. Informed of our advance, Napoleon visited the vanguard, surveyed the battlefield from the mountains, and ordered Murat not to persist in the defence of Raussnitz and pull back.

The vanguard action at Wischau is recalled in the Biography of Emperor Alexander: here, for the first time He came under fire and was within sight of Napoleon. Alexander's lessons in victory were tough, and had covered a huge sweep before his final meeting with Napoleon on the battlefield, which took place nine years after the Wischau action, at Arcis, 150 *versts* [160 km or 100 miles] from Paris.

He was waiting for nine years, full of labour, defeat, triumph, all the occasions of changeable fortune in gigantic wars. In the morning, upon hearing the gunfire, the Tsar joined the vanguard. It was a festive moment. The soldiers' jubilation drowned the noise of the guns. Initially in a cheerful mood the Emperor followed the offensive movements of the columns, but when the firing subsided he walked silently around the battlefield and peered through his lorgnette [a type of spectacles] at the prone bodies, and ordered aid to be given to those in whom he noticed the spark of life. Saddened at the sight of those struck by death and wounds, the Emperor did not eat anything all day and by the evening felt unwell.

The army was located in front of Wischau, where the headquarters were set up, 30 *versts* [32 km or 20 miles] from Brünn. A clash with the enemy seemed almost inevitable, but opinions differed on further operations. Initially they wanted to continue pushing down the highway, and attacking the French near Brünn, but then it was decided to leave the Olmütz road, choose a new operational route from Hungary, make an oblique march to the left drawing closer to Archduke Charles and cutting Napoleon's route to Vienna.

On that evening, 16 [28] November, Napoleon, upon returning from the vanguard, met Graf Haugwitz in Brünn, who had secret orders from his Court to dawdle *en route*, giving the Prussian army time to concentrate.[1] Indeed, he was in no hurry. The Potsdam Treaty was signed on 22 October [3 November]. Graf Haugwitz left Berlin on 3 [15] November, stayed for several days in Dresden for imaginary negotiations with the Elector of Saxony and in Prague under the guise of an illness that had stricken him, and arrived in Brünn no earlier than 16 [28] November. Greeted immediately by Napoleon, Graf Haugwitz, fearing to annoy him, surprisingly decided not to announce all the demands with which he was sent from Berlin, and during the first audience limited himself to talking about the need to guarantee peace in Europe, by offering the mediation of Prussia for a general reconciliation.[2] Napoleon, as mentioned above, already knowing the real purpose of the embassy of Graf Haugwitz from the papers of an intercepted courier, did not reject mediation, but said that as he was facing a Russian army in full offensive, he had no time to engage in diplomacy. He invited Graf Haugwitz to go to Vienna, to begin negotiations with Talleyrand. Of course, Napoleon saw that the impending battle would be the best response, since the vanquished could not expect the indulgence of Prussia and it would be easy for the victor to restore relations with them.

Having sent Graf Haugwitz to Vienna, Napoleon only temporarily postponed the thunderous breach with Prussia and did not eliminate the fear of war with them, however, he decided to turn to Emperor Alexander again. At night, he sent General Savary to Wischau to offer the Tsar a personal meeting between the vanguards, pausing hostilities for a day. Savary arrived in Wischau at dawn on 17 [29] November. The Emperor did not accept the invitation, he sent Adjutant-General Prince Dolgorukov to Napoleon while he followed the army himself. That same morning, the left wing departed from the Olmütz road, and after eight *versts* [8.4

1 Count Stackelberg's [Gustav Ernst von Stackelberg] report from Berlin, dated 10 [22] July 1806.
2 Alopeus' report, dated 7 [19] December.

km or 5½ miles], they stopped at Kutscherau [Kučerov]. The vanguards were: Prince Bagration ahead of Raussnitz, Kienmayer in sight of Austerlitz.

During this manoeuvre, Prince Dolgorukov arrived at the front line of the French army, where Napoleon soon arrived, accompanied by two squadrons. Seeing our *parlementaire*, he got off his horse, greeted him cordially, and went to him along the highway. Inquiring about the health of Emperor Alexander, he stopped and said suddenly: 'how long do you think we will fight?' To the reply that the issue could not be resolved quickly, Napoleon objected: 'What do they want from me? Why is Emperor Alexander fighting me? What does He require? Let Him extend the borders of Russia at the expense of His neighbours, especially the Turks, then all his quarrels with France will be over.' Prince Dolgorukov replied that the Emperor was not seeking acquisitions for Russia, did not harbour hostility towards France, respected them, and wished them all possible happiness, but had armed himself for the independence of Europe. He further stated that the Emperor could not look indifferently at the French occupation of Holland, at the misfortunes of the Sardinian King, deprived of his property by the French, without receiving the compensation promised to him by the treaties between Russia and France. Napoleon replied; 'Russia needs to follow a completely different policy and think about its own interests.' Again he objected that Emperor Alexander only wished for lasting peace for all Powers. The conversation continued in this manner on the road for no more than an hour. Seeing no hope of rapprochement, Napoleon said: 'Well then, we will fight!' Without answering and, throughout the meeting avoiding addressing Napoleon as 'Your Imperial Majesty,' Prince Dolgorukov remounted his horse and left.[3] French historians have written that returning from the vanguard, Napoleon said of the Allies: 'Strange people! They want me to give up all our conquests without a fight and pull back behind the Rhine, yet they cannot take Vienna from me.' Mentioning his conversation with Prince Dolgorukov in bulletins, Napoleon said of it: 'Even then I would not accept the proposals he brought if the Russians were standing on the heights of Montmartre.' Napoleon thought and acted differently when Alexander actually approached Montmartre!

Returning to Kutscherau, Prince Dolgorukov talked about the discouragement he had noticed in the French army. He said; 'Our success is undoubted, we only need to advance and the enemy will withdraw, as they withdrew from Wischau.' His words were believed. Eyewitnesses unanimously claim that the intelligence Prince Dolgorukov brought about the French army, and even, according to him, the shaky morale of Napoleon himself, was one of the reasons for the Allies to push for an attack without delay.

The next morning, 18 [30] November, the army continued to move its left wing, stopping at Merhof [Marefy], 12 *versts* [12.6 km or 8 miles] from Kutscherau. Prince Bagration occupied Posorschitz [Pozořice] and Kienmayer held Austerlitz. The slowness of our two-day march arose from a shortage of food, waiting for supplies and the complete lack of knowledge of the enemy situation. Although we were in a land friendly to us, we had no informants. The movements were clumsy along

3 Prince Dolgorukov's report to the Tsar, dated 13 [25] December.

bad country roads, and served Napoleon as an indication of the true intentions of the Allies: targeting his right wing. He had carefully examined the surroundings of Austerlitz, and ordered the marshals to study them, repeating: 'There will be a battle here!' Seeing the advance of Prince Bagration to Posorschitz and Kienmayer to Austerlitz, Napoleon drew his vanguard back, leaving patrols ahead of the army, and concentrated the army between Austerlitz and Brünn, behind lakes, a marshy river and villages. These orders, apparently betraying Napoleon's fears, filled the Allies with greater hope of success, since his previous operations were always marked by bold movements, and now his vanguard had been withdrawing for several days, and he took no action, meekly waiting in defensive positions. In the evening, we received a new subordination of regiments to columns, following which the composition in which the troops advanced the next morning to Austerlitz and then acted in battle was as follows:

1st Column
Dokhturov's
Units;
5th Jägers [later detached to Bagration] and one battalion from 7th Jägers.
Novoingermanland Musketeers.
Yaroslavl Musketeers.
Vladimir Musketeers.
Bryansk Musketeers.
Vyatka Musketeers.
Moscow Musketeers.
Kiev Grenadiers.
2 Battery Companies of Artillery.
1 Pioneer Company.
2½ Sotnia of Cossacks.

Ahead of Dokhturov's
Kienmayer's Detachment
2 Cossack Regiments.
3 weak Hungarian Cavalry Regiments.
5 Croat Battalions.

2nd Column
Count Langeron's
Units;
8th Jägers.
Vyborg Musketeers.
Perm Musketeers.
Kursk Musketeers.
Ryazhsk Musketeers.
Fanagoria Grenadiers.
1 Pioneer Company.
2½ Sotnia of Cossacks.

3rd Column
Przhibyshevsky's
Units;
2 battalions of 7th Jägers.
Galits Musketeers.
Butyrsk Musketeers.
Podolsk Musketeers.
Narva Musketeers.
Avoz Musketeers.
1 Pioneer Company.

4th Column
Kolowrat's [Vincent Maria Graf Liebsteinsky von Kolowrat]
15 weak Austrian battalions
Miloradovich's
Units;
Apsheron Musketeers.
Smolensk Musketeers.
Novgorod Musketeers.
Malorussia Grenadiers.
1 Battery Company of Artillery.
1 Pioneer Company.

5th Column
Prince Liechtenstein's
Units;
Yelisavetgrad Hussars.
Kharkov Dragoons.
Chernigov Dragoons.
His Highness' Ulans.
32 Austrian squadrons.

Prince Bagration's Detachment
Pavlograd Hussars.
Mariupol Hussars.
St Petersburg Dragoons.
Tver Dragoons.
Her Majesties Leib Cuirassiers.
6th Jägers.
Staroingermanland Musketeers.
Arkhangelogorod Musketeers.
Pskov Musketeers.
8 Sotnia of Cossacks.
2 Horse Artillery Companies.
1 Foot Artillery Company.

Reserves
Tsarevich's
Units;
Chevalier Guard Regiment.
Lifeguard Horse Regiment.
Lifeguard Hussars.
Lifeguard Cossacks.
Preobrazhensky Regiment.
Semyenovsky Regiment.
Izmailovsky Regiment.
Lifeguard Jäger Battalion.
Leib Grenadier Regiment.
Lifeguard Artillery Regiment.

It was the eve of the Battle of Austerlitz, 19 November [1 December]. At noon, the Allied army left the camp at Merhof, and having crossed Austerlitz, settled down at four o'clock, as follows: Dokhturov's 1st Column in Hostieradek [Hostěrádky-Rešov], with Kienmayer's detachment in front, at Aujest [Újezd u Brna]; Count Langeron's 2nd on Dokhturov's right wing; Przhibyshevsky's 3rd at Pratzen [Prace]; Kolowrat's 4th behind them; Prince Liechtenstein's 5th Cavalry to the left of the 3rd and 4th Columns; Prince Bagration's on the Brünn highway near Posorschitz; the Lifeguard in front of Austerlitz. There was a total of not more than 80,000 men in the army.

During this movement beyond Austerlitz it was still light, and Napoleon was watching for the alignment of our columns, being in the forward outposts, where there was some minor skirmishing. The French were falling back everywhere, but slowly, and finally withdrew to the positions where their troops occupied the following places: on the left wing astride the road from Brünn to Olmütz, Lannes' Corps; three infantry divisions and one of cavalry, having a supporting battery of 18 guns ahead of them on the Santon hill; in the centre at Jirschikowitz [Jiříkovice], Bernadotte's Corps of two infantry divisions and one of cavalry; on the right wing at Puntowitz [Ponětovice] and Kobelnitz [Kobylnice], Soult's Corps of two infantry divisions and one of cavalry. In the second line, Murat's *Réserve de cavalerie* of two dragoon divisions and two of cuirassiers, behind them, Oudinot's ten grenadier battalions; in the rear line, the foot and horse of the *Garde* of ten battalions and 14 squadrons. Thus, Napoleon's main forces were concentrated in the space of four *verst* [4.2 km or 2½ miles], between Kobelnitz and the Santon hill. On the extreme right wing, between Sokolnitz [Sokolnice] and Telnitz [Telnice], behind the Goldbach [Říčka] stream, stood Legrand's [Étienne Legrand] infantry division and Margaron's [Pierre Margaron] light cavalry; four *versts* [4.2 km or 2½ miles] behind them, at Raigern [Rajhrad], was Marshal Davout, with one infantry and one cavalry division. In total, there were some 90,000 men in the French army.

Having reviewed Napoleon's position, adjoining the mountains to the left, and covered frontally by ponds, villages and streams, the Allies intended to envelope his right wing, passing a significant number of troops over the Goldbach at Telnitz and Sokolnitz. For these reasons, at the end of the survey, they began to make a disposition, but at that time Napoleon was preparing for an offensive battle himself, and when it got dark, he pushed Soult's and Bernadotte's corps over the stream, placing them in front of Jirschikowitz, Puntowitz, and Kobelnitz, pushing the reserves up behind them and assigning all these troops to strike at our centre. At ten o'clock in the evening in darkness the movement ended, but with great precision, because, on Napoleon's orders, the generals had previously examined the ground.

As the corps were taking up their new positions, Napoleon rode along the bivouacs and looked at our campfires. The French camp was roused. The soldiers raised lit straw torches, and vowed to Napoleon to celebrate the anniversary of his coronation, coming the next day, with victory. Returning to his headquarters, Napoleon issued orders, announcing that tomorrow the great question of the honour of France would be decided: which is the best infantry in the world, French or Russian? Boosting the courage of the troops, he did not conceal his decisions, saying: 'We will take advantage of the Allied manoeuvre as they envelope our right wing.' Military historians unanimously acknowledge the decision to put two corps ahead of a defile before the battle as one of Napoleon's boldest operations. They also attribute a hunch about the intention of the Allies to attack him on his right to his great genius. Fictional praise is not necessary for this amazing commander. The movements he made in the evening, and his orders for the Battle of Austerlitz in general, were based on his knowledge of our decisions.[4]

The huge glow, a reflection of the festive greeting of Napoleon by his army, led us to the conclusion that the French intended to withdraw; it was thought that the enemy increased their campfires deliberately, wanting to hide their retrograde movement. Adjutant-General Prince Dolgorukov visited the outposts of Colonel Count O'Rourke, and ordered him to observe which direction the French would withdraw, saying that we probably knew about their decision to pull back.[5] That was almost the unanimous opinion in our headquarters. It was feared that Napoleon would not accept battle, and dispositions were hurriedly drawn up. In essence, these were as follows: Dokhturov's 1st Column would leave Hostieradek, cross Aujest towards Telnitz, occupy the village and turn to the right, level with the head of Count Langeron's 2nd Column, which was assigned to break through between Telnitz and Sokolnitz; Przhibyshevsky's 3rd Column was to descend from the Pratzen heights towards Sokolnitz and occupy it, in alignment with the first two columns. All these troops would be under the direction of Count Buxhoeveden. Kolowrat's 4th Column was to break through at Kobelnitz, then join its left flank to the third column and push back the enemy right wing towards Latein [Líšeň] together. At the start of the battle, Prince Bagration was to hold in front of Posorschitz and maintain this position at all costs, and on seeing the success of the four columns, act offensively, at least not allowing himself to be be enveloped on the left. To strengthen his left wing, they sent him the Yelisavetgrad Hussars, Chernigov Dragoons and Kharkov Dragoons entrusted to Adjutant-General Uvarov [Fëdor Petrovich Uvarov] from

4 *On amena l'armée de Votre Majesté plutôt pour la livrer à l'ennemi, que pour le combattre, et, ce qui achève cette infamie, c'est que nos dispositions étoient connues de l'ennemi, ce dont on a des preuves certaines.* Prince Dolgorukov's report to the Tsar, dated 6 [18] December.

5 From the Notes of Count O'Rourke.

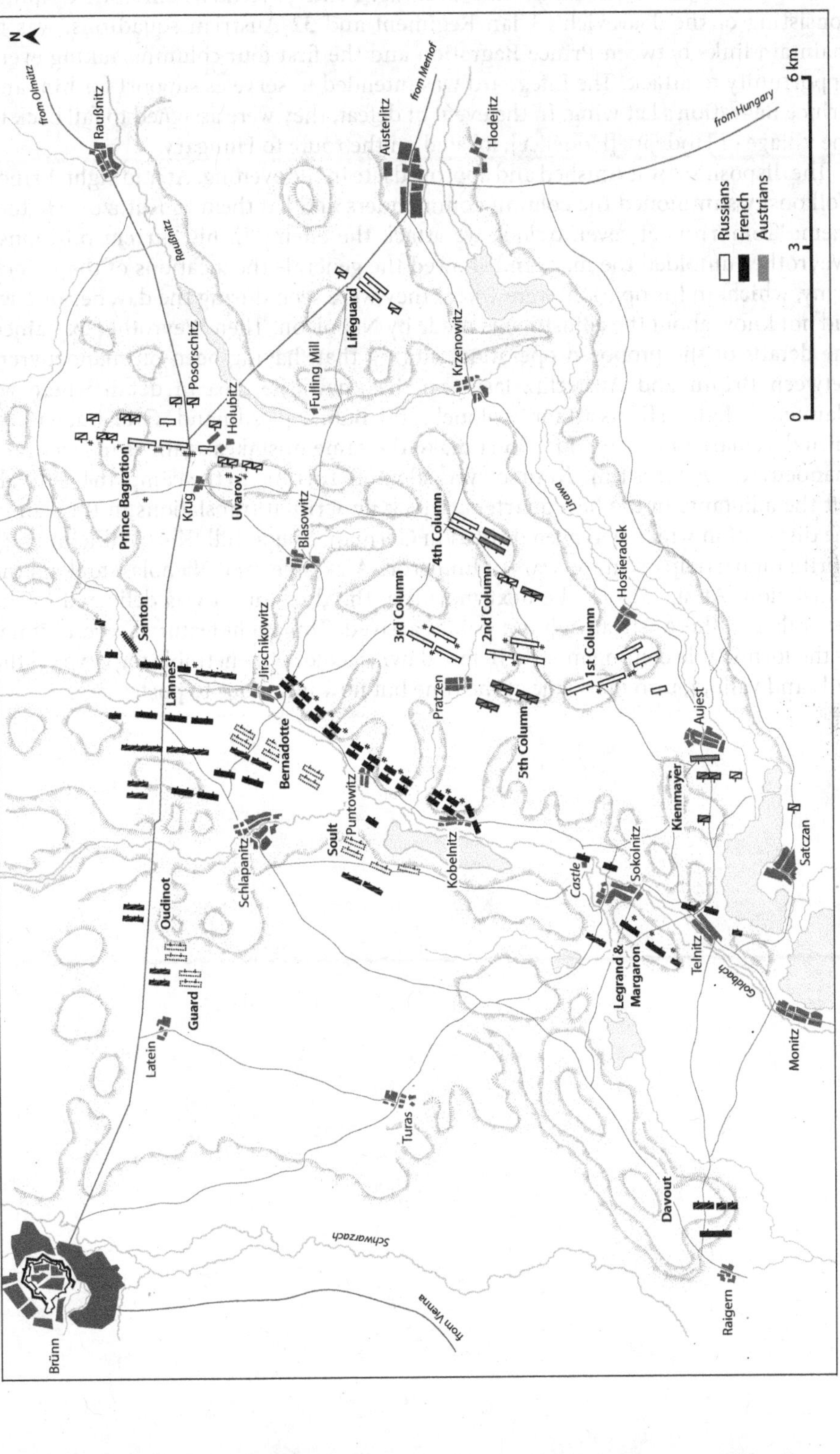

Plan of troop deployments prior to the Battle of Austerlitz.

Prince Liechtenstein's Column, that evening. Prince Liechtenstein's 5th Column, consisting of the Tsarevich's Ulan Regiment and 32 Austrian squadrons, was to maintain links between Prince Bagration and the first four columns, taking every opportunity to attack. The Lifeguard was intended to serve as support for him and Prince Bagration's left wing. In the event of defeat, they were assigned to fall back to the village of Hodejitz [Hodějice], located on the route to Hungary.

The disposition was finished and approved late in the evening. At midnight, Prince Volkonsky summoned the column commanders and led them to Kutuzov. He told them: 'Tomorrow at seven o'clock we attack the enemy in his current positions.' Weyrother unfolded the map, and showed the generals the locations of the French army, which, in his opinion, were where they were seen during the day, because we did not know about the adjustments made by Napoleon. Then Weyrother explained the details of the proposed operation, adding that, having been on manoeuvrers between Brünn and Austerlitz last year, he knew the area in detail where we planned to fight. His assistant, Colonel Graf Bubna [Ferdinand, Graf Bubna von Littitz], remarked to him: 'Just don't make the same mistakes again as in last year's manoeuvres.' All this time Kutuzov was silent. Returning to the camp, the generals left the adjutants in the headquarters to pick up written translations in Russian of the disposition which had been drafted in German. Major Toll [Karl Wilhelm Toll], a brilliant participant in the wars of Emperors Alexander and Nicholas, took up the translation. At six o'clock the next morning, the disposition was delivered to the generals and the Austrian column guides arrived. This night featured several times in the formidable coming month. Before dawn, a cold, impenetrable fog covered the hills and valleys, unremarkable at the time but now infamous to posterity.

13

The Battle of Austerlitz

Napoleon's dispositions. – The initial operations of Dokhturov, Count Langeron and Przhibyshevsky. – The arrival of the monarchs on the battlefield. – The defeat of our centre. – Count Kamensky's battle. – The exploits of Prince Volkonsky. – The actions of the Lifeguard. – The actions of the Allied cavalry. – The defeat of the Lifeguard. – Prince Bagration's operations. – The defeat of Count Langeron and Przhibyshevsky. – Dokhturov's exploits. – Withdrawal. – Napoleon's conversations with Russian prisoners of war. – Troop locations at the end of the battle.

Today [1844], forty years after the battle of Austerlitz, it would simply be unforgivable not to tell the whole truth about it, how strange it would seem if an historian intended to keep silent about the Russian defeat at Narva during the reign of Peter the Great. We will relate Austerlitz's bloody day, as impartially as we talk about Alexander's victories.

On 20 November [2 December], at 8 o'clock in the morning, the first three columns emerged from their overnight camps: Dokhturov set off for Telnitz; Count Langeron followed on his right wing; Przhibyshevsky descended from Pratzen towards Sokolnitz. Napoleon stood on the mound at Schlapanitz [Šlapanice], surrounded by his marshals, summoned to him even before dawn. Our movements were initially hidden from him by the fog. As the sun illuminated the mountain peaks, Napoleon saw that the heights we had occupied were stripped of troops and our columns had taken the directions that completely agreed with what he had announced in his orders to the army. Obviously knowing that, he gave the marshals their final orders: Bernadotte and Soult were to occupy the Pratzen heights, cutting our army in two, and to start the attack in half an hour, hoping that by then the allied forces would be even more divided; Murat's *Réserve de cavalerie*, Oudinot's grenadiers, and Bessières' [Jean-Baptiste Bessières] *Garde* were to follow Soult and Bernadotte; Lannes and Davout were to operate on the defensive on the flanks until success in the centre was certain. The bivouac smoke and fog covering the valleys prevented us from seeing the troops concentrated by Napoleon the previous evening on our side of the defile, and we were of the opinion that the enemy was standing behind the streams and ponds.

The first musket shots rang out on our left wing, where Kienmayer's detachment was closest to the French, at Aujest, who was required to take Telnitz and clear the way for Dokhturov's 1st Column. In front of Telnitz, Kienmayer encountered some of Legrand's and Margaron's divisions, located on the extreme right wing of the French army. The village of Telnitz, surrounded by vineyards and ditches, gave the enemy a strong defence. Having already distinguished himself with Suvorov at Rymnik and full of courage, Kienmayer broke into the village twice, but could not establish a foothold in it. An hour later, Count Buxhoeveden appeared with Dokhturov's Column, and sent a battalion of the 7th Jäger Regiment and Löwis' [Fëdor Fëdorovich Löwis] brigade, the Novoingermanland Musketeers and Yaroslavl Musketeers, to reinforce the Austrians. Kienmayer and Löwis attacked and took Telnitz. Count Buxhoeveden, sticking to the assignment given to him in the disposition to stay level with the head of Count Langeron's second column, limited himself to capturing Telnitz and halted any further advance by Dokhturov, waiting for the arrival of Count Langeron.

As soon as the fire died down, Davout arrived from Raigern, with Friant's [Louis Friant] infantry division and Bourcier's [François Antoine Louis Bourcier] cavalry, and took command of Legrand's and Margaron's divisions. He marched on Telnitz in the midst of a dense fog and charged with the bayonet at the battalion of the 7th Jäger Regiment and the Austrian infantry occupying the village. The Allies fell back in disorder. The Novoingermanland Musketeers, sent to support them, ran into those running back and became mixed up with them. The French also could not escape disorder. Unable to distinguish between objects in the damp half-light, they fired on each other. When it cleared up, they began to advance from Telnitz in our direction, but were overrun by the Hessen-Homburg Hussars, after which Count Buxhoeveden again took possession of Telnitz and established himself in it.[1] These were the initial actions of Dokhturov's Column.

Count Langeron left the overnight camp at the same time with Dokhturov on his left flank. In the lead was the 8th Jäger Regiment; behind them marched the Vyborg Musketeers, Perm Musketeers and Kursk Musketeers; Count Kamensky 1st [Sergey Mikhailovich Kamensky] followed with the main body of the Ryazhsk Musketeers and Fanagoria Grenadiers. At half-past nine, as Dokhturov was launching his attack on Telnitz, Count Langeron was approaching the Goldbach, he was blocked by skirmishers and batteries set up on the other side of the stream, and started to engage the enemy.

Przhibyshevsky's column set off from Pratzen towards Sokolnitz, also on the left flank: in the lead were two battalions of the 7th Jäger Regiment; following them were the Butyrsk Musketeers, Galits Musketeers, Narva Musketeers, Podolsk Musketeers and Azov Musketeers. Vineyards, ditches and ravines slowed the march. Approaching to within musket range of Sokolnitz, our men noticed that the castle, besides which ran the road over the stream, was occupied by the French. Przhibyshevsky ordered Major-General Miller 3rd [Ivan Ivanovich Miller] to attack the castle with the Galits Musketeers and two battalions of the 7th Jägers. Miller successfully completed the mission, drove the enemy off and took two guns, but was seriously wounded. Major-General Strich took his place. Przhibyshevsky supported him with the Butyrsk Musketeers, and attacked the high ground to where the French

1 Buxhoeveden's report to Kutuzov.

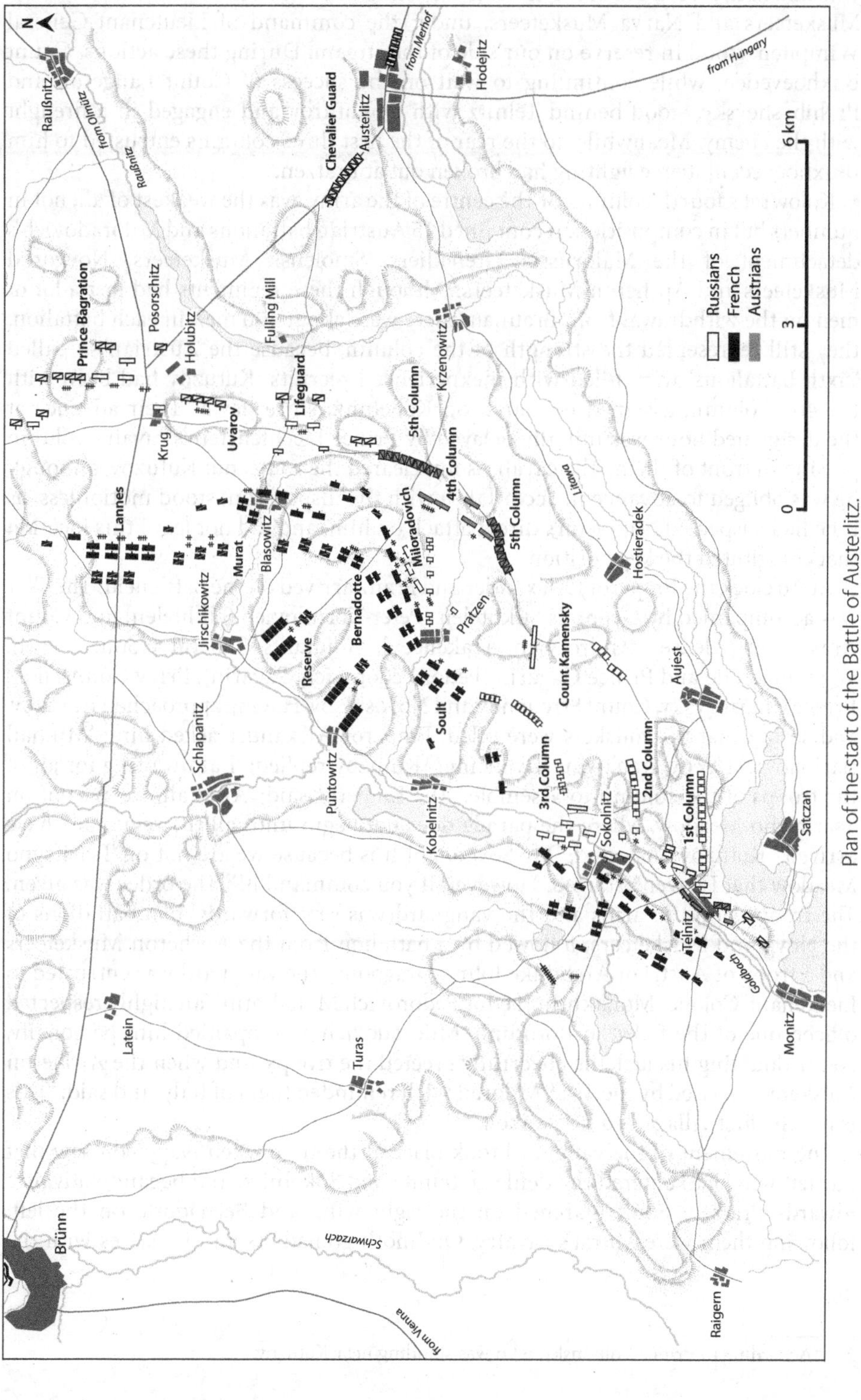

Plan of the start of the Battle of Austerlitz.

who had been forced out of the castle had fallen back. The Podolsk Musketeers, Azov Musketeers and Narva Musketeers, under the command of Lieutenant-General Wimpffen, stood in reserve on our side of the stream. During these actions, Count Buxhoeveden, while continuing to wait on the success of Count Langeron and Przhibyshevsky, stood behind Telnitz with Dokhturov and engaged in a firefight with the enemy. Meanwhile, to the rear of the first three columns entrusted to him [Buxhoeveden], fierce fighting had broken out at Pratzen.

Kolowrat's fourth column, or the centre of the army, was the weakest of all, not in numbers but in composition. It contained 15 Austrian battalions and Miloradovich's detachment of the Malorussia Grenadiers, Smolensk Musketeers, Novgorod Musketeers and Apsheron Musketeers. Although these regiments had lost a lot of men on the withdrawal from Braunau, there were about 400 men in each battalion, they still represented the strength of the column, because the Austrian so-called 'sixth battalions' were filled with inexperienced recruits. Kutuzov had been with the 4th Column, assigned to march on Kobelnitz, since dawn. Their advance at the designated hour was initially delayed by Prince Liechtenstein's cavalry column passing in front of them. The cavalry soon cleared the route, but Kutuzov, although he was obliged to advance in accordance with the disposition, stood motionless, as if he had suspected Napoleon's direct attack on him, and did not leave this location that constituted the key position.

At 9 o'clock the Emperors Alexander and Franz arrived on the battlefield. The Tsar was accompanied by Generals Sukhtelen [Peter Kornilovich Sukhtelen] and Count Arakcheev [Aleksey Andreevich Arakcheev], Adjutants-General Count Lieven, Wintzingerode and Prince Gagarin [Fëdor Fëdorovich Gagarin], Privy Counsellors Prince Chartorysky, Count Stroganov and Novosiltsov. Having approached Kutuzov, and seeing that the muskets were piled, Emperor Alexander asked him: 'Mikhail Ilarionovich! Why aren't you advancing?' Kutuzov replied; 'I am waiting for all of the troops of the column to assemble.' The Emperor said; 'After all, we are not on Tsaritsyno Meadow, where the parade does not begin until all the regiments have arrived.' Kutuzov answered; 'My Sovereign! It is because we are not on Tsaritsyno Meadow that I haven't started. However, if you command it!'[2] The order was given. The troops stood to arms and the vanguard was sent forwards: two battalions of the Novgorod Musketeers, followed by a battalion from the Apsheron Musketeers and a troop of Austrian Archduke John's Dragoons. The vanguard was entrusted to Lieutenant-Colonel Monakhtin [Fëdor Fëdorovich Monakhtin], an highly respected officer, one of the fallen at Borodino. Miloradovich accompanied him personally. Never doubting his luck, he cheerfully greeted the troops, and when the Apsheron Musketeers passed by the Tsar, Miloradovich reminded them of Italy, and said: 'This is not the first village you have taken.'

The movement of the vanguard took place at the time when Napoleon saw that our left wing had entered the defile at Telnitz and Sokolnitz, and began to advance towards Pratzen: Soult marched on the right wing and Bernadotte on the left; following them were Murat's cavalry, Oudinot's grenadiers and Bessières with the

2 According to Prince Volkonsky, who was standing near Kutuzov.

Garde. Napoleon rode between the fighting corps and the reserves. No sooner had Miloradovich and the vanguard passed through the village of Pratzen and begun to enter more open ground, than they witnessed the formidable French advance. Encountering fierce fire, two battalions of the Novgorod Musketeers, 'not resisting even a little, turned back,'[3] mixed with the Apsheron battalion behind them, fled past Emperor Alexander, to the left flank of the column and, not recognizing the Monarch, ignored his pleas. Having been continuously and personally trained by Napoleon to manoeuvre in the camp at Boulogne for two years in a row, the French gracefully and quickly ascended the slopes, and attacked the fourth column frontally and from the flanks.

Thus from the very beginning the battle took on a different character in the centre: from an offensive posture, we were turned to the defensive, and were attacked as we went to attack. The veil that had concealed Napoleon's plans from us rose and revealed his intention to cut our army in two. In order to prevent his attempt at our destruction, it was necessary, at all costs, to keep the Pratzen heights and not to allow Napoleon to break our centre; it was necessary to take new precautions and decide on them instantly. The Emperors Alexander and Franz, Kutuzov, the Russian and Austrian generals, who were accompanying the Monarchs and the fourth column were located in the very place where the storm had suddenly broken. Miloradovich led into action the Malorussia Grenadiers, Smolensk Musketeers and Apsheron Musketeers and the grenadier battalion of the Novgorod Musketeers, which had not formed part of the vanguard. The mass of French poured onto the heights from various directions. Kutuzov rushed forward and was wounded by a bullet in the cheek. Emperor Alexander sent the Lifeguard surgeon, Wylie [Sir James Wylie], to him. Kutuzov said to the doctor, pointing at the French; 'Thank the Tsar, and report that my wound is not dangerous, but the mortal wound is right here!' The enemy were so close that Kutuzov could see their faces. Drenched in blood and under small-arms fire, he issued orders, poorly understood in the confusion. The Austrian General Jurczek [Franz von Jurczek], the Commanders of the Malorussia Grenadiers, Berg [Grigory Maximovich Berg], and the Novogorod Musketeers, Repninsky [Sergey Yakovlevich Repninsky], were wounded. Kutuzov's beloved son-in-law, *Flügel-Adjutant* Count Tiesenhausen [Fëdor Ivanovich Tiesenhausen], led one shaken battalion forward with their colour in his hands and fell shot through by a bullet. The widespread French offensive, the deaths and wounding of many commanders led the troops into confusion. Miloradovich tried to hold on until the Austrians could form up behind him, and after incredible personal efforts from officers and soldiers, he was overwhelmed. He began to rally and reform his detachment behind the Austrians, but showered with lethal fire, having lost 2,388 men in the shortest possible time, they fled and swept Miloradovich's detachment from the heights. Witnessing the disaster, Emperor Alexander ordered Miloradovich to round up his men and fall back to Austerlitz.[4]

3 Kutuzov's own words from his secret report to the Tsar, dated 28 December [9 January, 1806].

4 *Quand deux bataillons qui étaient en avant se sont trouvés surpris en marche par l'ennemi, j'ai marché avec le reste en avant, et j'ai soutenu le combat jusqu'à ce que les Autrichiens ont pris leurs positions derrière moi. M'ayant ensuite replié sur eux, ils ont quitté leur position, et mes*

During these operations, which lasted two hours, the Allies lost much of their regimental artillery. The Austrian battery, which was on the right wing of the fourth column, mistook the Frenchmen, who were enveloping us on the right, for the Russian army and stopped firing.[5] The French seized them. The Russian Battery Company, which was standing on the left wing of the column, first went ahead with Miloradovich, but with the infantry moving backward, sent back for their limbers, firing at everything but at the wrong ranges. Soon they were left unsupported and French skirmishers quickly closed on them. The company commander ordered them to pull back and came out of action with the officers. Pulling back a short distance, the lower ranks, despite the absence of officers, halted and resumed firing. At that moment Miloradovich arrived and greeted this handful of the brave. The voice of the beloved commander encouraged them once more. But the French quickly rushed the battery and took two guns; while the rest of them galloped away, overtaking each other and got onto a country road. Two guns were saved and on the fourth day they reunited with the army with their *Feuerwerkers*, while four were taken the next morning by the French.[6] In general, when the defeat of the fourth column took place, the confusion was so great that the Tsar's entourage lost sight of Him, lost their way, and joined Him after nightfall and some a day or even two later. Thereafter, during the course of most of the battle, only His Lifeguard surgeon, Wylie, bodyguard, Ene, a horse and two Cossacks accompanied the Emperor.

When the French overwhelmed us on the heights, from then on it was impossible to defeat them with the disruption and small numbers of allied troops in the centre, lacking reserves, Kutuzov rode to the left wing of the fourth column. Ascending the heights, he found there Count Kamensky 1st's brigade, with the Fanagoria Grenadiers and Ryazhsk Musketeers, finding themselves on the heights for the following reason: marching in the main body of Count Langeron's column towards Sokolnitz, Count Kamensky saw the French ascending the Pratzen heights to his right. Informing Count Langeron, he stopped the brigade, formed them at right angles to the French right wing and attacked, wishing to assist the 4th Column.[7] At that moment, as Kutuzov arrived with the Duty General, Prince Volkonsky, Count Kamensky's brigade was being overwhelmed. Prince Volkonsky grabbed the colour of the Fanagoria Grenadiers, ordered the assembly to be beaten, and rallied the brigade. Fiercely attacking the enemy, the Fanagoria Grenadiers took two guns, but were forced back again with the loss of the cannon captured from the French, and were rallied by Prince Volkonsky once more. For a third time the brigade attacked the French and after failing it was again restored to order. This feat marked his first

gens s'étant dispersés, j'avais toute la peine possible à les réunir devant les yeux de l'Empereur, et sous le feu de mitrailles. C'est alors que j'ai reçu l'ordre de Sa Majesté de me retirer sur Austerlitz. Miloradovich's letter to Kutuzov.

5 *Die Östereichische Artillerie, der Ähnlichkeit der Kleidung wegen, sah die feindliche Infanterie für Russen an, und stellte ihr Feuer ein, in dem Augenblicke, wo es am wirksamsten hätte werden sollen. Östereichische Militair-Zeitschrift, 1822, p. 283.*

6 These details were taken from Count Kamensky 2nd's report, who was instructed to investigate the commander of the Battery Company, who was put on trial. Count Kamensky 2nd's report to Kutuzov, dated 13 [25] June 1806.

7 Count Langeron's report to Kutuzov, dated 23 November [4 December].

steps on the field of battle, of one who occupies one of the top places in the military History of Emperor Alexander, during the enormous wars of 1813, 1814 and 1815, was the Chief of His General Staff, the closest, most trusted General and inseparable companion of the Blessed Monarch from the age of 20 until His death.[8]

The actions of the Fanagoria Grenadiers and Ryazhsk Musketeers on the right flank of the enemy kept some of Soult's corps from attacking the centre for a considerable time,[9] but could not stop them. Seeing the impossibility of withstanding with two regiments, which were joined in the meantime by two squadrons of St Petersburg Dragoons and a *Sotnia* of Cossacks from Isaev 3rd's Regiment, Kutuzov, cut off from Austerlitz, retreated to Hostieradek and went down the Litawa valley, while sending an order to Count Buxhoeveden to fall back with the first three columns. Thus, bearing the title of Commander-in-Chief, Kutuzov remained with only one brigade, and had no further influence on the battle. Not knowing the fate that had befallen Kutuzov, the Tsar sent in all directions to search for him, but met him after the battle.[10]

Kutuzov had barely left with Count Kamensky's brigade, when Count Langeron arrived with the Kursk Musketeers at the very place where they had fought. The following factors brought him here: approaching the Goldbach, Count Langeron received a report from Count Kamensky 1st that the French were climbing the Pratzen heights, and that as a result of this movement, he had halted the Fanagoria Grenadiers and Ryazhsk Musketeers, and could not lead them to Sokolnitz following the second column. Count Langeron doubted the accuracy of this report, but soon hearing a cannonade from Count Kamensky's Brigade, he rode towards him, wanting to personally verify what was happening. Realizing the truth of Count Kamensky's report, Count Langeron led the Kursk Musketeers from Sokolnitz to help him, but as he proceeded to the place where Count Kamensky's Brigade had been, Kutuzov was already withdrawing with them. The French attacked the Kursk Musketeers coming face to face with an enemy incomparably superior in strength. The Kursk Musketeers were completely overwhelmed, losing some 1,600 men.

During the rout of our centre and Count Buxhoeveden's operations at Telnitz and Sokolnitz, a battle was also taking place on the right wing. Prince Liechtenstein's fifth cavalry column of His Highness the Tsarevich's Uhlan Regiment and 32 Austrian squadrons was supposed to occupy the ground between Pratzen and Prince Bagration, having the Lifeguard in reserve. Prince Liechtenstein was late in arriving at his appointed place, having encountered Przhibyshevsky's column passing in front of him during his departure from the overnight camp. As a result of this delay, there was nobody holding the gap between the centre and the right wing

8 In the Battle of Austerlitz, Prince Volkonsky showed accomplishments, which in defeat are more visible than in a fortunate battle. He was not only distinguished by courage, but prudence and the preservation of all the composure that is needed in such cases, contributing three times to the rallying of the men of the Fanagoria and Ryazhsk regiments under enemy fire, with whom I could withdraw in reasonable order'. Kutuzov's report, dated 30 November [12 December].

9 Kutuzov's secret report to the Tsar, dated 28 December [9 January, 1806].

10 After the withdrawal of the 4 Column, I remained with Count Kamensky's Brigade until the end of the action and until nightfall'. Kutuzov's letter to Count Lieven, dated 18 [30] June 1806.

– a circumstance that did not escape Napoleon's experienced gaze. He ordered some of Rivaud's [Olivier Macoux Rivaud] division, from Bernadotte's Corps, originally sent towards Pratzen, and two divisions from Lannes' Corps, Caffarelli's infantry, and Kellerman's [François Étienne Kellerman] Dragoons, to march on Blasowitz [Blažovice] and occupy the ground designated for Prince Liechtenstein's operations. With these troops Napoleon intended to cut off Prince Bagration from our centre, but they unexpectedly encountered the Lifeguard. The details of the action are as follows:

After spending the night in front of Austerlitz, Tsarevich Konstantin Pavlovich, in a white Lifeguard Horse tunic and helmet, led the Lifeguard out at the hour appointed in the disposition. The column guide was the Austrian Colonel Buol [(Joseph) Ignaz von Buol zu Berenberg]. The Lifeguard crossed the stream at the fulling mill, and stopped marching a further *verst* [1,050 metres or 1,170 yards] towards Blasowitz, where Prince Liechtenstein should already have been. Ahead of the Lifeguard were troops that had initially been taken to be Prince Liechtenstein's Column. The Tsarevich formed the Lifeguard infantry in two lines with a deployed front: at the front were the Preobrazhensky and Semyenovsky regiments having Grand Duke Mikhail Pavlovich's Artillery Company front and centre; in the second line were the Izmailovsky Regiment and Lifeguard Jäger Battalion. On the right flank of each battalion were two guns. Behind the infantry were the Lifeguard Hussars and Lifeguard Horse. Malyutin's [Peter Fedorovich Malyutin] independent detachment of the Chevalier Guard, the Leib Grenadiers and the Lifeguard Cossacks, were in the rearguard of the army and came into action later. As soon as the formation was complete, round shot flew from the battery of the force standing in front of the Lifeguard, initially thought by us to be Austrians, and tore a file from the Preobrazhensky regiment. The error was revealed. The shot was proof that it was the enemy in front of us. The Tsarevich ordered the Lifeguard Jäger Battalion, under Count Saint-Priest [Emmanuel Saint-Priest] – killed in 1814 at Rheims – to occupy the village of Blasowitz, and he sent to inform Prince Bagration, his colleague from the Italian campaign, about his situation. Prince Bagration replied that His Highness had decided for the best: to hold Blasowitz until the reason for the non-arrival of Prince Liechtenstein was explained. In Blasowitz a fierce firefight ensued. The Tsarevich reinforced the Lifeguard Jägers with a battalion of the Semyenovsky Regiment. Having received orders from Emperor Alexander, already under attack in the centre, to send reinforcements to Pratzen, the Tsarevich detached a battalion of the Izmailovsky Regiment under Colonel Khrapovitsky [Matvei Yevgrafovich Khrapovitsky] – now [1844] General-of-Infantry. Khrapovitsky arrived on the scene during the rout of the 4th Column, and fell back to Austerlitz with them.

The French ejected our troops from Blasowitz and began to bombard the Lifeguard. Only then did Prince Liechtenstein appear. Unable to take up his start positions as they were already occupied by the French, he attached himself to the left flank of the Guard. Seeing the French advancing on the left, towards Pratzen, and on the right, towards Blasowitz, he decided to attack them, and started to deploy his troops. The Tsarevich's Ulan Regiment at the head of the column was the first to charge at the French cavalry, scattered them and chased them through the intervals of their infantry, but in the heat of the moment ran into a battery, was greeted with canister fire, and fell back, pursued by cavalry and enduring the fire of the infantry stood on either side. Having suffered 400 casualties, their commander, Meller-Zakomelsky [Yegor Ivanovich Meller-Zakomelsky], and 16 officers captured, the Ulans did not return to their original location, but joined up with Prince Bagration. Following the Ulan's attack, Prince Liechtenstein led the Austrian cavalry forward. Trying to hold the French, he made attacks to the right and left, sometimes successfully, sometimes not, and held on as long as he could, while the French, having overwhelmed our centre, turned the fire from there into Prince Liechtenstein's left flank, threatening to cut off his line of retreat. Whereupon Prince Liechtenstein pulled back to Austerlitz, which was the conclusion of his participation in the battle.

Not receiving any news of the progress of the battle from anyone, left with just his own forces, consisting of six infantry battalions and ten cavalry squadrons, without reserves, with inexperienced generals and officers, Grand Duke Konstantin Pavlovich was in a most difficult situation. But fighting spirit was not lacking in this Royal protégé of Suvorov's. He did not want to withdraw without orders, and sent detachments to the left, to the broken centre, covering the movement with skirmishers. After advancing a little, they saw French columns to the right. The Lifeguard faced their front, charged with bayonets fixed and crushed the first two columns but in pursuit of them were engaged by batteries, became disordered and lost one gun. The French cavalry attacked the Semyenovsky Regiment, was repulsed, and a French colonel who had jumped into their ranks was caught on their bayonets. Napoleon's Mamelukes hacked at the Preobrazhensky Regiment, but not well, as the regiment was in the vineyards. A bloody fight ensued with cold steel. The Preobrazhensky, standing like giants, stabbed many of the Mamelukes. The Lifeguard Horse freed the infantry from the enemy horsemen. The first two squadrons, under the command of Colonel Olenin [Yevgeny Ivanovich Olenin], hit the flank of the French, turned them back, and in pursuit they galloped into a battalion of the *4e Régiment de ligne*, cut them down and took their eagle – the only Allied trophy of the battle of Austerlitz.[11] Freed from enemy cavalry, the Tsarevich hastily rallied the Lifeguard, and began to fall back, harassed by the French. Soon after, the cavalry attacked him again, and disordered several battalions. Our men crossed over the stream in disarray. At that moment, the Chevalier Guards and the Lifeguard Cossacks arrived, who had received orders to hurry at the trot at the beginning of the fighting. The commander of the Chevalier Guard Regiment, Depreradovich [Nikolai Ivanovich Depreradovich] ordered the first two squadrons to attack the French right flank, the third squadron was sent down the centre, and the 4th and 5th to the enemy left wing. The Lifeguard Cossacks also went into action. The attacks lasted for a quarter of an hour, and cost the Chevalier Guards 15 officers, 200 privates and 300 horses killed and wounded, but having said that, they gave time for the Lifeguard infantry to cross the ravine.[12] The 4th and 5th squadrons were particularly affected when they attacked the French cavalry during their hand-to-hand combat with the Semenovsky regiment. They liberated the infantry, but suffered terrible casualties themselves, caught from two directions by *Grenadiers*

11 This brilliant attack by the Lifeguard Horse is depicted in a painting located in Strelna Palace.
12 Depreradovich's report to Malyutin.

à cheval and *Chasseurs à cheval de la Garde impériale*. The 4th squadron of the Chevalier Guards was almost completely destroyed: only 18 men survived. Their commander, Prince Repnin [Nikolai Grigorievich Repnin], and several officers, all wounded, were captured. Overwhelmed, the Chevalier Guards galloped behind the stream, and lined up as Major-General Lobanov [Vasily Mikhailovich Lobanov] arrived with the Leib-Grenadier Regiment. He placed all three battalions with a deployed front ahead of Austerlitz. Seeing the Leib-Grenadiers, and believing that they formed the head of Essen's corps, Napoleon anticipated the imminent arrival of his entire corps. Such an assumption forced Napoleon to stop further pressure on the Lifeguard and on the fourth column, by then already back behind the stream.

Having seized all the ground from Blasowitz to Pratzen and Aujest, and having driven our army from the heights lying in front of these villages, Napoleon ended his offensive actions against our centre. He placed batteries on the heights, opening fire from there, scattered skirmishers along the stream and ordered the following attacks: Lannes on Prince Bagration, while Marshal Davout was to take on our first three columns, sending some of Soult's corps, the *Garde* and the grenadiers to their rear. The attacks on our flanks began the second phase of the battle of Austerlitz. It was one o'clock in the afternoon. Already having no general communications, the battle was a spectacle of individual independent actions, as always happens when the middle of an army is broken through and separated from the flanks.

In the morning, after reading the disposition delivered to him from the headquarters, Prince Bagration told the Austrian officers of the General Staff who were with him: 'We will lose this battle.' Whereupon he deployed his troops as follows: in the centre, infantry astride the road in two lines under the command of Adjutant-General Prince Dolgorukov; the 6th Jägers in the villages of Holubitz [Holubice] and Krug [Kruh]. On the left wing, Adjutant-General Uvarov with the Yelisavetgrad Hussars, Chernigov Dragoons and Kharkov Dragoons, ahead of a ravine; on the right the Mariupol Hussars and Pavlograd Hussars; in reserve Her Majesty's Cuirassiers, Tver Dragoons and St Petersburg Dragoons. The cavalry of the right flank and reserve were commanded by Count Wittgenstein and Chaplitz [Yefim Ignatievich Chaplitz]. The fighting soon began. Marshal Lannes, the Bayard of Napoleon's Army, who was facing Prince Bagration, was ordered to operate on the defensive at the beginning of the battle. As Napoleon succeeded at Pratzen, Lannes moved forward. Then, upon learning of Napoleon's decisive victory, and having given the order to advance, he went on doggedly. Uvarov twice attacked the cavalry that was on the French right wing, and held the enemy, while at the same time, Prince Bagration stopped the French in the centre and on his right wing. When Caffarelli's infantry division and Kellerman's dragoon division returned to Lannes, having originally been assigned to Blasowitz, where they had been in action against our Lifeguard, Lannes intensified the attack. Uvarov led a general attack with his three regiments and was thrown back behind the ravine with the loss of his horse artillery. Lannes fed more forces against Prince Bagration's left wing, weakened by Uvarov's withdrawal, and threw the 6th Jäger Regiment out of Krug and Holubitz. Prince Bagration sent Count Kamensky 2nd [Nikolai Mikhailovich Kamensky] – hero of the Finnish War, with the Arkhangelogorod Musketeers forward from the second line. Kamensky's resistance was stubborn but short lived. Several times cavalry surrounded him, attacking from all sides; in the pauses between the attacks the French smashed him with artillery. In one hour 1,600 men became casualties in the Arkhangelogorod Musketeers. The regiment fell back in disorder and Count Kamensky almost died here – the bright hope of Russia at the time. In the general confusion, he fell after his horse was hit by round shot. The Battalion Adjutant Zakrevsky [Arsenii Andreevich Zakrevsky] – now [1844] General-of-Infantry – offered him his horse, and Count Kamensky escaped on it, removing the remains of his regiment from under fire. Then, seeing the unfortunate turn of events in the centre, Prince Bagration began to pull back, maintaining his usual composure – the subject of astonishment to the Austrians even now.[13] He withdrew to Raussnitz, stopping in three positions. Lannes followed on his heels and was preparing to attack the Raussnitz position when he received the order from Napoleon to stop, and to stay in the same alignment as the rest of the army until the defeat of our left wing was completed.

Here we left things in the following situation:

1. Count Buxhoeveden, having made his way with Dokhturov's column to Telnitz, was awaiting the success of the 2nd and 3rd columns ahead of this village;
2. Count Langeron, deprived of the assistance of the Ryazhsk Musketeers and Fanagoria Grenadiers which had gone with Kutuzov, and of the defeat of the Kursk Musketeers as they were going to their rescue, had returned to Sokolnitz, where Olsufiev [Zakhar Dmitrevich Olsufiev] fought on with the 8th Jägers, Perm Musketeers and Vyborg Musketeers;
3. Przhibyshevsky had captured Sokolnitz castle and was attacking the French who stood on the high ground.

Operating on the defensive, Davout skilfully supported the fighting. After the defeat of our centre he was ordered to attack our left wing and Napoleon informed him that some of Soult's corps were moving into the rear of our troops from the Pratzen heights, and he was on the march to Aujest himself with the *Garde* and the grenadiers, on our line of retreat.

Holding Dokhturov and Count Langeron, Davout turned the main force against Przhibyshevsky, who stood on both sides of the Goldbach; the 7th Jägers, Galits Musketeers, Butyrsk Musketeers and two battalions of the Narva Musketeers, under the command of Major-General Strich, were beyond the stream in front of Sokolnitz, while on our side of the stream in reserve was Lieutenant-General Wimpffen with one battalion of the Narva Musketeers, the Azov Musketeers and Podolsk Musketeers, which had lost a lot of men at Schöngrabern, so that in both there were no more than 1,700 men.

As Davout launched the attack, Przhibyshevsky learned about the approach of the French to the rear of Sokolnitz, and sent to inform his situation to the Commander-in-Chief and Count Langeron, who was to his left, but the messengers could not fulfil the orders given to them, as Davout had already managed to cut the communications of the 3rd Column with Count Langeron and the right wing. Not receiving orders

13 *Der Fürst Bagration entwickelte in solchen Augenblicken einen seltenen Grad von Standhaftigkeit und Geistesgegenwart. Östereichische Militair-Zeitschrift. 1822, p. 291.*

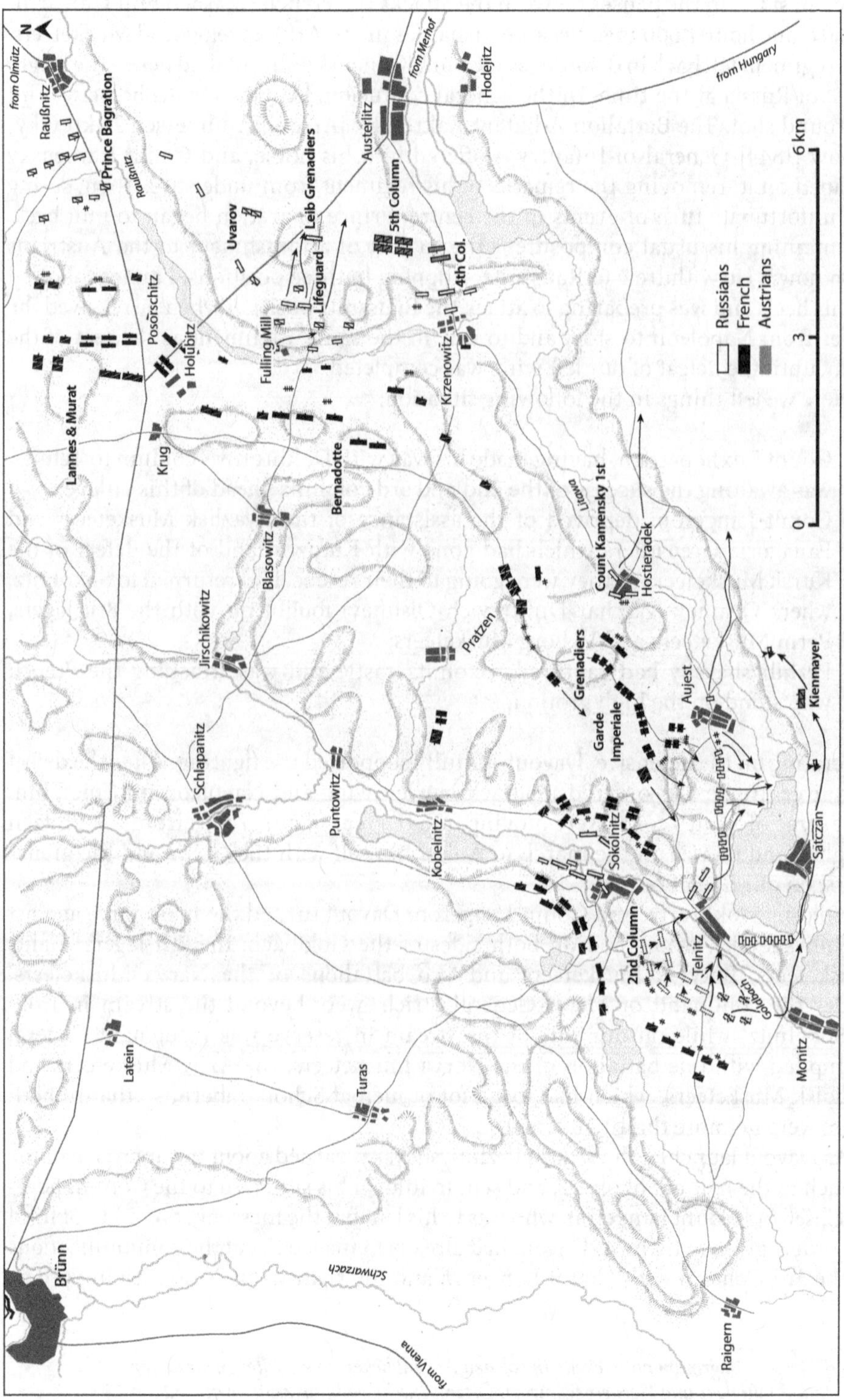

Plan of the later stages of the Battle of Austerlitz.

from anyone, not having information about the course of the battle and seeing that the troops had fired their cartridges and every minute were getting more and more disordered, Przhibyshevsky tried his best to maintain order and did not dare to fall back without orders. His situation was all the more difficult, in that he had taken command of the column only a day before the battle and not knowing his subordinates or even the generals, was completely unknown to the troops entrusted to him. Meanwhile, Davout pressed on him. With colours in their hands, our officers rushed forward and died. While Przhibyshevsky endured the bloody combat, Soult attacked and smashed Wimpffen's reserve, and captured this general, who was bleeding from the wounds he had received. Selekhov took his place, turned towards the village of Sokolnitz, cluttered with men, guns, caissons, but there was no passage through the crowded streets and according to Przhibyshevsky and Selekhov, 'everything was suddenly mixed up.' The French broke into Sokolnitz, cut the line of retreat of the column, and captured Major-General Miller who had been wounded at the beginning of the action and was in Sokolnitz Castle. Przhibyshevsky decided to move with his mixed crowd of men to the right, to Kobelnitz, hoping to meet Kolowrat's 4th Column there, which had been assigned to take possession of Kobelnitz in the disposition. At every step our ranks were thinned, smashed by cannon and musket fire. The swiftness of the attack grew from the French conviction of their undoubted success. Pursued and surrounded by the enemy, covering two *versts* [2.1 km or 1½ miles], our men were at Kobelnitz before twilight. Here the French cavalry cut into the crowds and completed the disorder, capturing Generals Przhibyshevsky, Strich and Selekhov. The soldiers did not give up. Having perceived troops at Kobelnitz, and mistaking them for Austrians, our men rushed to their imaginary Allies, but instead of Allies they met the French and were completely dispersed.[14] Casualties in the regiments of the 3rd Column were as follows:

	Strength	**Casualties**
7th Jäger Regiment	1,125	700
Galits Regiment	1,478	1,100
Butyrsk Regiment	1,709	1,600
Narva Regiment	1,552	1,300
Podolsk Regiment	709	180
Azov Regiment	990	400
Total:	7,563	5,280

The desperate and prolonged resistance of the 3rd Column facilitated the withdrawal of Dokhturov and Count Langeron, since Soult, engaged in combat with Przhibyshevsky, could not move his troops behind them. Although Count Buxhoeveden had already received orders to pull back, but not knowing positively that the battle had been irretrievably lost to us in the centre, he hoped to gain an

14 From the business of the Auditor-General, and the Journal of the State Council, 1810.

advantageous turn of affairs by throwing back the French right wing. The views of Count Buxhoeveden were shared by the Austrian Generals Stutterheim [Wilhelm von Stutterheim] and Kienmayer, summoned by him to a council of war. But when Count Buxhoeveden saw the French descending behind him, he became convinced of the futility of any further exchange of fire beyond Telnitz, and began to fall back through Telnitz with Dohturov's column, also ordering Count Langeron to fall back. Count Langeron could only extract two regiments from combat, the 8th Jägers and Vyborg Musketeers; the Perm Musketeers, being in the lead, were surrounded by the enemy and after a courageous defence were overwhelmed losing five field-officers and 39 subalterns, 1,684 lower ranks killed, wounded and captured, and lost six guns.[15] Among such a huge waste of men, testifying to the terrible situation in which the regiment found itself, the soldiers tore the two colours from their poles, and then presented them to Kutuzov: clear evidence that the blame for the death of the Perm Musketeers was not the timidity of the troops. Also in the Azov Musketeers, in the midst of a scene of destruction, the wounded NCO Starichkov tore the colour from its pole, and when captured, knew to hide it under his clothes. Lying on his deathbed in Brünn, he handed the colour to one of his comrades and he presented it to his superiors on his return to Russia. This colour is in the St Petersburg Arsenal. Grenadier Nesterov of the Narva Musketeers, seeing the Sub-Ensign killed, tore the colour from its pole and hid it on himself. He was soon captured, but took his chance to escape, rejoining the army during its return to Russia, and presented the banner to Kutuzov, who returned the colour to the regiment, ordering it to be nailed to its pole.[16] There were many examples of courage at Austerlitz. They were preserved for a long time in oral traditions but no one wrote them down and time has erased the feats from memory.

Count Buxhoeveden and Count Langeron were in a hurry to reach Aujest, laying on their line of retreat but only managed to pass the two leading battalions through the village, as the enemy was already approaching there from the Pratzen heights, cutting off the entrance to Aujest from our battalions. Gathering these troops, Dokhturov turned back, disordered by the *Artillerie de la Garde impériale*, positioned personally on the high ground at Aujest by Napoleon. Remaining the overall commander, Dokhturov ordered Löwis to form a rearguard at Telnitz with three battalions and hold the French, preventing them from striking him from behind, and the remaining troops to go along two roads: either across the bridge over the Litawa between the Aujest and Satczan [Žatčany] ponds or along a causeway between two ponds to the village of Satczan. The bridge collapsed under the weight of the guns. Our men rushed over the frozen pond, but the ice did not always hold. The same disastrous fate befell those who took to the causeway. It was so narrow that only two men could walk abreast. Seeing it crowded with men and artillery, some of the unit commanders led their troops and guns over the ponds. And then the ice began to crack; men, horses and guns were stuck in the ponds, while Napoleon continued the destructive cannon fire. Round shot and shells rained down on our troops; the ice disappeared under their feet, and they plunged into icy water; but

15 Battle note, dated 1 [13] December.
16 Kutuzov's report to the Sovereign Emperor, from Dubno, dated 28 February [12 March] 1806.

nobody discarded their weapons; everyone tried to help each other and even to save the guns. The efforts of the brave to overcome obstacles that were not commensurate with human muscle were futile. As the regiments crossed the causeway and ponds, Dokhturov reformed the troops into columns. Fearing that the French would cross the Litawa and Aujest, and would cut his route, he ordered Kienmayer, with the Austrian cavalry and Cossacks, to gallop around the ponds and sit opposite Aujest; then he sent several more infantry battalions, who had managed to cross the causeway before the rest. Showing unemotional composure here – a distinguishing feature of his glorious military bearing – Dokhturov led his troops out of the valley and ponds, and arrived in Neudorf [Nesvačilka] after dark, where he was joined by Löwis, falling back step by step with the rearguard. The French wrote:

> At the end of a lost battle and in a desperate position one cannot show more determination than that of General Dokhturov.[17]

Darkness was falling. Kutuzov and Prince Volkonsky were on the road to Hungary with the Fanagoria Grenadiers and Ryazhsk Musketeers; The Counts Buxhoeveden and Langeron, having passed Aujest with two battalions, crossed the Litawa, and were following the left bank towards Austerlitz; the Lifeguard was behind Austerlitz; Prince Bagration was holding at Raussnitz; to the left of him was Uvarov's cavalry detachment; Prince Liechtenstein's cavalry and the remains of the 4th Column were between Austerlitz and Krzenowitz [Křenovice]. Napoleon's army occupied almost the exact locations where the Allies had assembled before the battle. Lannes and Murat were within sight of Raussnitz; Bernadotte was on the Pratzen heights; Soult was in the Aujest area, with a second line formed from the *Garde* and grenadiers; Davout was between Telnitz and Sokolnitz. The Raussnitz stream [Rakovec] and the Litawa separated the belligerent armies. The final musket shots were heard on the left wing near Dokhturov, on the right by Prince Bagration, in the centre near Miloradovich. At six o'clock, when complete darkness covered the bloody mountains and plains, the firing subsided, and the camp fires of the victors lit up. The French loudly and merrily settled down for the night, greeting Napoleon when he circled the battlefield and thanked the regiments. In response to their bombastic leader, a roar of enthusiastic exclamations was heard, similar to what we heard when Alexander appeared among the troops after His victories in Germany and France.

Having issued orders, Napoleon went to spend the night in Posorschitz. On the way he was passing the prisoners and when he heard that there were Russian Lifeguard officers amongst them, he asked: 'where is the senior officer?' Colonel Prince Repnin was summoned. 'You commanded Emperor Alexander's Chevalier Guards?' Napoleon asked him. – 'I am a squadron commander in this regiment.' Prince Repnin replied. – 'Your regiment has done its duty nobly.' Said Napoleon. – 'The approval of a great captain is a good reward for a soldier.' Came the reply. – 'I grant it to you with pleasure.' Napoleon retorted and asked: 'Who is this young man

17 *On ne peut à la fin d'une bataille perdue et dans une position désespérée faire une plus belle contenanace que celle du général Doctouroff.* Dumas, *Précis des événemens militaires. Tome XIV, p. 201.*

next to you?' – Prince Repnin introduced Lieutenant Sukhtelen [Pavel Petrovich Sukhtelen],[18] barely out of his youth. Looking at him, Napoleon said smiling: 'He's very young to be rubbing up against us.' – 'You don't have to be old to be brave.' Sukhtelen answered boldly and with passion. 'Well answered, young man.' Said Napoleon. 'You will go far.' Saying goodbye to the captives, Napoleon ordered them to be taken to his bivouac and have their wounds bandaged.[19] The order was carried out. The wounded were taken to the huts built for Napoleon's headquarters, where they were warmly welcomed. The senior French generals were especially friendly towards them.

Emperor Alexander was by then in front of Austerlitz, with Miloradovich's detachment and impatiently awaited Kutuzov, wanting to consult with him about further orders. After waiting a long time, and not finding Kutuzov, the Emperor ordered the troops to take the road to Hungary, to Hodejitz, the place designated the day before for the army, in case of a lost battle; Miloradovich was to stay ahead of Austerlitz until relieved by Prince Bagration, who was ordered to hurry from Raussnitz to Austerlitz to form the rearguard. Having entrusted the safeguarding of the march to Count Wittgenstein, late in the evening Prince Bagration replaced Miloradovich, and deployed the army to be protected from a night attack. The night passed peacefully.

18 Died [1833] whilst serving as Military Governor of Orenburg.

19 The actual conversation went like this: '*Vous commandiez les chevaliers gardes de l'Empereur Alexandre?*'
'*Je suis chef d'escadron dans ce régiment.*'
'*Votre régiment a fait noblement son devoir.*'
'*C'est une belle recompense pour un soldat, que l'approbation d'un grand capitaine.*'
'*Je vous l'accorde avec plaisir. Qui est ce jeune homme à côté de vous?*'
'*Souchtelen, lieutenant dans mon escadron.*'
'*Il est venu bien jeune se frotter à nous.*'
Sukhtelen: '*On n'a pas besoin d'être vieux pour être brave.*'
Napoleon: '*Bien répondu, jeune homme. Vous ferez votre carrière. Qu'on aie soin de ces messieurs, qu'on les mène à mon bivouac, et qu'on dise à Larrey, qu'il visite leurs blessures. Au revoir, prince Repnin!*'
From Prince Repnin's Notes.

14

Consequences of the Battle of Austerlitz

Casualties of the Allied and enemy armies. – Austrian accusations against the Russians. – Kutuzov rejects responsibility for the defeat. – Emperor Alexander's opinions on Kutuzov. – The Emperor's displeasure with Count Langeron. – The trial of Przhibyshevsky. – Punishments. – Details.

At Austerlitz the Russian army suffered some 21,000 killed, wounded and captured,[1] and lost 133 guns.[2] The Austrians suffered 5,922 casualties.[3] The number of guns lost by them is unknown to us, due to the non-publication of information about it. According to French historians, there were less than 8,000 killed and wounded in Napoleon's army and 760 men missing, but Marshal Bernadotte – later the King of Sweden – returning from Austerlitz to the Rhine, said that the French casualties were as high as 12,000 men.[4] Immediately after the battle, our losses seemed much greater than they actually were, due to the fact that, in addition to the 21,000 men mentioned above, many more thousands were counted as believed to be killed or left for dead. Thousands of these were stragglers or in captivity. Taking advantage of the long November night and the situation of the French army, spread out over 13 *versts* [13.6 km or 8½ miles] from Raussnitz to Telnitz, the prisoners escaped individually or several men together. There were 5,600 men including escapees and stragglers who later rejoined the army and the supply train;[5] Others found themselves in Bohemia and Silesia, or otherwise making their way to Russia. The great waste of artillery occurred as much from the disruption that occurred in our columns, as from a battlefield intersected by ravines, ditches and vineyards, the viscous, rain-soaked ground, and the exhaustion of horses who had been fed for several days only with straw.

When Allied armies are defeated, they usually blame one another for the failure. This happened after Austerlitz. Paying respect to the courage of the Russian army,

1 Kutuzov's strength returns.
2 The return filed by the Chief-of-Artillery, Bogdanov, to Count Arakcheev, on the third day after the battle of Austerlitz.
3 *Östereichische Militair-Zeitschrift, 1822, p. 229.*
4 Report by the Russian Envoy to Berlin, dated 18 [30] December.
5 Kutuzov's report to the Tsarevich, dated 3 [15] December and to the War Ministry, dated 18 [30] March, 1806.

the Austrians attributed the defeat to our inability to manoeuvre, the awkwardness of our infantry, and the dead weight of our guns. But is it true that in the six years before the Battle of Austerlitz, when the Russians won victories in Italy with them, our guns were lighter, the troops more mobile, more skilful in manoeuvres? The reason for the victories in Italy was that the Commander-in-Chief of the Allied army was Suvorov, and at Austerlitz the Austrians led operations. Here is the key to the successes of 1799 and the failures of 1805. The provision of magazines lay with the Austrians, since the war was fought on their territory, but there was neither bread nor fodder. The Austrians brought the Russian army to places familiar to them, where they carried out training exercises annually. It turned out, on their own admission, that they were mistaken even in calculating distances.[6] Unaware of the spaciousness of the battlefield, they stretched the army out over 14 *versts* [14.7 km or 9 miles], did not bother to form a reserve, and finally were so inefficient that even after the war they were surprisingly unaware of their orders. Six weeks after the Battle of Austerlitz, Kaiser Franz told our ambassador, Count Razumovsky: 'What will surprise you, is that at this time, I do not yet know the plan of this battle.'.[7]

Kutuzov rejected responsibility for the defeat. The day after the battle, he rode up to the Izmailovsky Regiment, and talking about it with the officers, said (there are still witnesses to this speech):[8] 'I wash my hands of it'. Seven years later, at Krasny, having turned Napoleon's army into disordered, unarmed crowds of confused men, Kutuzov sat on a bench. The weather was inclement, and a memorial was laid out before him from the French colours captured that day. On one was written in golden letters: 'For the victory at Austerlitz'. Looking at the inscription, Kutuzov told us: 'Gentlemen! You are young; you will outlive me and hear stories about our warriors. After everything that is happening now, before our eyes, one victory I have won, or one failure I have suffered more or less, is still my glory, but remember: I was not to blame for the Battle of Austerlitz.' So said Kutuzov. However, the general opinion in the army condemned him, because, seeing the flawed orders by persons entrusted to Emperors Alexander and Franz, he did not stubbornly refute them using all his persuasion drawn from his many years of experience and deep understanding. Emperor Alexander expressed himself in a similar manner. After the triumph over Napoleon, the glory of our Monarch could not be increased by one victory won by Him, or overshadowed by one defeat suffered by Him. He once said: 'On the Austerlitz Campaign I was young and inexperienced. Kutuzov told me that we needed to operate differently, but he should have been more persistent in his opinions'. Here the curtain falls. The investigation cannot extend beyond the graves of the great Monarch and His leading commander, and remains forever covered in obscurity: the extent to which the provision of resources were made, on the one hand by Kutuzov and on the other, allowed by the Tsar.

---

6 *Das Terrain nahm eine weit größere Ausdehnung ein, als die Disposition voraussetzte. Östereichische Militair-Zeitschrift, 1822, p. 285.*

7 *Ce qui vous surprendra, me dit l'Empereur François, c'est qu'à l'heure qu'il est, je ne connois pas encore le plan de cette bataille.* Count Razumovsky's report, dated 11 [23] January, 1806.

8 Among the witnesses is a member of the Military Council, General Khrapovitsky.

In the absence of unity of command, it remained for unit commanders to deploy at their discretion, and each performed his duty to the best of his ability, with more or less success and skill. Least successful were the operations by Count Langeron and Przhibyshevsky. The former was ordered to resign. The letter written to him on this occasion by Count Lieven, and signed by the Tsar himself, testifies to Alexander's mild treatment even with those who were unfortunate enough to incur His justifiable anger. Count Lieven's letter read as follows:

> The consequences of the day of 20 November [2 December] having been particularly disastrous for the column which was under the orders of Your Excellency, and His Majesty being unhappy with the way in which this column was conducted, to spare your sensitivities, by my office, grants you permission to request your retirement.[9]

Subsequently, Emperor Alexander returned His favour to Count Langeron, seeing his glorious service on countless battlefields. Przhibyshevsky, upon returning from captivity, was put on trial, accused of having surrendered too early in the battle. The Auditor-General acquitted him, being sure he was captured at the end of the battle. The case was ordered to be transferred to the State Council, and here they accused Przhibyshevsky of 'not providing the generals of his column with proper instructions for the precise execution of the disposition, not following the line of retreat given in advance as the road to Hungary, not maintaining continuous communications with the other columns or with his reserves, splitting his forces, so that he had no means to support the sections detached from them, not supplying the men with cartridges, not linking up with his reserves, not falling back to the designated rendezvous, and moving with a mob of disordered men in the opposite direction to the disposition, where in complete disorder, surrounded by the enemy, he surrendered'. Based on these findings, the State Council sentenced Przhibyshevsky to reduction to the ranks for a month and dismissal from service. Emperor Alexander approved the verdict.[10] Colonel-in-Chief of the Galits Musketeers, Major General Loshakov, was also put on trial and reduced to the ranks for absence without leave from the regiment after the battle with the supply train and then in Lemberg [Lvov].[11] Two battalions of the Novgorod Musketeer Regiment, in the words of Emperor Alexander, 'covered themselves with ignominy, taking flight'. The Tsar ordered the field-officers and subalterns of both battalions to carry swords without sword-knots, the lower ranks could not carry hangers, and had five years added to their service obligation; equally, he ordered the publication of a printed list of the officers and soldiers found with the supply train, he barred such officers from promotion and would not dismiss them from service until they atoned for their misconduct, and added five years to the

9 *Les suites de la journée du 20 Novembre ayant été particulièrement facheuses pour la colonne qui s'est trouvée sous les ordres de Votre Excellence, et Sa Majesté étant peu satisfaite de la manière dont cette colonne a été conduite, pour ménager votre délicatesse, vous accorde par mon organe la permission de demander votre retraite.*

10 Supreme command, dated 25 November [7 December] 1810.

11 Report by the Auditor-General, dated 19 [31] August 1807.

service obligation of lower ranks separated from their regiments, and deprived them of the right to receive the insignia of the Order of St Anne.[12]

With the few exceptions of those who did not fulfil their duty, the battle of Austerlitz did not overshadow the courage of the Russian army, although in the confusion of battle, not controlled by one mind, by one will, individual efforts were lost. Napoleon himself was our impartial judge. Talking with his companions on the island of St Helena about past events, he used to say that the Russians showed more courage at Austerlitz than in other battles with him, moreover, more than at Borodino.[13] To conclude with the following line: the year 1820, on 20 November [2 December], Emperor Alexander, meeting Miloradovich in the palace, told him: 'Remember Mikhail Andreevich! Fifteen years ago today, a miserable day for our army?' Miloradovich replied; 'Allow me to disagree with Your Majesty I can't call the day miserable for the army, when officers and soldiers fought like lions.'[14] The Emperor smiled and shook the hand of the bravest of the brave.

12 Supreme command, dated 16 [28] March, 1806.

13 *L'armée russe d'Austerlitz n'auroit pas perdu la bataille de la Moskwa. Mémoires de Ste Hélène, par Las Cases, Tome IV.*

14 Words of Miloradovich, I heard his conversation with the Tsar, taking place in the hall, near the small court chapel.

15

The Withdrawal From Austerlitz

Reasons for withdrawing to Hungary. – Discussions. – Alexander at the battle of Austerlitz. – His illness. – Rumours of the Tsar's wounds. – Napoleon's orders. – Emperor Alexander's not to Marshal Davout. – The mistaken belief of the possibility of the capture of Emperor Alexander. – Concentrating the army at Czejtsch. – The scattering of our wagons. – The arrival of Essen's corps.

During our preparations for the Battle of Austerlitz, in the event of a lost battle, it was necessary to withdraw along the road to Hungary, where it might be possible to find food and enter into communications with Archduke Charles. It was thought that linking up with him and the resources of Hungary would give us the opportunity to continue the war even after a failure. But it was soon learned that there were no reserves in Hungary, and there was nothing for the army to survive on there. Taking advantage of this circumstance, the constant advocates for peace in the Viennese Cabinet recognised and declared peace as the only way to save Austria. Their meetings took place in Prince Kaunitz's castle in Austerlitz, while the battle was raging, death flew over the head of Alexander, reaping thousands of victims around Him, and Russian blood flowed in rivers. After the battle ended, Kaiser Franz expressed to the Tsar his desire to send Prince Liechtenstein to Napoleon, with a proposal to end hostilities and begin peace negotiations. Alexander replied that once he had sent Grafs Stadion and Gyulay from Olmütz to Napoleon, He provided the Austrian Court with measures to be taken, which he recognised would be useful for Austria's welfare, and therefore, in the present, woeful circumstances, the negotiators would not be prevented from leaving. Provided with instructions from his Monarch, Prince Liechtenstein went to Napoleon that very evening. This was the first, direct consequence of the Battle of Austerlitz.

Meanwhile the rain poured down. The army was streaming towards Hodejitz in the darkness. Emperor Alexander rode with them in silence. In the morning, coming under fire, He deployed them under round shot, canister and bullets. Beside Him, Lifeguard Surgeon Wylie's horse was wounded by canister shot; a horse 30 *sazhens* [63 metres or 70 yards] behind the Tsar was killed by a shell; a round shot struck two paces in front of him and showered Him with earth. The Emperor had remained with the 4th Column until their final defeat. When the army fled, He crossed the marshy, steep banked stream with some difficulty, and then issued orders. Eyewitnesses testify to His constant composure, and add that His facial expression was visibly heavy with sadness and the pallor of death. Speaking with Count Razumovsky about the Battle of Austerlitz, Kaiser Franz said: 'He had admired the courage of our men in general, and the stamina of some regiments, in the midst of the greatest dangers; that the fearlessness of the Emperor Alexander had also struck him, as well as the brilliant and cool manner in which He had shown himself in the hottest places. Especially since this was His first battle.'[1]

Before midnight, Emperor Alexander arrived in the village of Hodejitz, as happens in such circumstances, full of wounded, stragglers and transport. A room was found for the Emperor, with some difficulty. At the time there were only three members of his retinue with him: the Lifeguard Surgeon, Wylie, the bodyguard, Ene, and the *Feldjäger* [military courier], Prokhnitsky. Then, by chance Uvarov's Adjutant, Chernyshev, turned up. During the battle he had been sent to the Tsar with a report on the operations of the right wing. Not finding his aides de camp, the Emperor kept Chernyshev with him, sent him with orders and on his arrival in Hodejitz, said to him: 'Do for me one last service today: find Kutuzov'. Events depended on the successful execution of this mission, in the dark and amongst moving troops. Chernyshev was fortunate enough to find Kutuzov quickly, who on his part had sent out everywhere to find out: where is the Emperor? Having talked with Kutuzov, and not finding His carriage in Hodejitz, the Tsar went on horseback towards Czejtsch [Čejč], but could not get further than seven *versts* [7.3 km or 4½ miles].

For four days since the time of the action at Wischau, he had felt unwell. The difficulties endured in the battle, the unfortunate feeling of failure, emotional excitement, the inclement weather at night, in other words, a combination of mental and physical exhaustion worsened the Tsar's painful condition, and he was forced to stop in the village of Uhrschitz [Uhřice], in a peasant's hut, where his only comfort was some straw. His head was burning, and he was showing symptoms of cholera. A preparation of chamomile and 30 drops of opium calmed the Tsar. He fell asleep. It was necessary to revive the patient with wine, which, despite all efforts, could not be had in the village. Upon learning that Kaiser Franz had arrived not long before in Uhrschitz, and stopped at the priest's house, they sent there for wine. Everyone there was asleep. They woke *Ober-Hofmarshal* Lamberti, and asked him for wine for the sick Monarch. He refused, responding that he barely had enough wine for Kaiser Franz. Finally they managed to buy wine from an Hungarian officer, and it eased the Emperor's condition. Thus, part of the night was spent by our Monarch on the straw in a peasant's hut.

After three hours of restful sleep, before dawn, the Emperor mounted his horse and rode to Czejtsch, the army's assembly area for that day, 21 November [3 December]. Passing by the troops, the Tsar tried to hide his illness, questioned the generals he met about their casualties in the battle, and he saluted

1 *L'Empereur François me dit, de ce ton qui n'admet ni fard, ni composition, qu'il avait admiré la valeur de nos gens en général, et la contenanace de quelques corps, au milieu des plus grands dangers; que l'intrépidité de L'Empereur Alexandre l'avait également frappé, ainsi que la manière brillante et froide, dont Il s'était montré aux endroits les plus chauds. Que cependant c'étaient Ses premières armes; que sans doute, cela ne pouvait pas être autrement, mais que cela étonniat, parceque c'était assez rare.* Count Razumovsky's report, dated 11 [23] January, 1806.

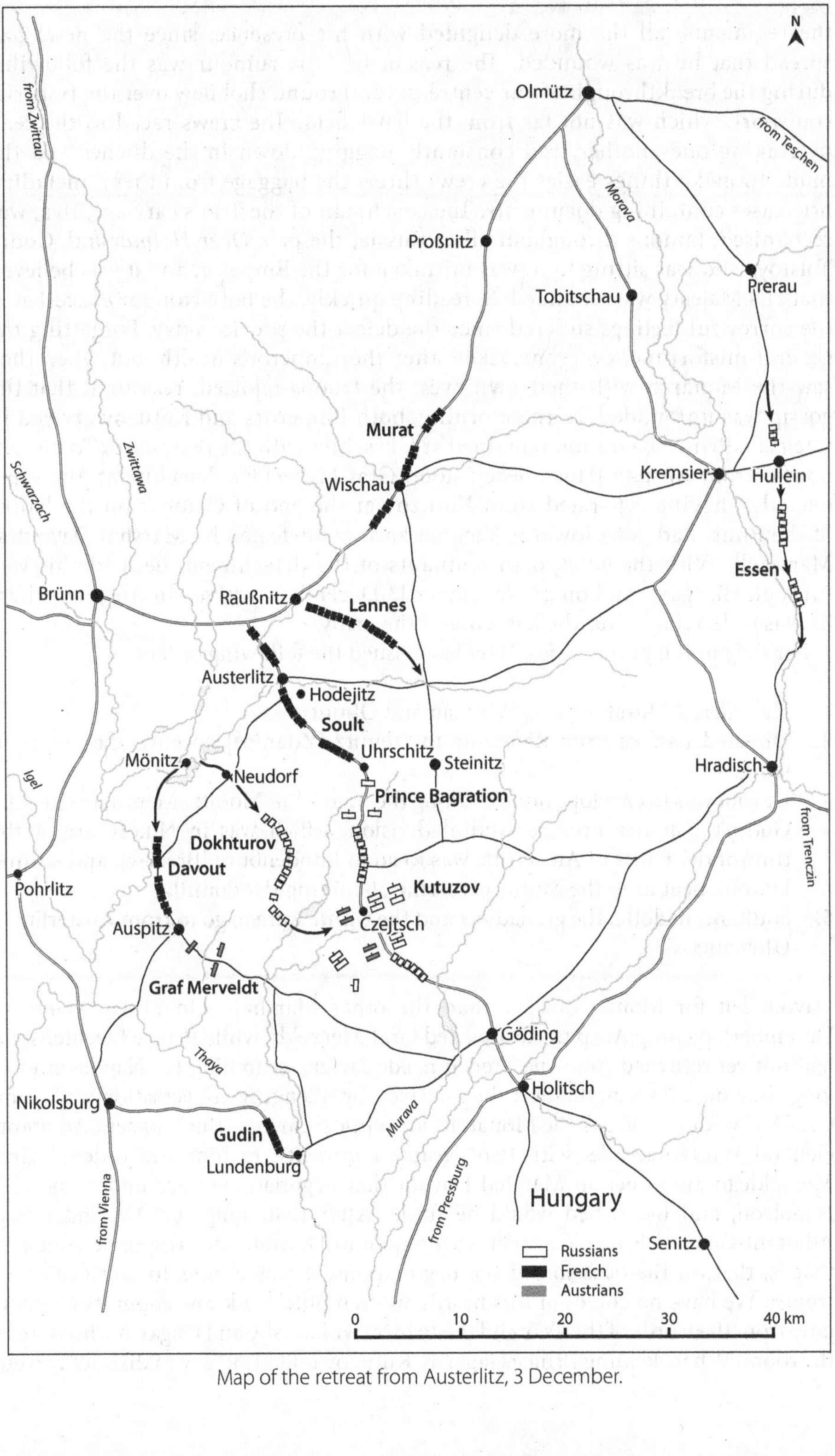

Map of the retreat from Austerlitz, 3 December.

the regiments, all the more delighted with his presence, since the news had spread that he was wounded. The reason for this rumour was the following: during the breakthrough of our centre, several round shot flew over the Imperial transport, which was not far from the battlefield. The crews raced to the rear, overtaking one another, and constantly bogging down in the ditches and the mud. To make things easier the crews threw the baggage from them, including briefcases containing documents. The coachman of the Tsar's carriage, Ilya, was recognised, famous throughout all of Russia; the pale *Ober-Hofmarshal*, Count Tolstoy, who was sitting in it, was mistaken for the Emperor, and it was believed that His Majesty was wounded. Spreading quickly, the false rumour exacerbated the sorrowful feelings suffered since the defeat the previous day. Forgetting the general misfortune, everyone asked after the Emperor's health, but when they saw the Monarch with their own eyes, the troops rejoiced, reassured that the gossip was unfounded. In the morning, both Emperors and Kutuzov arrived in Czejtsch. Prince Bagration remained at Uhrschitz with the rearguard. To his left, not far from Auspitz [Hustopeče], stood Graf Merveldt's detachment, the same one who, having separated from Kutuzov at the end of October on the banks of the Enns, had gone towards Vienna, and was defeated by Marshal Davout at Mariazell. With the 4,000 man remnants of the detachment, he made his way through Hungary, and on 21 November [3 December] arrived in Auspitz, where he was ordered to cover the left wing of the army.

For the pursuit of the Allies, Napoleon issued the following orders:

1. He ordered Murat to go to Wischau and Olmütz;
2. Directed Lannes from Raussnitz to Steinitz [Ždánice], to envelope our right wing;
3. Davout was to envelope our left, along the road from Mönitz [Měnín] to Auspitz;
4. Gudin's [Charles Étienne Gudin] division, which was in Nikolsburg at the time of the Battle of Austerlitz, was to go to Lundenburg [Břeclav], and joining Davout, beat us to the Murava crossing at Göding [Hodonín];
5. Soult, Bernadotte, the grenadiers and the *Garde* were to go to from Austerlitz to Uhrschitz.

Davout left for Mönitz quicker than the other Marshals. On 21 November [3 December], passing Auspitz, he attacked Graf Merveldt, while Prince Liechtenstein had not yet returned from the French headquarters, searching for Napoleon for a long time on a dark night, and then delayed by a lengthy conversation with him. Graf Merveldt sent to ask the Monarchs for reinforcements. The Tsar sent Adjutant-General Wintzingerode, with two cavalry regiments, to him and ordered Graf Merveldt to announce to Marshal Davout that negotiations were underway with Napoleon, and bloodshed would be futile. After that, Emperor Alexander sent Adjutant-General Prince Gagarin with a note to Davout, with the same contents, that is, that on the occasion of the negotiations, it was useless to sacrifice brave troops. We have no copies of this hastily written note; we know about its contents only from the words of the Tsar and the Princes Volkonsky and Gagarin who were in the room. When sending Prince Gagarin, Kutuzov told him: 'Try to distract Davout in conversation for longer, and gain time.'[2] Then Kutuzov asked the Monarchs to go to Holitsch [Holíč], and leave him in Czejtsch to deploy the troops. Their Majesties set off, escorted by three regiments; the Lifeguard Hussars were in front, followed by the Emperors, the Chevalier Guard and the Lifeguard Horse walked in the main body. On the way the answer from Marshal Davout arrived, who, upon reading the Tsar's note, expressed his readiness to stop the vanguard action.

Without exception, all historians consider the captivity of Emperor Alexander to have been inevitable if Davout had not stopped, and taking advantage of his superior numbers, continued to press Graf Merveldt. No one took the trouble to investigate the case, and everyone believed the writers but their unanimous testimony is destroyed when looking at the map. From Czejtsch, where the Emperor was, to the Murava River is 15 *versts* [15.8 km or 10 miles]. Davout was further away, and, in order to reach the bridge over it, not only had to break our rearguard, but, so to speak, leapfrog over it: impossible, because the army was close and could strengthen the rearguard and stop Davout. After such obvious evidence of a mistaken view on the subject, it would not be worth spreading it about had not Napoleon himself announced in print about the inevitable captivity of Emperor Alexander during the extension of Davout's advance. Napoleon did not stop there. In the Notes he composed on St Helena, he says that 'even after crossing the Murava in Holitsch, the Emperor would have been caught if he had not agreed to a truce.'[3] In Holitsch, a wide river separated the Tsar from the enemy, and the French were further from there than our army. Soon the army came to the river, crossed over it and had all the roads beyond it opening up for its unhindered withdrawal, and, consequently, for the passage of the Tsar. Where was the possibility for his capture? In none of the Descriptions of the Wars of Emperor Alexander did we refute the historians who preceded us when we found their testimony to be false, convinced that truth is the best objection, but it was impossible to remain silent here. Fallen from an immeasurable height, Napoleon's words will pass into posterity and require our explanation, so that the false expressions of the exile on an African rock, motivated by impotent vengeance towards Alexander, the author of his fall, would not be recognised as truth by future generations.

While the Monarchs were travelling to Holitsch, the troops of Kolowrat's and Miloradovich's 4th Column, Prince Lichtenstein's cavalry and the Guard concentrated in Czejtsch. Many regiments arrived mixed together and without backpacks, as they had removed them going into action, or when returning from combat, did not go to the locations where the backpacks were cached. They waited a long time for Dokhturov and the troops that made up Count Langeron's and Przhibyshevsky's columns. Although their overall commander, Count Buxhoeveden, was in Czejtsch, he could not convey anything positive to Kutuzov about the fate of the troops entrusted to him, escaping with only two of the 44 battalions under his command. Finally, at about noon, Dokhturov came along, leading with him the miserable remnants of the columns of Count Langeron and Przhibyshevsky who joined him,

2 As related by Prince Gagarin.

3 *Mémoires pour servir à l'histoire de France, publiés sur les manuscrits entièrement corrigés de la main de Napoléon, par Montholon. Tome II.*

and having lost a lot of men in the night march: some remained on the road from exhaustion; others got lost in the forests. Linking up with Dokhturov, Kutuzov withdrew from Czejtsch to Göding, on 22 November [4 December] crossed the Murava, and settled down at Holitsch. Prince Bagration's rearguard was attacked at this time by Soult but not strongly and withdrew in perfect order. This marked the end of military operations in the first war between Emperor Alexander and Napoleon. The honour of the last, parting shots belonged to Prince Bagration, as well as the honour of the first engagement with the enemy at Lambach.

Soon convoys began to arrive in Holitsch, led down country lanes from the Olmütz road in the wake of the army, having been directed there from Austerlitz. Many government and private carts did not have time to move off the Olmütz road and fell into Murat's hands. Other army heavy baggage and carriages were led by frightened guides down the lanes; including several of Emperor Alexander's staff; they found themselves in Teschen. Only his own carriage made it to Holitsch on the third day after the Battle of Austerlitz, so that the Tsar was left without servants for three days, and was unable to change shoes, underwear or clothes. The Tsarevich's baggage arrived in Holitsch on the sixth day. All the time, the personal staff of the Grand Duke consisted of one valet who did not lag behind him in the battle.[4] On 24 November [6 December], Essen's 12,000 man Corps joined the army. During the Battle of Austerlitz, he was 60 *versts* [63 km or 40 miles] from the battlefield, at Prerau [Přerov], from where he was directed through Hullein [Hulín] and Hradisch [Hradiště] to Holitsch. The corps consisted of the Alexandria Hussars, Starodub Dragoons, Siberia Dragoons, Yekaterinoslav Grenadiers, Moscow Grenadiers, and Schlüsselburg Musketeers. The troops were in excellent condition, but somewhat downhearted being too late to fight, as negotiations had already begun.

4 The valet was called Dmitry. Which old-timers do not remember him?

16

The Final Actions of Emperor Alexander and Napoleon

The truce. – Emperor Alexander's orders. – Prussia's fickleness. – The Emperor's relations with Austria, return to Russia, opinion on the campaign of 1805 and the desire to resume hostilities. – Napoleon's conversation with Prince Repnin. – Napoleon's treaty with Prussia. – The Peace of Pressburg. – Napoleon's return to Paris. – The Austerlitz Bridge. – Painting of the Battle of Austerlitz.

On the evening of the day when the Monarchs arrived in Holitsch, Prince Liechtenstein returned from the French Army and brought Kaiser Franz an invitation to see Napoleon. Kaiser Franz went to the vanguard, and on the 22 [4 December] met Napoleon between the forward outposts of the armies. Their conversation lasted two hours, and resulted in the cessation of hostilities between the French and the Austrians, on the conditions accepted by Kaiser Franz: not to allow foreign troops onto his territories, and to persuade Emperor Alexander to return the Russian army in Austria to Russia. Wanting to find out the Tsar's opinion on these conditions, Napoleon sent General Savary and Kaiser Franz sent General Stutterheim to him. At 5 o'clock on a dark morning, on 23 November [5 December], they arrived in Holitsch, and found the Tsar already dressed. He received Stutterheim first who, on behalf of his Monarch, asked for consent to the demands proposed by Napoleon. The Tsar replied: 'I have brought my army to the aid of Austria, and will send it back if your Monarch wishes to do without my assistance.'[1] He then gave orders for General Savary to be summoned, and gave him a verbal promise to return his troops to Russia. Notified of the Tsar's decision, Napoleon ordered his corps to halt, and Kaiser Franz sent Prince Liechtenstein to him to conclude a truce. It was signed on 26 November [8 December], with the conditions that they immediately agree on peace, and if peace does not take place, not to resume hostilities without giving each other 15 days notice. The ceasefire determined the line of demarcation between the warring armies, the Austrian Kaiser made an obligation not to mobilise the Hungarians, and set a date for the departure of Russian troops from Austrian

1 Supreme orders to Count Vorontsov in London, dated 24 November [6 December], from Holitsch.

territory, namely: from Moravia and Hungary within two weeks and from Galicia within a month.

Napoleon's readiness for a truce and the negotiations for peace that had begun after a brilliant victory, stemmed from his disadvantages. Standing on the border of Hungary, Napoleon saw the Prussian army gathering behind him, knowing that the King of Sweden was on the left bank of the Elbe, with the Russians, British and Swedes, and could march towards the Rhine, where there were few French troops. Archduke Ferdinand's corps in Bohemia was gathering strength daily. Bennigsen was hurrying to join him from Silesia. Archduke Charles was moving quickly towards the banks of the Danube, and Essen's corps was approaching us. Such an accumulation of allied forces was a portend to Napoleon of the likelihood of a continuation of the war against numerous armies, and he took advantage of the Viennese Court's tendency to negotiate, pushing for a glorious peace to scatter the clouds gathering against him.

During the negotiations between Napoleon and the Austrians on the armistice, Emperor Alexander, being in Holitsch, ordered:

1. Colonel Lanskoy [Sergei Nikolaevich Lanskoy], (who died a hero at Craonne in 1814), was to go to Napoleon's headquarters, confirm the number of our prisoners, and to ease their situation, hand to each captured general 200 *chervonets* [gold ducats], each field-officer 50, and subaltern 25.
2. General Lacy was to put Anrep's corps on ships in Naples and take some of the troops to Corfu, and the rest to Russia.
3. Count Stroganov was to go to London, discover the intentions of the British Government, and reassure them of the continuing alliance with Russia.
4. Adjutant-General Prince Dolgorukov was to go to Berlin, tell the King of Prussia the whole truth about the Battle of Austerlitz, and promise if Prussia decides to fight Napoleon, or if he is forced into war, to support them with all the forces of Russia, providing Bennigsen's and Count Tolstoy's corps at the disposal of the Prussian King in the first instance.

Following Prince Dolgorukov, the Tsar sent the Tsarevich, Konstantin Pavlovich, to Berlin to assure the King of Prussia of the immutability of his feelings. At the same time, Kaiser Franz sent General Stutterheim to Berlin to find out to what extent he could hope for Prussia's assistance if Napoleon's demands were to prove too burdensome for Austria, promising to delay negotiations, pending the decision of the Berlin Court.

In Berlin, there was already rumour about a battle that took place in the vicinity of Brünn, but they did not know who won. Suddenly there was a rumour about the defeat of Napoleon. The joy was general, but short-lived. A few hours after the spread of the false message about our success, a report came from Graf Haugwitz, describing the defeat of the Allies and a request, on the occasion of changed circumstances, to provide him with new instructions. The King decided to remain faithful to the Potsdam Treaty, and ordered:

1. Colonel Phull was to hurry to the headquarters of Emperors Alexander and Franz to find out about the current state of affairs and agree with them on a military plan of operations;
2. To move the army onto Austrian territory, once the one month deadline designated to receive a response from Napoleon had elapse and there being no answer;
3. Graf Haugwitz was to act in respect of previous instructions with Russia and Austria in turn.[2]

They had not yet had time to execute the orders regarding the movement of the army when Prince Dolgorukov and Stutterheim arrived in Berlin with the news of the ceasefire, which had barred the entry of foreign troops over the borders of the Austrian Monarchy. After listening sorrowfully to the story of the Battle of Austerlitz, the King of Prussia reproached us for having ventured into battle without waiting the remaining few days for the deadline to receive an answer from Napoleon to Graf Haugwitz's proposals, and for making a truce without the knowledge of Prussia, thus depriving the King of the opportunity to send troops onto Austrian territory. The King said that the orders for the army to march had been written and were ready to be despatched when the news of the ceasefire put a stop to all measures taken for war with Napoleon. Prince Dolgorukov and General Stutterheim, as well as the envoys Alopeus and Graf Metternich, exhausted all arguments to persuade the King to declare war immediately, even the personal gains for Prussia. For his part, the French ambassador Laforêt, exaggerating Napoleon's already great successes, persuaded Prussia to remain at peace with him, promising them greater benefits. It is easy to comprehend the hesitation of the Berlin Court caused by the sudden change of circumstances. With all his heart devoted to the Emperors Alexander and Franz, sharing with them the conviction that it was necessary to stop Napoleon's encroachments, the King did not dare to fight against him after the Battle of Austerlitz, and deferred making a decision until he had received reports from Graf Haugwitz on the progress of the negotiations. Anticipating, however, the possibility of war with Napoleon, the King asked Emperor Alexander, for Bennigsen's and Count Tolstoy's corps to be placed at his disposal and to add Essen's corps, ordering him to go to Silesia to join Bennigsen.

Meanwhile, informed by Kaiser Franz of the conclusion of a truce, the Tsar replied that by signing the given peace, he promised, wherever acceptable:

1. To completely maintain neutrality between Austria and France, or whichever Power might be at war with Austria;
2. Not to conclude commitments with France or any other Power harmful to Austria's interests, and to inform them secretly of any Russian actions that are disadvantageous to Austria;
3. Upon bringing the army and internal affairs of Russia into an arrangement, to go to the aid of Austria if it is at war with France.

2 Alopeus' report, dated 28 November [10 December].

In conclusion, the Tsar asked Emperor Franz 'I beg Your Majesty to accept these commitments as just as binding on me as if they were listed in the most solemn treaty.'[3]

The next day, 27 November [9 December] Emperor Alexander said goodbye to his Ally, and went from Holitsch to St Petersburg, via Trentschin [Trenčín] and Teschen, ordering Kutuzov to lead the army concentrated around Holitsch to Russia via the camp at Senitz [Senica]. Thus, the activities of Emperor Alexander in his first war with Napoleon were concluded. He said 'I did everything humanly possible. If Mack had not lost his army at Ulm, if the King of Prussia had declared war immediately after the French had violated his neutrality, if the King of Sweden hadn't impeded the movement of troops in the north, if the British had arrived in time in the theatre of war, and in general, if the London Court had been more active from the moment when they had nothing more to fear from a French landing, then we would have held Bonaparte, would not have allowed him to concentrate all his forces against us, and things would have taken a different turn.'[4]

Thus, upon the departure of Emperor Alexander from Holitsch, all hope for the success of the allies seemed lost. Suddenly, an opportunity presented itself to re-launch the war, and Emperor Alexander was in a hurry to seize the opportunity to enter combat with Napoleon again. These were the circumstances: when meeting with Kaiser Franz after the Battle of Austerlitz, Napoleon gave assurances that he would offer moderate terms to Austria, but having barely signed the truce, hardly as soon as the Russian troops departed on their return march and negotiations began on peace, Napoleon presented the conditions to Austria itself, and included Venice among the territories required from it. On the way to St Petersburg, knowing about the cruelty of the Victor, the Tsar wrote to Berlin whilst on the road about the need to help Austria. He said; 'Austria will be forced to agree to Napoleon's excessive demands, after which it will cease to be an independent State. With the weakening of Austria, the opportunity to maintain the balance between the Powers collapses, and the acquisition of Venice by Napoleon will gift it into Turkey's hands.' To avert such a general disaster for Europe there was, according to the Emperor, one way: Prussia's determination to force Napoleon to accept the terms of the Potsdam Treaty, and in case of refusal to declare war on him. The Emperor promised to support Prussia with all the forces of Russia, adding that meanwhile, Kutuzov's army would deploy and take revenge for the battle of Austerlitz,[5] Austria could gather its scattered troops, Archduke Charles could open hostilities, and the militia [Honvéd] be mobilised in Hungary.[6] The call of Emperor Alexander did not find an echo in the Berlin Court, but the memory of this act of the Tsar must be held as evidence that the Battle of Austerlitz did not shake him, did not stop the intention to fight Napoleon until his

3 *Je prie Votre Majesté d'agréer ces engagemens tels que je les lui adresse par la présente lettre, et je promets sur ma parole Impériale de les envisager comme tout aussi obligatoires pour moi, que s'ils étoient énoneés dans le traité le plus solennel.*

4 Supreme orders to Count Vorontsov in London, from Holitsch, dated 24 November [6 December].

5 '*L'armée de Koutousoff prendra sa revanche.*'

6 Supreme orders to Alopeus in Berlin, dated 3 [15] December.

strength was exhausted, with strong confidence in the power of Russia, and the holy calling to be the deliverer of Europe.

On the other hand, Napoleon did not stop looking for opportunities to get closer to Emperor Alexander. The polite, cold response of the Tsar to his letter brought to Olmütz by General Savary, and the Tsar's refusal to invite Napoleon to meet before the Battle of Austerlitz, did not stop Napoleon's desire, even after his victory, to enter into relations with Emperor Alexander. Immediately upon the conclusion of a truce with the Austrians, Napoleon gave orders for Prince Repnin to be summoned and, asking about his wounds, he said: 'I want to send you to Emperor Alexander, and again offer him peace. We have nothing to fight over. Tell him that if he accepted my invitation and came to meet with me, I would submit to his magnificent soul. After hearing the thoughts of Emperor Alexander about ways to restore peace in Europe, I would agree with him. Instead of Himself, he sent a young man who talked to me impertinently and where? Amongst my columns! What was going on? We fought, and now I have the right to announce offers. We can still be close. Let the Emperor appoint a plenipotentiary to Vienna, but not the kind of men who are in his headquarters. The truth is kept from Monarchs. Alexander was born to the Throne, and I myself became a Monarch, and so what? My former comrades, even my former commanders, dare not tell me the truth. Let's move on to the battle. What a strange idea to be stretched out over a vast space, to separate the columns? It is necessary to keep the army together, so to speak, in a fist so that everything can be suddenly thrown into the face of the enemy. However, Emperor Alexander was to lose the battle. This was his first, and my fortieth battle. Farewell! Pass my words on to the Emperor, and say that I want to renew friendly relations with him.' Not exactly knowing Emperor Alexander's location, Napoleon advised Prince Repnin to go to Olmütz. Here he found the Head of our Ministry of Foreign Affairs, Prince Chartorysky, who sent Prince Repnin back to Brünn, and ordered him to say that in managing political affairs, he knows the Tsar's ever-present inclination towards peace, but not otherwise than accepting as the basis for negotiations, the proposals with which Novosiltsov was sent to Paris in June, making some amendments to them, however. Returning to Brünn, Prince Repnin could not find the French headquarters there, and the answer given to him in Olmütz by Prince Chartorysky was communicated to Marshal Berthier in writing. That ended the matter.[7]

Having sent Prince Repnin to Emperor Alexander, Napoleon went from Brünn to Vienna and, after the conclusion of the armistice, paying most attention to the army of Archduke Charles, who was then at Kermern, 100 *versts* [105 km or 66 miles] from Pressburg. Murat's, Bernadotte's and Lannes' corps remained in Moravia; Soult, the grenadiers and the *Garde* marched to Vienna, to link up with the garrison made up of Mortier's consolidated corps; Marshal Davout turned towards Pressburg, where peace negotiations had begun. Upon arrival in Vienna, Napoleon summoned Graf Haugwitz, announced to him that he was aware of the secret communications between the Prussian King and the Emperors Alexander and Franz and, that having dealt with the Russians and Austrians, he could immediately invade Silesia, raise

7 From Prince Repnin's Notes.

the Poles who were Prussian subjects and begging him for the restoration of Poland, to force the Berlin Court to peace, whichever he wants, and brutally avenge the recent, malicious intentions of Prussia against him. Furthermore, Napoleon said that he forgave the Prussian King and wanted him for an ally, but a strong ally, and offered him Hanover, demanding Neuchâtel and Kleve for France in exchange, and Ansbach for Bavaria. To Graf Haugwitz's objection that he lacked the authority to agree to such an important matter, Napoleon gave him 24 hours to think, after which he should either agree to the required conditions, or carry a declaration of war to Berlin. Graf Haugwitz bent to the will of the victor and concluded the treaty on the terms he desired, quickly ratified by the King of Prussia, which resulted in a cooling of relations between Emperor Alexander and Prussia and a declaration of war by the British King. For an unauthorised action, without the authority to sign such a document that completely changed the political relations of Prussia, Graf Haugwitz was motivated on the one hand by Napoleon's threats and on the other by his conviction that an alliance with France was as necessary for the good and benefit of Prussia as an alliance with Russia was harmful.

The treaty between Prussia and Napoleon robbed Austria of any hope of help from the Berlin Court. Austria, already defenceless under the terms of the ceasefire, deprived of the assistance of Emperor Alexander, occupied by a victorious enemy army and having neither arsenals nor reserves, could not argue any longer and on 14 [26] December signed the Peace of Pressburg. Napoleon acted towards them, in his own expression; 'as with a conquered fortress, which was to be secured and if not completely demolished, then at least disarmed.' Austria recognized all Napoleon's appropriations in Italy, ceded Tyrol, Venice and several possessions in Germany to him, lost 2,785,000 subjects, and paid 200 million francs in indemnities. Napoleon elevated the Electors of Bavaria and Württemberg to Kings, as it said in the bulletin; 'rewards deserved by the loyalty and friendship that they showed to the Emperor,'[8] declared the King of Naples deprived of his Throne, and reproached his wife [Maria Karolina von Österreich], the sister of Kaiser Franz, calling her 'this criminal woman.'[9] There was no precedent to such an impudent assault on the sanctity of the dignity of a Monarch: showering a Queen with curses, taking away a throne, distributing royal crowns as a reward, by order of the army. And how much more shame faced would the Monarchs be, if Alexander had not saved them, had not broken Napoleon!

Notifying the Tsar of the conclusion of peace, Kaiser Franz wrote: 'The treaty of Pressburg became a capitulation to an enemy who used the full extent of his advantages. This state of affairs forced me to give up some of my provinces to preserve the existence of those I retain. I had to succumb to the power of circumstances which gathered against me. However, I will not have lost everything if your Imperial

8 *Les Electeurs de Bavière et de Wirtemberg vont prendre le titre de Roi, recompense qu'ils ont méritée par l'attachement et l'amitié qu'ils ont montrés à l'Empereur dans toutes les circonstances.*

9 *Le général Saint-Cyr marche à grandes journées sur Naples, pour punir la trahison de la reine, et précipiter du trône cette femme criminelle, qui, avec, tant d'impudeur, a violé tout ce qui est sacré parmi les hommes.Trente septième bulletin de la grande armée.*

Majesty's friendship remains with me and, if so, it is due to the ties that unite us.'[10] The appeal of friendship found an echo. The Tsar repeated the promise made to Kaiser Franz in Holitsch: under no circumstances to lose sight of Austria's interests, not to make commitments with anyone contrary to their interests, debate everything secretly with Kaiser Franz, go to his aid if an attack is launched upon him, and make every effort to return territory lost to Austria under the terms of the Peace of Pressburg.[11]

On the way from Vienna to France, Napoleon entered multi-national agreements with the Bavarian and Badenese Courts, forming the Confederation of the Rhine [*États confédérés du Rhin*] and laid the foundation for his dominion over Germany, which quickly expanded and made these countries tributaries to France, until eight years later, in 1813, Alexander liberated them. In Paris, Napoleon celebrated his victories magnificently; scattered awards on the troops, saying in an order to the army that he did not have sufficient promotions, medals or money to be worthy of distribution to the brave; honoured the memory of those who fell on the battlefield, recognised the orphaned children as his children, and wishing to perpetuate the recent feat with a monument, ordered the construction of a bridge over the Seine, named for Austerlitz. The ruler of Western Europe, already dreaming of conquering Tsarigrad [Istanbul] and the expulsion of the British from India, could he have imagined that after a few years, the erected monument served as an occasion for Emperor Alexander to reveal a new example of generosity to the conquered and Blessed Realm of France? Upon our entry into Paris, it was proposed to the Emperor that the Austerlitz bridge should be blown up. He replied; 'No need to touch it; it's enough for us for History to record that the Russian army marched across the Austerlitz bridge.' Then, visiting the Tuileries Palace, the Tsar stopped in a hall decorated with portraits of Napoleon's Marshals and a painting of the Battle of Austerlitz. Looking at the picture, he said to us; 'It is not shameful to remember Austerlitz here.'[12]

---

10 *Le traité de Presbourg est devenu une capitulation avec un ennemi qui a usé de toute l'étendue de ses avantages. L'état des choses m'a forçé de renoncer à une partie de mes provinces pour sauver l'existence de celles que je conserve. J'ai du succomber à la force des circonstances qui se sont réunies contre moi. Cependant je n'aurai pas tout perdu si l'amitié de Votre Majesté Impériale me reste et si Elle tient aux liens qui nous unissent.* Letter dated 4 [16] January, 1806.

11 Tsar's letter to Kaiser Franz of April 1806.

12 Overheard personally.

17

Kutuzov's Return to Russia

Kaiser Franz's letter to Kutuzov. – The reply. – The march of the army through Hungary and Galicia. – Arrival in Russia. – The losses in men during the campaign. – Entry of the Lifeguard in St Petersburg. – Awards.

While Napoleon triumphantly returned to France, accepted by the German Courts as the sovereign leader of them all, Kutuzov led the army to Russia. On 27 November [9 December] he set off from the camp at Senitz on the return march, having received the following rescript from Kaiser Franz on the day of his departure:

> A series of unfortunate events have brought about our separation at an earlier point in time than I and you and anyone who was concerned about the common good, could only hope would come later and in more favourable circumstances. I use these last moments of your presence to tell you that you take with you my respect and my thanks equally. I certainly do not ignore your efforts, your zeal and your devotion to me and the Emperor, your Lord, and our common interest, and I know how sensitive it is to you that your sincere efforts have not been as successful as they deserve. I only wish that these assurances of mine may help to comfort you. If, incidentally, I am unable to ensure that the remembrance of me does not also awaken those adverse moments that we experienced together, that you will always rejoice in me, and I ask you for this, just as I assure you of my remembrance, my respect and favour. You may say the same to your subordinate generals and the entire army.[1]

---

1 *Lieber General en Chef Koutousoff! Eine Reihe unglücklicher Ereignisse haben den Zeitpunkt früher herbeigeführt, den Ich und Sie und jeder, dem die gemeinschaftliche gute Sache am Herzen war, erst später und nach günstigeren Umständen, wünschen und erwarten konnte, nehmlich jenen unserer Trennung. Ich benutze diese letzten Augenblicke Ihrer Anwesenheit, um Ihnen zu sagen, daß Sie in gleichem Grade Meine Achtung und Meinen Dank mitnehmen. Ich verkenne Ihre Bemühungen, Ihren Eifer und Ihre Ergebenheit für Mich und den Kaiser, Ihren Herrn, und unser gemeinsames Interesse gewiß nicht, und weiß wie empfindlich es Ihnen fällt, daß diese Ihre aufrichtigen Bemühungen nicht jenen Erfolg hatten, den sie verdienten. Ich wünsche nur, daß diese Meine Versicherungen Ihnen zu einiger Beruhigung dienen mögen. Wenn Ich übrigens nicht besorgen darf, daß die Erinnerung an Mich auch zugleich jene an die widrigen Momente erweckt, die wir zusammen erlebten, so wird sie Mich immer freuen, und Ich ersuche Sie darum, so wie Ich Sie auch hiemit Meines Andenkens, Meiner Achtung und*

Kutuzov replied to Kaiser Franz;

> Your Majesty's gracious rescript will remain a precious assurance of your just feelings for me and my family. Sire! I dare to repeat: I am one of the most diligent servants of the just cause, which is the constant concern of my Monarch and of Your Majesty. If my efforts, labours and hopes were unsuccessful, then, of course, it was thus pleasing to God, who controls the destinies of Kings and nations. I obey Him with a broken and distressed heart. No matter what happens, I will not forget the good deeds with which Your Majesty showered me over the whole campaign, when I had the joy of being at your behest. The remembrance of them will remain forever in my memory and that of my descendants. They will never utter your name, or the name of my Monarch, without the liveliest gratitude. I will declare Your gracious feelings to all generals and troops subordinate to me. Sire! I fall at your feet with gratitude and deepest respect to you.

Kutuzov marched from Senitz through Hungary and Galicia via Kaschau [Košice], Eperies [Prešov] and Lemberg, in three columns: infantry in the first, cavalry in the second and artillery in the third, meeting greater obstacles while crossing the Carpathian mountains, where the guns had to be drawn by oxen. By order of the Hungarian Palatine [Joseph Anton Johann Baptist von Österreich], former spouse of Grand Duchess Alexandra Pavlovna, and the unlimited zeal of the Hungarians, all possible benefits were provided to our troops. Kutuzov was honoured magnificently. In many places, the entire corps of officers was entertained free of charge. They showed kindred care for the sick, and lovingly rested them in their homes. The Archduke Palatine himself visited Kutuzov to find out if the army had any needs.[2] Five days' march from Senitz, Kaiser Franz sent General Strauch to Kutuzov to ask: 'If he was authorised to resume operations against the French if circumstances were to prompt the Viennese Court to break the ceasefire?' The question was raised because Napoleon's demands during the negotiations in Pressburg seemed unbearable to Austria. Kutuzov replied that he did not have the power to return, and would continue the march, having orders to lead the troops to Russia, for which Emperor Alexander had given his word to Napoleon via General Savary.[3] Then a personal decree was brought to Kutuzov, as a result of the wish expressed by the Prussian King to send Essen's corps to Silesia to join Bennigsen. Kutuzov did not comply with the decree, reporting: 'Essen's movements could not be carried out covertly; upon learning of his march, Napoleon, all things permitted to him, would probably send an army along the direct route to block his path. These new circumstances would put Austria in great difficulty, and things could take a most disadvantageous turn

---

Gewogenheit versichere. Ein gleiches sagen Sie Ihren untergebenen Generals und der ganzen Armee.

Holitsch, den 6-ten December 1805.

Franz.

2 Kutuzov's report to the Tsar, dated 26 December [7 January, 1806].

3 Kutuzov's report to the Tsar, dated 3 [15] December.

for them.' Moreover, Kutuzov suggested that it would be more convenient and faster to send troops from the reserves located within Russia to Bennigsen.

Crossing from Hungary to Galicia, Kutuzov thanked the Palatine on behalf of the army for his care of our troops and the hospitality provided to us at every turn. The Palatine replied; 'Orders made during the march of Russian troops through Hungary have no cost other than that accepted by you. Happy to pay it themselves if the Emperor of all Russians graciously accepts the willingness of the Hungarians to fulfil their duty.'[4] Almost the same cordial welcome awaited our men in Galicia, and eased the march amid the onset of frosts. Throughout the march to Russia, soldiers who had been separated from the army at Austerlitz rejoined. Some brought colours torn from their poles by them during the battle; others brought guns that were considered lost via almost impassable roads.[5] Wanting to prevent the squandering of money abroad, Kutuzov did not pay the troops before entering Russia,[6] but he made calculations with the Austrian Government for the rations for the army during its four-month stay in Kaiser Franz's territories.[7] Finally, after difficult winter marches, the troops entered Radsywyliw on 26 December [7 January, 1806]. From the last Austrian border town, Kutuzov once again thanked Kaiser Franz for his grace to the Russian army, the care from the civil authorities and the friendly disposition of the population, and recommended the rewarding of Austrian officers of the General Staff who were with him since the opening of the war.

All losses incurred during the campaign by the troops under Kutuzov's command were broken down as follows:

During the withdrawal from Braunau to Brünn	5,840 men.
At Austerlitz	21,000 men.
Total:	26,840 men.
Left in Austrian hospitals	7,200 men.

Emperor Alexander ordered an immediate re-manning of the army so that by March 1806 it would consist of 2,754 field-officers and subalterns and 92,404 lower ranks.[8] But while the troops and recruits were being replenished, a new disaster appeared – contagious disease. Kutuzov placed the regiments in widely scattered quarters and sent the Lifeguard to St Petersburg. Three months later, on 29 March [10 April], they arrived in the area of the capital, and settled there for several days, preparing for their ceremonial entry into St Petersburg. On 9 [21] April, the army marched on a ceremonial parade from the Moscow Gate to the Winter Palace. Here they stopped in the square, and medals were distributed to all Lifeguard officers,

4 The Archduke Palatine's letter to Kutuzov, dated 24 December.
5 Kutuzov's report to the Tsarevich, dated 3 [15] December.
6 Kutuzov's report to Intendant-General Prince Volkonsky [Dmitry Petrovich Volkonsky], dated 26 December [7 January, 1806].
7 Kutuzov's report to the Austrian General Graf Haller, dated 26 December [7 January, 1806].
8 Kutuzov's report to the Governor of Volhynia [*Prince Mikhail Nikolaevich Volkonsky*], dated 8 [20] February [1806].

without exception; moreover, the lower ranks were granted one rouble per man, not as credit of a third of their pay; the Lifeguard Horse were given St George standards for the Eagle they had captured at Austerlitz.

The *Duma* of the Knights of St George sought to present the Emperor with the insignia of the Military Order, first class. The senior Knight, Prince Prozorovsky [Alexander Alexandrovich Prozorovsky], presented a report on this to His Majesty, signed by all available knights; insignia of the order were presented by the Chancellor of orders, Prince Kurakin [Alexander Borisovich Kurakin]. The sovereign thanked the *Duma*, and said that the first class of the Military Order was a reward presented to commanders and that he had shared danger with the troops, but had not commanded them, and brought the army to the aid of his Ally, who directed all operations for their particular purposes. As proof of his respect for the Military Order, the Tsar accepted only the insignia of the 4th class. The Emperor granted the 3rd class of this order to Grand Duke Konstantin Pavlovich, on the recommendation of Kutuzov, who reported: 'I would not dare to speak of the courage and firmness of spirit of the Sovereign Tsarevich in the Battle of Austerlitz, but I would dare to present the general opinion of the army and mine that the glory of the Military Order would be enhanced by adding His Highness to this class.' The Order of St George was granted for the Battle of Austerlitz, and generally for the campaign of 1805: 2nd class to Prince Bagration; 3rd class to Miloradovich, Dokhturov, Count Wittgenstein, Quartermaster-General Gerard, Chaplitz, Ulanius, two Depreradovichs [Nikolai Ivanovich Depreradovich and Leonty Ivanovich Depreradovich], and Adjutant-Generals Uvarov, Wintzingerode, Count Lieven and Princes Dolgorukov and Volkonsky; 4th class to 32 field-officers and subalterns, including 16 from the Lifeguard. Kutuzov was awarded two decorations for the entire war: Order of Vladimir 1st class and, for one of his daughters, the Freylinsky Monogram [brooch worn by Maids of Honour to the Empress or Dowager Empress]. Soon afterwards, a new military deployment followed. Kutuzov was appointed Military Governor of Kiev. But Kiev was not the end of his career. Providence protected Kutuzov for the most dangerous of times, when the fate of Russia was to be fulfilled. It was waiting for 1812 for the Peace of Bucharest and the Patriotic War.

18

Operations of the Independent Corps in Hanover

The composition of Count Tolstoy's corps and the Fleet. – The voyage. – The objective of operations by land and maritime forces. – Emperor Alexander's orders to Count Tolstoy to go on the offensive. – Count Tolstoy's advance from Pomerania towards the Weser. – The arrival of the British and Swedes in the theatre of war. – Council of war. – Deployment of the Army of the North. – The new deployment of the Allied forces. – The return of Bennigsen and Count Tolstoy to Russia. – Inspections in Schwedt and Stettin.

Having described the event in the main theatre of the war, it remains for us to depict the operations of independent corps in Hanover and Naples.

Three days after the departure of Emperor Alexander from St Petersburg, on 12 [24] September, Count Tolstoy's corps sailed from Kronstadt and Reval for Swedish Pomerania. It was composed of His Majesty's Cuirassiers, Kurland Dragoons, Izyum Hussars and two Cossack regiments and the Lifeguard Ural *Sotnia*; Pavlov Grenadiers, St Petersburg Grenadiers, Belozersk Musketeers, Ryazan Musketeers, Kexholm Musketeers, 3rd Marines, 1st Jägers and 20th Jägers, in all 20,363 combatants. Under Count Tolstoy's command were the generals Count Osterman [Alexander Ivanovich Osterman], Kozhin [Sergei Alexeevich Kozhin], Verderovsky [Nikolai Ivanovich Verderovsky], Prince Shakovsky [Ivan Leontovich Shakovsky], Lieven [Ivan Andreevich Lieven?], Neverovsky [Dmitry Petrovich Neverovsky]. The Quartermaster-General was Berg [Burkhard Maksimovich Berg], the Brigade-Major was Vorontsov [Mikhail Semënovich Vorontsov] (now [1844] General-of-Infantry), and as *Flügel-Adjutant* Benckendorf [Alexander Khristoforovich Benckendorf], later General-of-Cavalry. The fleet, assigned to transport Count Tolstoy's corps, was commanded by Admiral Tate [Yegor Yegorovich Tet or George Tate]. Under his command were the ships of the line: *Blagodat, Gavriil, Rafail, Silny, Vsevolod, Omgeten, Zachatie St Anna, Arkhistratig Mikhail, Yanuary, Prince Charles* and *Evropa*. Frigates were: *Bogoyavlenie Gospodne, Schastlivy, Tikhvinskaya Bogoroditsa, Theodosy Totmensky, Emmanuil, Legky, Konstantin* and *Nikolai*, and several minor vessels. When it proved impossible to load the entire corps aboard warships, they hired as many as 140 private merchant ships. Initially the voyage was carried out safely, towards the end a storm lashed the fleet and transport ships; more than 400

Cossacks were drowned; a cuirassier platoon became castaways on a distant island; several guns and ammunition caissons were lost. When the sea calmed down, the ships anchored in various places off Pomerania and the island of Rügen where the troops disembarked and assembled at Stralsund.

The purpose of sending Count Tolstoy's corps to Pomerania, as it was not known in which direction Prussia would turn, was initially as follows:

1. Count Tolstoy was to unite with Mikhelson's army, which was assigned to operate in northern Germany if the King of Prussia gave consent for it to pass through his territory;
2. If the Berlin Court opposes Mikhelson's transit through Prussia, Count Tolstoy was to enter Prussian territory and act offensively, as a diversionary force for our other armies;[1]
3. If Prussia declared war on us, then Admiral Tate, having landed Count Tolstoy's corps in Pomerania, was to sail the fleet towards the coast of Prussia, pinning down its forces by threatening landing parties and potentially inflicting harm on its trade through the blockading of Prussian harbours, and sending cruisers in various directions to capture Prussian merchant ships. Tate was particularly instructed to try to launch a raid on Danzig [Gdańsk], so that, in addition to exerting influence on Prussian trade, we might acquire a suitable place to shelter our cruisers from the Northwest gales raging in the autumn.[2]

Soon after the arrival of Count Tolstoy in Stralsund, events took a favourable turn for us when, offended by the French march through Ansbach, the King of Prussia concluded an agreement with Emperor Alexander in Potsdam. While in Berlin, the Emperor summoned Count Tolstoy there and, not worrying any more about Prussia and not waiting for Mikhelson, ordered him to persuade the Swedish King to start the campaign as soon as possible and to drive the French out of Holland together with the Swedes and the British expected at any moment. Moreover, the Tsar ordered Count Tolstoy that if the Swedish King, distracted by disputes with Prussia, were to delay his departure, separate from him and march on Hanover, stripped of French troops, occupying just the Hamelin fortress in this area.[3] Returning from Berlin to the Swedish King, Count Tolstoy, together with the Russian and British envoys, urged him to set off. Gustav Adolf did not agree, and wanted to wait until the conclusion of his business with the Berlin Court, fearing that the Prussians would take possession of his German territory once he went off on campaign.[4] His military resources in Pomerania were also very limited: the regiments lacked transport; there were only six horse and 13 three-pounder guns in the artillery; the cavalry was not fit for purpose, often having agricultural horses instead of war horses. Not wanting to waste time waiting for the Swedish troops to deploy and the feud between Prussia and Sweden to end, Count Tolstoy took advantage of Gustav Adolf's departure from

1 Supreme orders to Count Tolstoy.
2 Decree to Admiral Tate, dated 6 [18] September.
3 Supreme orders to Count Tolstoy, dated 23 September [5 October] and 4 [16] October.
4 Report of the Russian Envoy to the Swedish Court, dated 31 October [12 November].

Stralsund to the island of Rügen, and at the beginning of November marched on Hanover, assigning the vanguard to Count Osterman – the hero of Kulm.

The troops crossed the Elbe at Lauenburg and proceeded on to Lüneburg. It was compared to a triumphal march. The Duke of Mecklenburg [Friedrich Franz I] and other sovereign Princes came to meet us; the population of the nearby villages flocked to see the Russians, who had not appeared in northern Germany since the Seven Years War. Everyone was astonished, as Count Tolstoy's corps was in a most brilliant state. Our officers were entertained everywhere; balls were held in our honour in the larger towns. Having occupied Hanover, Count Tolstoy kept a vanguard on the left bank of the river Weser, and sent Verderevsky's detachment to observe the Hamelin Fortress in anticipation of the British deploying an army on the right bank of the Weser. Our corps was quartered in Nienburg. On the day of the Battle of Austerlitz, 20 November [2 December], the British generals Don [Sir George Don] and Cathcart [William Schaw, 1st Earl Cathcart] arrived in Nienburg, with the news that their corps, the first of 10,000 men, and the second of 14,000, had arrived at the mouth of the Weser from England. Both came under the command of Count Tolstoy, and on his orders they moved their corps to Bremen.

Finally, the King of Sweden stirred himself from inaction, having received a guarantee of the security of his territory from Prussia via Emperor Alexander. Reassured by the Tsar, Gustav Adolf set out with 12,000 men from Pomerania, crossed the Elbe and stopped in Lüneburg. Thus, an army of 56,000 Russians, British and Swedes was formed in northern Germany. The Hanover Legion, assembled by Colonel Arentschildt [Wilhelm Daniel von Arentschildt] on the island of Rügen, by the will of Emperor Alexander and the King of Sweden, at Russian expense, from the Hanoverian troops disbanded by the French after occupying Hanover, was soon to join them.[5] Upon arrival in Lüneburg, on 7 [19] December, the Swedish King invited Count Tolstoy, Lord Cathcart and General Don to join him, and in a council of war they unanimously adopted the following plan of action: while waiting for the roads to dry out, confine ourselves to the defence of the crossings over the Ems and taking possession of Hamelin, and once the ground has frozen, to advance on the lower Rhine. Belated decisions!

No sooner had the council of war ended, than Adjutant-General Prince Gagarin arrived in Lüneburg, sent from Holitsch by Emperor Alexander, with the sad news of the Battle of Austerlitz, the negotiations between Austria and Napoleon and a decree for Count Tolstoy that he was no longer under the command of Gustav Adolph, but at the disposal of the King of Prussia. Listening to Prince Gagarin's story about the defeat, our officers did not believe him at first, took his words for fiction, not comprehending the possibility of a Russian defeat.[6] Soon afterwards, Lord Cathcart and General Don received orders from London to return to England at the earliest opportunity. The King of Sweden, left alone with his troops, angrily led them back to the right bank of the Elbe. Thus the Northern Army, established just a few days

5 Instructions to Arentschildt from the Minister of Foreign Affairs, dated 29 September [11 October] 1804.

6 According to eyewitnesses, now [1844] Adjutants-General Count Vorontsov and Naryshkin [Levin Alexandrovich Naryshkin], and from manuscript notes by Count Benckendorf.

previously, was divided and the hopes placed in it at the beginning of the campaign crumbled. The Russians had been ready to depart from Pomerania at the end of September, almost two months before the Battle of Austerlitz. Consequently, if the British and Swedes had been equipped for the campaign at that time, the Northern Army, of almost 60,000 men, skilfully led, could have had a strong influence on Napoleon's operations, would probably have stopped his rapid pursuit to Vienna, and allowed time for the Russian forces and Archduke Charles to draw closer to the heart of Austria. Instead, the British were landing at Bremen in late November, and the Swedes came to the left bank of the Elbe in December, when the roads were impassable and operations in the main theatre of war were being decided, depriving the northern army of an opportunity to participate in the war.

Meanwhile, the King of Prussia, having not yet received a report from Count Haugwitz on the agreement concluded with Napoleon, ordered Count Tolstoy not to go into combat at all against the French, to withdraw Verderevsky's observation detachment from Hamelin, and to submit his further plans to the Prussian General, Graf Kalckreuth for approval. In a meeting with him, on 15 [27] December, it was proposed to Count Tolstoy and the English generals:

1. The British and Russians remain on the right bank of the Weser, the former from Bremen to Verden, and the latter from Verden to Nienburg, occupying Hanover as a garrison;
2. The 8,000 man corps under Graf Kalckreuth was to cover them, forming a vanguard along the river Ems and having a detachment at Hamelin.

By arranging the troops in this way, it was hoped to avoid a clash between the Anglo-Russians and the French, on the assumption that the French would not attack the Prussians, because Napoleon was negotiating with Prussia, and therefore was not at war with them.

The unilateral adoption of these measures seemed to Count Tolstoy, Don and Lord Cathcart insufficient protection for their troops from French attack. They did not place much reliance on Prussia's shaky policies, especially when they learned that Graf Kalckreuth often corresponded with the Commander-in-Chief of the French army assembling in Holland and kept his relations with the enemy secret from them. When asked what he intended to do in the event of an attack by the French, Graf Kalckreuth answered that there would be no attack and, if against all expectation the French attacked, he would meet them with weapons in hand. This was the situation in the middle of December 1805, when the King of Prussia received the treaty signed by Graf Haugwitz and Napoleon, and ordered Bennigsen and Count Tolstoy to return to Russia. Bennigsen immediately moved from Silesia to Russia, but Count Tolstoy was reluctant to set off, under various pretexts, not wanting to leave our allies, the British, alone, until transport ships could sail from England to Bremen to load the British troops aboard them. A few days later, the ships arrived in Cuxhaven. The British sailed to their homeland, and Count Tolstoy went to Russia, leaving in the memory of the inhabitants for many years the exemplary discipline that distinguished the Russian army in this two-month stay in Hanover.

When Count Tolstoy's corps approached the river Oder, preparing to cross at Schwedt and Stettin, the King of Prussia and the Queen wanted to inspect our troops, and arrived in Schwedt. The Guards officers who accompanied them in large numbers at the first meeting treated our men arrogantly. The battle of Austerlitz had humbled the Russians in their eyes; the Prussians considered only themselves capable of defeating Napoleon. Their hour of disappointment was soon to come. Our men held their peace. The next morning, after the arrival of the Prussian Monarchy in Schwedt, the Izyum Hussars, 1st Jägers and 3rd Marines entered. Amazed by the harmony of movement, the beauty and physical strength of the troops, the Prussians became more respectful towards us. At the parade in Stettin, our men made the same impression on the Prussians as in Schwedt. The regiments greeted the Monarchy of Prussia with relentless shouts of 'Hurrah!' The Queen was moved to tears, seeing the explosion of joy amongst the troops produced by her presence. From general to soldier, we all idolised the Queen, knowing her liking for Russia; all eyes were fixed on the Queen, radiant with beauty. She once appeared in front of the ranks in a green Amazonian dress with red edging – in imitation of the colours of Russian uniforms. Our musicians escorted her from the parade square to the palace. The Queen rode ahead of them. Throughout the parades, she showered our generals and officers with unspoken signs of goodwill. Even now, after forty years, they speak with tenderness about her mercies. After examining Count Tolstoy's entire corps, the King presented decorations to the generals and expressed a wish for three Russian soldiers to be sent to Berlin as an example. Upon the return of these soldiers to Russia (selected from the Kexholm Musketeers), the Queen gave them necklaces and earrings, ordering them to hand these gifts over to their wives on behalf of Her Majesty.[7]

The details given here about the parades in Schwedt and Stettin should not be considered unimportant. They are intentionally mentioned as events that held important consequences. The Prussian King and his wife, who had a great influence on affairs, personally ascertaining the excellent condition of the Russian troops, had high hopes for their courage and fortitude, were filled with confidence that with the help of such an army Prussia could successfully compete with Napoleon. This confidence was one of the reasons for the decision made shortly afterwards by the Berlin Court: to get close to Russia, to raise a strong voice against Napoleon's arbitrariness in Germany after the Peace of Pressburg and finally declare war on him in September 1806.

7 From Count Benckendorf's hand-written notes.

19

Operations in Naples

General Lacy's departure to Naples. – The situation in the Kingdom of Naples. – The Russians and British arrive in Naples. – The Allied offensive. – Council of war. – The return of the Russians to Corfu and Russia.

In preparation for war in 1805, Russia, Britain and the King of Naples had the intention of driving the French out of southern Italy, and then turning their forces on Lombardy to join with the Austrians. Assigning an army to a land so remote from Russia, Emperor Alexander recognized the need to first find out the situation in Naples through an experienced military man. The choice fell on the retired General Lacy living near Grodno. Secretly and without letting his orders be known in the army, he was informed of his acceptance back into service, with the appointment as Commander-in-Chief of Russian forces in Corfu, and those who would later come to Italy from Russia. He was ordered: to avoid publicity, not to call into St Petersburg, and to go from Grodno to Naples under the guise of a tourist. Upon arrival, he had to collect accurate information about the Neapolitan armed forces; agree with the British when and how many troops they will send from Malta; agree with the Neapolitan Court on the plan of action, food and supply for our corps with draught and artillery horses, and upon receipt of the news of the outbreak of war in Germany from the Russian Ambassador in Vienna, Count Razumovsky, to order General Anrep to immediately leave Corfu with his corps for Naples. The Engineer, Major-General Opperman [Karl Ivanovich Opperman], was selected to help Lacy, who went to Naples under the pretext of restoring his poor health, with a secret mission to inspect arsenals, fortresses and positions.

The King and Queen of Naples received General Lacy extremely graciously, told him of their gratitude towards Emperor Alexander and hatred for Napoleon. But their military resources were insignificant. Throughout the Realm there were only 6,000 infantry, with old, heavy muskets, 1,100 cavalry on unsuitable horses, and 500 artillerymen who had not produced a gunpowder specialist in three years. Horse artillery and a general staff were non-existent. Gunpowder and ammunition was limited. Many fortresses had no construction drawings; the main two fortresses, Gaeta and Capua, were dilapidated and weakly armed. The officers, with no passion for their service and overwhelmed by disagreements in policy matters, did not know their chain-of-command; commanders and soldiers were decidedly unmilitary; desertion was a daily occurrence in the regiments. The nobility and the people showed complete indifference to the adverse situation of their fatherland, they were afraid of the French and had no faith in the Government. Incredible abuses occurred in the management of the War Ministry. To make matters worse, General Saint-Cyr's 17,000 man French Corps occupied several regions of the Kingdom.

Having learned in detail about everything, Lacy considered it folly to have even a little faith in the Neapolitan armed forces, and Anrep's Corps insufficient for operations in Italy. He requested that several regiments be sent from Russia to Corfu, but meanwhile he used all means to increase and improve the Neapolitan troops – this was a very difficult matter, due to the Government's fear of raising French suspicions.[1] However, no one knew the real purpose of Lacy's and Opperman's visit to Naples. Even the ministers did not know, except for Medici [Luigi de Medici]. Lacy directed all his activities through the offices of the Queen. She supplied him with the information he needed and he informed her alone of his decisions. It is easy to imagine what kind of feelings the Queen harboured for the French, remembering that she was the sister of the ill-fated Marie Antoinette, the wife of Louis XVI.

At the end of August, foreseeing a breach with Austria, Napoleon demanded that the King of Naples be bound by an agreement to maintain neutrality in an actual war. If the proposal were accepted, he promised to withdraw Saint-Cyr's corps from Neapolitan territory, and in the event of a refusal he threatened to occupy Naples with French troops. Deprived of the means to resist the threat with an armed response, on 9 [21] September, the King accepted the conditions required of him, and Saint-Cyr departed for Lombardy. Secretly informing our Envoy of the pressing reasons for signing the agreement, the Queen told him that her husband would be faithful to their former obligations to Russia, ready to act in union with Emperor Alexander.[2] Once Saint-Cyr had set off for northern Italy, Lacy received notice from Count Razumovsky in Vienna that war was inevitable. With the consent of the Neapolitan Court, he immediately sent out couriers: one to Anrep ordering him to leave the necessary garrisons on the Ionian Islands and to sail to Naples with the rest of the troops, and another to Malta with the same requirement for the British General Craig [James Henry Craig], having previously been in secret relations with this General, equipped with orders from the London Court to leave for Naples on receipt of notice from General Lacy.

Anrep arrived in Naples on 7 [19] November, and Craig on the 8 [20], the day Kutuzov and Count Buxhoeveden linked up between Brünn and Olmütz. Our corps was composed of the Siberia Grenadiers, Vitebsk Musketeers, Kozlov Musketeers, Kolyvan Musketeers, one battalion from the Alexopol Musketeer Regiment, 13th Jägers, 14th Jägers and one company of Battery Artillery, in total 11,250 men, and the legion formed in Corfu from Souliotes, Albanians and Shimariotes, 1,624, bringing the total to 12,874 men. There were 6,640 other ranks in the British detachment. General Craig was subordinated to Lacy, invested by the King of Naples with the rank of Commander-in-Chief of his troops, as many as 7,500 men. The King promised to increase their numbers to 15,000 within two months. It seemed that the fulfilment of this promise would have no obstacles, because from the day the Russians entered Naples, the Neapolitan's fear of the French disappeared, the spirits

1 Lacy's reports, dated 2 [14] May and 9 [21] June.
2 Count Razumovsky's report from Vienna, dated 17 [29] October.

of the nobility, people and troops were completely reborn. All came to life with refreshed memories of Suvorov and his friend, Admiral Ushakov [Fëdor Fëdorovich Ushakov], which were rooted in contempt for the French in Italy, from Calabria to the Alpine mountains and a decisive belief in the impossibility of the French resisting the Russians. Suvorov's recent victories in Piedmont and Lombardy, and Ushakov's in southern Italy, when he restored the legitimate authority of the King of Naples in the shortest time, 600 Russians had taken possession of Naples and 1,000 of our men formed the garrison, or more justly, the stronghold of Rome only, having resurrected the fallen morale of the Neapolitans, fulfilling their inflamed imaginations with their undoubted conviction of success. The Court exhausted themselves in expressing favour for our generals and officers; the populace honoured our soldiers; thousands of curious people flocked daily to admire the Russian camp, spread out at the foot of Vesuvius.

Amid the general delight, the news spread about the Austrian defeat at Ulm, and then about Archduke Charles's withdrawal from Lombardy. The people did not falter in their hope of deliverance by the Russians, according to the Government they were frightened by the consequences of the conditions they had agreed with Napoleon about maintaining neutrality, and they prepared to operate on the defensive. Fearing that Massena would detach more forces against Naples after the retreat of the Austrians from Italy, they intended to confine themselves only to the defence of the Kingdom of Naples, placing troops in strong positions within its frontier with the Papal territories, and waiting there for a turn of events in Germany, the main theatre of war, as well as for the reinforcements promised to General Lacy from Russia and from the King of Naples.

Before departing from Naples, Lacy was brought orders sent by Emperor Alexander in Olmütz, to embark the troops on ships, sail to Trieste and go from there to join Archduke Charles, who was travelling from Italy to the banks of the Danube. Archduke Charles wrote to General Lacy in the same vein as Emperor Alexander, depicting the futility of the allied forces' further presence in Italy and the need to concentrate more strength in the centre of the Austrian Realm, where hostilities had shifted after the Austrian disaster at Ulm and the capture of Vienna by Napoleon. Fearing sailing on the stormy Adriatic Sea in late autumn, Lacy did not agree to the Archduke's call, and did not follow the Supreme Command, the execution of which was given, however, at his discretion. In accordance with the views adopted by the Neapolitan Government, he decided to go to the border with the Papal territories. On the day of departure from Naples, the Allied forces, comprising 23,000 men, were lined up on the magnificent Chiaia Embankment in front of a huge gathering of the populace. The Russians stood on the right wing, the Neapolitans on the left, the British in the middle. The King and Queen, in a gilded carriage drawn by 12 horses, drove around the army and blessed them with prayers for victory on campaign.

On the third day of marching, near Gaeta, Lacy received intelligence of the movement of 35,000 men sent against him by Massena, stopped the columns and gathered the generals for a meeting. Before receiving orders from their Courts, almost everyone suggested: to withdraw to Calabria, and wage a defensive war from there. General Craig advised that, with the apparent hopelessness of the situation, the

Russians and the British immediately return to Naples, board their ships and leave Italy. Only Anrep was of the opposite opinion (he was killed at Mohrungen [Morąg] in 1807, to the sincere sorrow of Emperor Alexander and the Russian army, who saw the talent of a general of paramount importance in him). Anrep did not see a need to rush into a withdrawal and offered to find out more about the enemy forces and their movements, and to wait to see if there was any chance of successfully opposing the French. His opinion was not accepted and according to the majority of voices, Lacy ordered the withdrawal. At this time, *Flügel-Adjutant* Shepelev [Dmitry Dmitrievich Shepelev] arrived from Holitsch with news of the Battle of Austerlitz, and with orders: to send back the number of troops needed to defend the Ionian Republic, and to sail with the rest to Black Sea harbours as soon as possible.[3] Lacy led the corps to Naples, not getting within a hundred *versts* [105 km or 66 miles] of Rome, where they had eagerly awaited the Russians, preparing for them the same festive welcome with which they had greeted our compatriots on the banks of the Tiber six years before, when Paul's colours flew over the Eternal City. In Naples, the Allied corps was split up: the British went to Malta, the Neapolitans set off for Calabria, the Russians went to the picturesque harbour of Baiae, and there they boarded the ships of Vice Admiral Senyavin's [Dmitry Nikolayevich Senyavin] squadron. The French quickly advanced on Naples, meeting no resistance, and the King of Naples left for Sicily with his family. He was escorted by the Russian ship-of-the-line *Praskovya*, on which was the King of Sardinia, deposed by Napoleon and in poor fortune overshadowed by the flag of Alexander. Wanting to help the King of Naples in unfortunate circumstances, the Tsar refused the subsidy that came to us from Britain for the maintenance of our troops located in Naples in his favour,[4] and ordered Senyavin, having taken Anrep's corps to Corfu, to return to Sicily and cruise off its coast, preventing the French from landing there. A month later, upon learning of Napoleon's hostile intentions towards Sicily, the Tsar ordered General Lacy, should the King of Naples request it, to send several regiments from Corfu to Messina, or Palermo to guard him.[5]

3 Supreme orders from Holitsch, dated 24 November [6 December].
4 Supreme orders to Count Vorontsov in London, dated 5 [17] March 1806.
5 Instructions to Lacy, dated 30th December 1805 [11th January 1806].

20

Conclusions

Throughout the month of December, 1805, Russian troops returned to their homeland from various parts of Europe. Most of them, the corps of Essen, Count Tolstoy, Bennigsen and Anrep, had no chance to fire a single shot in the campaigns we described. They marched back, but how did they march? With regret, seeing the impossibility of drawing swords, fighting Napoleon and punishing the French for their momentary triumph in Moravia. Everywhere the Russians heard condolences, while departing from Italy and Germany, where they were the most valued guests in nobles' castles and in the homes of ordinary residents. In spite of our defeat at Austerlitz, the health cups were drained and songs thundered in the name of young Alexander. Everyone was sure that the first failure in the war would not shake him: in him they saw a Monarch sent by Heaven for the good of mankind. But Alexander's happiness was also great. Since his appearance on the political horizon, due to some secret attraction, the hearts of all in Europe had turned to him. Everyone expected salvation from him, the erstwhile, calm, independent being. Time lived up to expectations, although in the first war with Napoleon, fortune betrayed Alexander.

The immediate consequences of the war of 1805 were the surrender of vast areas by Austria; Napoleon's alliance with Prussia; his decisive predominance in Holland, Italy, Switzerland and the German states, from the Rhine to the Inn and the Weser. The general opinion was that his power was unlimited, demonstrated by the humiliation of Austria, the timid objections of Prussia, the arbitrary distribution of royal crowns by Napoleon and especially by his fortunate battle with the Russians. The skill with which Napoleon exploited the errors of the Allies and treachery increased his already great military renown, especially since at Austerlitz, for the first time appearing on the battlefield as a Crowned Sovereign, he triumphed over a Russian army revered as invincible and under Suvorov's leadership had quite recently defeated the French. The battle of Austerlitz was endowed with special gravity, taking place in the presence of the two most powerful Monarchs on the continent, Alexander and Franz. Therefore, following all of Napoleon's earlier victories, for many years the French called it the 'battle of the three emperors.' Any of the French military who were not at Austerlitz considered themselves disadvantaged; they were regarded as inexperienced soldiers, novices, it being said of them: 'He has not fought against Russians!' The glory of our armed forces was so strong in general opinion that the first news of the Russian defeat at Austerlitz was met with disbelief everywhere. When the French put the guns that we lost in this battle on the glacis at Vienna, the locals honoured them as Austrian guns taken from the Vienna arsenal, the carriages and wheels having been painted green on Napoleon's orders as a deception. Raising the morale of Napoleon's forces, the Battle of Austerlitz inflated Napoleon himself. Having tested his strength against the forces of Russia, from that time on he began to broadcast his views on affirming his influence on the destiny of the world, dreamed that he had overcome the inconstancy of fortune forever, and was led astray by this conceit until Alexander proved the possibility of defeating Napoleon.

The battle of Austerlitz made a particular kind of impression in Russia. That generation had grown up and matured with the victories of Catherine and Paul. Certainly believing in their invincibility, the Russians longed for a clash with Napoleon. Convinced that they were destined to put an end to his successes, they looked enviously at him, as if these victories overshadowed the centuries-old brilliance of the Russian armed forces. When, in September 1805, they learned about the movement of troops abroad, a common saying among our people was: 'We throw our hats at Bonaparte!' Contemporaries will still recall these words. Such self-confidence was supported by Kutuzov's stubborn actions during his withdrawal from Braunau, where every Russian step was marked by the skill of generals and the courage of our officers and soldiers. Soon after, news came to Russia about the unification of our armies near Olmütz and the probability of a battle. From day to day, they eagerly awaited notification of victory which, up until then, had been the inevitable outcome for the Russian armed forces, then the rumour spread about the defeat at Austerlitz. Following a century, heralded by victories, Russia was shaken, but did not falter in the conviction of the courage of their sons, blaming the failure on the timidity of our allies and on treachery, and on Kutuzov, reproaching him for not having the courage of his convictions. Honouring this war, not only as a matter of the State, but also as a matter of national pride, the Russians burned with thirst for a bloody vengeance on Napoleon. The hour of new battles was not far off. A year after the Battle of Austerlitz, the Russian army met the expectations of the Fatherland at Pultusk, Golymin, Eylau [Bagrationovsk], Heilsberg [Lidzbark Warmiński], all clashes with the French in the war of 1806 and 1807.

Having impartially described the campaign that ended in the Battle of Austerlitz, how should the significance of this battle in the history of Emperor Alexander be determined? In his reign, Austerlitz takes the same place as Narva in the reign of Peter the Great: the unsuccessful wish to achieve an objective and a short delay in completing the work entrusted by Providence to Peter and Alexander. With what intention did they fight? Peter wanted to affirm Russia's place among the European States and protect his State; Alexander wanted to curb Napoleon and affirm the security of Russia and Europe. Both stumbled at the first hurdle: one with Charles XII, the other with Napoleon. But Charles's triumph at Narva and Napoleon's at Austerlitz, gave them only fleeting success and did not prevent the Russian Monarchs from accomplishing the feat for which they had taken up arms – Peter, to establish Russia in Europe, Alexander to save Russia and liberate Europe. In the commonality of events of the twenty-year war of Peter the Great with Charles XII, the massacre of Narva disappears under the splendour of Poltava and the boundless consequences of the Treaty of Nystad [Uusikaupunki]. In the ten-year long struggle between Alexander and Napoleon, the Battle of Austerlitz is destroyed by the victories at Kulm [Chlumec], Leipzig, Fère-Champenoise, Paris, the fall of Napoleon, the restoration of the legitimate Throne, and the establishment of world peace. The Austerlitz disaster does not overshadow the glories of Alexander, but elevates them. Having suffered a bloody failure at his first appearance on the battlefield, the following year he had no doubts about competing with Napoleon again, then fought with him for many years until he wiped his opponent from the face of the earth, and showed in the fight against him the strength and determination with which Peter the Great was motivated in the fight against Charles XII.

THE END

Appendix

Kutuzov's Army – Order of Battle

1st Column – Major-General Prince Bagration's 7,733 men
Pavlograd Hussar Regiment
Kiev Grenadier Regiment
Azov Musketeer Regiment
6th Jäger Regiment
2 Artillery Companies
Cossack Regiment

2nd Column – Lieutenant-General Essen 2nd's 8,116 men
Chernigov Dragoon Regiment
Malorussia Grenadier Regiment
Apsheron Musketeer Regiment
Smolensk Musketeer Regiment
½ Company of Horse Artillery
2 Companies of Foot Artillery
1 Pioneer Company
1 Cossack Regiment

3rd Column – Lieutenant-General Dokhturov's 6,948 men
Mariupol Hussar Regiment
Butyrsk Musketeer Regiment
Moscow Musketeer Regiment
8th Jäger Regiment (1 battalion)
2 Artillery Companies
½ Company of Pontoniers

4th Column – Lieutenant-General Shepelev's 6,881 men
Novgorod Musketeer Regiment
Narva Musketeer Regiment
Podolsk Musketeer Regiment
2 Artillery Companies

5th Column – Lieutenant-General Baron Maltitz's 8,572 men
Her Majesty's Lifeguard Cuirassier Regiment
Vyatka Musketeer Regiment

Bryansk Musketeer Regiment
Yaroslavl Musketeer Regiment
8th Jäger Regiment (2 battalions)
1 Horse Artillery Company
2 Foot Artillery Companies
1 Pioneer Company
1 Cossack Regiment

6th Column – Lieutenant-General Baron Rosen's 8,455 men
St Petersburg Dragoon Regiment
Tver Dragoon Regiment
Novoingermanland Musketeer Regiment,
Vladimir Musketeer Regiment
Galits Musketeer Regiment
1 Horse Artillery Company
2 Foot Artillery Companies
½ Company of Pontoniers
1 Cossack Regiment

Total combatants of all ranks; 46,405

Index

From Reason to Revolution – Warfare 1721-1815

http://www.helion.co.uk/series/from-reason-to-revolution-1721-1815.php

The 'From Reason to Revolution' series covers the period of military history 1721–1815, an era in which fortress-based strategy and linear battles gave way to the nation-in-arms and the beginnings of total war.

This era saw the evolution and growth of light troops of all arms, and of increasingly flexible command systems to cope with the growing armies fielded by nations able to mobilise far greater proportions of their manpower than ever before. Many of these developments were fired by the great political upheavals of the era, with revolutions in America and France bringing about social change which in turn fed back into the military sphere as whole nations readied themselves for war. Only in the closing years of the period, as the reactionary powers began to regain the upper hand, did a military synthesis of the best of the old and the new become possible.

The series will examine the military and naval history of the period in a greater degree of detail than has hitherto been attempted, and has a very wide brief, with the intention of covering all aspects from the battles, campaigns, logistics, and tactics, to the personalities, armies, uniforms, and equipment.

Submissions

The publishers would be pleased to receive submissions for this series. Please contact series editor Andrew Bamford via email (andrewbamford@helion.co.uk), or in writing to Helion & Company Limited, Unit 8 Amherst Business Centre, Budbrooke Road, Warwick, CV34 5WE

Titles

No 1 *Lobositz to Leuthen: Horace St Paul and the Campaigns of the Austrian Army in the Seven Years War 1756-57* (Neil Cogswell)

No 2 *Glories to Useless Heroism: The Seven Years War in North America from the French journals of Comte Maurés de Malartic, 1755-1760* (William Raffle (ed.))

No 3 *Reminiscences 1808-1815 Under Wellington: The Peninsular and Waterloo Memoirs of William Hay* (Andrew Bamford (ed.))

No 4 *Far Distant Ships: The Royal Navy and the Blockade of Brest 1793-1815* (Quintin Barry)

No 5 *Godoy's Army: Spanish Regiments and Uniforms from the Estado Militar of 1800* (Charles Esdaile and Alan Perry)

No 6 *On Gladsmuir Shall the Battle Be! The Battle of Prestonpans 1745* (Arran Johnston)

No 7 *The French Army of the Orient 1798-1801: Napoleon's Beloved 'Egyptians'* (Yves Martin)

No 8 *The Autobiography, or Narrative of a Soldier: The Peninsular War Memoirs of William Brown of the 45th Foot* (Steve Brown (ed.))

No 9 *Recollections from the Ranks: Three Russian Soldiers' Autobiographies from the Napoleonic Wars* (Darrin Boland)

No 10 *By Fire and Bayonet: Grey's West Indies Campaign of 1794* (Steve Brown)

No 11 *Olmütz to Torgau: Horace St Paul and the Campaigns of the Austrian Army in the Seven Years War 1758-60* (Neil Cogswell)

No 12 *Murat's Army: The Army of the Kingdom of Naples 1806-1815* (Digby Smith)

No 13 *The Veteran or 40 Years' Service in the British Army: The Scurrilous Recollections of Paymaster John Harley 47th Foot – 1798-1838* (Gareth Glover (ed.))

No 14 *Narrative of the Eventful Life of Thomas Jackson: Militiaman and Coldstream Sergeant, 1803-15* (Eamonn O'Keeffe (ed.))

No.15 *For Orange and the States: The Army of the Dutch Republic 1713-1772 Part I: Infantry* (Marc Geerdinck-Schaftenaar)

No 16 *Men Who Are Determined to be Free: The American Assault on Stony Point, 15 July 1779* (David C. Bonk)

No 17 *Next to Wellington: General Sir George Murray: The Story of a Scottish Soldier and Statesman, Wellington's Quartermaster General* (John Harding-Edgar)

No 18 *Between Scylla and Charybdis: The Army of Elector Friedrich August of Saxony 1733-1763 Part I: Staff and Cavalry* (Marco Pagan)

No 19 *The Secret Expedition: The Anglo-Russian Invasion of Holland 1799* (Geert van Uythoven)

No 20 *'We Are Accustomed to do our Duty': German Auxiliaries with the British Army 1793-95* (Paul Demet)

No 21 *With the Guards in Flanders: The Diary of Captain Roger Morris 1793-95* (Peter Harington (ed.))

No 22 *The British Army in Egypt 1801: An Underrated Army Comes of Age* (Carole Divall)

No 23 *Better is the Proud Plaid: The Clothing, Weapons, and Accoutrements of the Jacobites in the '45* (Jenn Scott)

No 24 *The Lilies and the Thistle: French Troops in the Jacobite '45* (Andrew Bamford)

No 25 *A Light Infantryman With Wellington: The Letters of Captain George Ulrich Barlow 52nd and 69th Foot 1808-15* (Gareth Glover (ed.))

No 26 *Swiss Regiments in the Service of France 1798-1815: Uniforms, Organisation, Campaigns* (Stephen Ede-Borrett)

No 27 *For Orange and the States! The Army of the Dutch Republic 1713-1772: Part II: Cavalry and Specialist Troops* (Marc Geerdinck-Schaftenaar)

No 28 *Fashioning Regulation, Regulating Fashion: Uniforms and Dress of the British Army 1800-1815 Volume I* (Ben Townsend)

No 29 *Riflemen: The History of the 5th Battalion 60th (Royal American) Regiment, 1797-1818* (Robert Griffith)

No 30 *The Key to Lisbon: The Third French Invasion of Portugal, 1810-11* (Kenton White)

No 31 *Command and Leadership: Proceedings of the 2018 Helion & Company 'From Reason to Revolution' Conference* (Andrew Bamford (ed.))

No 32 *Waterloo After the Glory: Hospital Sketches and Reports on the Wounded After the Battle* (Michael Crumplin and Gareth Glover)

No 33 *Fluxes, Fevers, and Fighting Men: War and Disease in Ancien Regime Europe 1648-1789* (Pádraig Lenihan)

No 34 *'They Were Good Soldiers': African-Americans Serving in the Continental Army, 1775-1783* (John U. Rees)

No 35 *A Redcoat in America: The Diaries of Lieutenant William Bamford, 1757-1765 and 1776* (John B. Hattendorf (ed.))

No 36 *Between Scylla and Charybdis: The Army of Friedrich August II of Saxony, 1733-1763: Part II: Infantry and Artillery* (Marco Pagan)

No 37 *Québec Under Siege: French Eye-Witness Accounts from the Campaign of 1759* (Charles A. Mayhood (ed.))

No 38 *King George's Hangman: Henry Hawley and the Battle of Falkirk 1746* (Jonathan D. Oates)

No 39 *Zweybrücken in Command: The Reichsarmee in the Campaign of 1758* (Neil Cogswell)

No 40 *So Bloody a Day: The 16th Light Dragoons in the Waterloo Campaign* (David J. Blackmore)

No 41 *Northern Tars in Southern Waters: The Russian Fleet in the Mediterranean 1806-1810* (Vladimir Bogdanovich Bronevskiy / Darrin Boland)

No 42 *Royal Navy Officers of the Seven Years War: A Biographical Dictionary of Commissioned Officers 1748-1763* (Cy Harrison)

No 43 *All at Sea: Naval Support for the British Army During the American Revolutionary War* (John Dillon)

No 44 *Glory is Fleeting: New Scholarship on the Napoleonic Wars* (Andrew Bamford (ed.))

No 45 *Fashioning Regulation, Regulating Fashion: Uniforms and Dress of the British Army 1800-1815 Vol. II* (Ben Townsend)

No 46 *Revenge in the Name of Honour: The Royal Navy's Quest for Vengeance in the Single Ship Actions of the War of 1812* (Nicholas James Kaizer)

No 47 *They Fought With Extraordinary Bravery: The III German (Saxon) Army Corps in the Southern Netherlands 1814* (Geert van Uythoven)

No 48 *The Danish Army of the Napoleonic Wars 1801-1814, Organisation, Uniforms & Equipment: Volume 1: High Command, Line and Light Infantry* (David Wilson)

No 49 *Neither Up Nor Down: The British Army and the Flanders Campaign 1793-1895* (Phillip Ball)

No 50 *Guerra Fantástica: The Portuguese Army and the Seven Years War* (António Barrento)

No 51 *From Across the Sea: North Americans in Nelson's Navy* (Sean M. Heuvel and John A. Rodgaard)

No 52 *Rebellious Scots to Crush: The Military Response to the Jacobite '45* (Andrew Bamford (ed.))

No 53 *The Army of George II 1727-1760: The Soldiers who Forged an Empire* (Peter Brown)

No 54 *Wellington at Bay: The Battle of Villamuriel, 25 October 1812* (Garry David Wills)

No 55 *Life in the Red Coat: The British Soldier 1721-1815* (Andrew Bamford (ed.))

No 56 *Wellington's Favourite Engineer. John Burgoyne: Operations, Engineering, and the Making of a Field Marshal* (Mark S. Thompson)

No 57 *Scharnhorst: The Formative Years, 1755-1801* (Charles Edward White)

No 58 *At the Point of the Bayonet: The Peninsular War Battles of Arroyomolinos and Almaraz 1811-1812* (Robert Griffith)

No 59 *Sieges of the '45: Siege Warfare during the Jacobite Rebellion of 1745-1746* (Jonathan D. Oates)

No 60 *Austrian Cavalry of the Revolutionary and Napoleonic Wars, 1792–1815* (Enrico Acerbi, András K. Molnár)

No 61 *The Danish Army of the Napoleonic Wars 1801-1814, Organisation, Uniforms & Equipment: Volume 2: Cavalry and Artillery* (David Wilson)

No 62 *Napoleon's Stolen Army: How the Royal Navy Rescued a Spanish Army in the Baltic* (John Marsden)

No 63 *Crisis at the Chesapeake: The Royal Navy and the Struggle for America 1775-1783* (Quintin Barry)

No 64 *Bullocks, Grain, and Good Madeira: The Maratha and Jat Campaigns 1803-1806 and the emergence of the Indian Army* (Joshua Provan)

No 65 *Sir James McGrigor: The Adventurous Life of Wellington's Chief Medical Officer* (Tom Scotland)

No 66 *Fashioning Regulation, Regulating Fashion: Uniforms and Dress of the British Army 1800-1815 Volume I* (Ben Townsend) (paperback edition)

No 67 *Fashioning Regulation, Regulating Fashion: Uniforms and Dress of the British Army 1800-1815 Volume II* (Ben Townsend) (paperback edition)

No 68 *The Secret Expedition: The Anglo-Russian Invasion of Holland 1799* (Geert van Uythoven) (paperback edition)

No 69 *The Sea is My Element: The Eventful Life of Admiral Sir Pulteney Malcolm 1768-1838* (Paul Martinovich)

No 70 *The Sword and the Spirit: Proceedings of the first 'War & Peace in the Age of Napoleon' Conference* (Zack White (ed.))

No 71 *Lobositz to Leuthen: Horace St Paul and the Campaigns of the Austrian Army in the Seven Years War 1756-57* (Neil Cogswell) (paperback edition)

No 72 *For God and King. A History of the Damas Legion 1793-1798: A Case Study of the Military Emigration during the French Revolution* (Hughes de Bazouges and Alistair Nichols)

No 73 *'Their Infantry and Guns Will Astonish You': The Army of Hindustan and European Mercenaries in Maratha service 1780-1803* (Andy Copestake)

No 74 *Like A Brazen Wall: The Battle of Minden, 1759, and its Place in the Seven Years War* (Ewan Carmichael)

No 75 *Wellington and the Lines of Torres Vedras: The Defence of Lisbon during the Peninsular War* (Mark Thompson)

No 76 *French Light Infantry 1784-1815: From the Chasseurs of Louis XVI to Napoleon's Grande Armée* (Terry Crowdy)

No 77 *Riflemen: The History of the 5th Battalion 60th (Royal American) Regiment, 1797-1818* (Robert Griffith) (paperback edition)

No 78 *Hastenbeck 1757: The French Army and the Opening Campaign of the Seven Years War* (Olivier Lapray)

No 79 *Napoleonic French Military Uniforms: As Depicted by Horace and Carle Vernet and Eugène Lami* (Guy Dempsey (trans. and ed.))

No 80 *These Distinguished Corps: British Grenadier and Light Infantry Battalions in the American Revolution* (Don N. Hagist)

No 81 *Rebellion, Invasion, and Occupation: The British Army in Ireland, 1793 -1815* (Wayne Stack)

No 82 *You Have to Die in Piedmont! The Battle of Assietta, 19 July 1747. The War of the Austrian Succession in the Alps* (Giovanni Cerino Badone)

No 83 *A Very Fine Regiment: the 47th Foot in the American War of Independence, 1773–1783* (Paul Knight)

No 84 *By Fire and Bayonet: Grey's West Indies Campaign of 1794* (Steve Brown) (paperback edition)

No 85 *No Want of Courage: The British Army in Flanders, 1793-1795* (R.N.W. Thomas)

No 86 *Far Distant Ships: The Royal Navy and the Blockade of Brest 1793-1815* (Quintin Barry) (paperback edition)

No 87 *Armies and Enemies of Napoleon 1789-1815: Proceedings of the 2021 Helion and Company 'From Reason to Revolution' Conference* (Robert Griffith (ed.))

No 88 *The Battle of Rossbach 1757: New Perspectives on the Battle and Campaign* (Alexander Querengässer (ed.))

No 89 *Waterloo After the Glory: Hospital Sketches and Reports on the Wounded After the Battle* (Michael Crumplin and Gareth Glover) (paperback edition)

No 90 *From Ushant to Gibraltar: The Channel Fleet 1778-1783* (Quintin Barry)

No 91 *'The Soldiers are Dressed in Red': The Quiberon Expedition of 1795 and the Counter-Revolution in Brittany* (Alistair Nichols)

No 92 *The Army of the Kingdom of Italy 1805-1814: Uniforms, Organisation, Campaigns* (Stephen Ede-Borrett)

No 93 *The Ottoman Army of the Napoleonic Wars 1798-1815: A Struggle for Survival from Egypt to the Balkans* (Bruno Mugnai)

No 94 *The Changing Face of Old Regime Warfare: Essays in Honour of Christopher Duffy* (Alexander S. Burns (ed.))

No 95 *The Danish Army of the Napoleonic Wars 1801-1814, Organisation, Uniforms & Equipment: Volume 3: Norwegian Troops and Militia* (David Wilson)

No 96 *1805 - Tsar Alexander's First War with Napoleon* (Alexander Ivanovich Mikhailovsky-Danilevsky, trans. Peter G.A. Phillips)

No 97 *'More Furies then Men': The Irish Brigade in the service of France 1690-1792* (Pierre-Louis Coudray)

No 98 *'We Are Accustomed to do our Duty': German Auxiliaries with the British Army 1793-95* (Paul Demet) (paperback edition)